WRITING THE GREAT WAR

CASS SERIES: MILITARY HISTORY AND POLICY
Series Editors: John Gooch and Brian Holden Reid
ISSN: 1465-8488

This series will publish studies on historical and contemporary aspects of land power, spanning the period from the eighteenth century to the present day, and will include national, international and comparative studies. From time to time, the series will publish edited collections of essays and 'classics'.

WRITING THE GREAT WAR

Sir James Edmonds
and the Official Histories
1915–1948

ANDREW GREEN

FRANK CASS
LONDON • PORTLAND, OR

First published in 2003 in Great Britain by
FRANK CASS PUBLISHERS
Crown House, 47 Chase Side, Southgate
London N14 5BP

and in the United States of America by
FRANK CASS PUBLISHERS
c/o ISBS, 920 NE 58th Avenue
Suite 300, Portland, OR
97213-3786

Website: www.frankcass.com

Copyright © 2003 Andrew Green

British Library Cataloguing in Publication Data

Green, Andrew
 Writing the Great War: Sir James Edmonds and the official
 histories 1915–1948. – (Cass series. Military history
 and policy; 11)
 1. Edmonds, Sir James E. (James Edward), 1861–1956. 2. World
 War, 1914–1918 – Historiography
 I. Title
 940.4'00722

ISBN 0-7146-5495-7 (cloth)
ISSN 1465-8488

Library of Congress Cataloguing-in-Publication Data

Green, Andrew, 1964–
 Writing the Great War: Sir James Edmonds and the official histories
1915–1948 / Andrew Green.
   p.   cm. – (Cass series – military history and policy, ISSN
1465–8488; no. 11)
Includes bibliographical references and index.
 ISBN 0-7146-5495-7 (cloth)
1. World War, 1914–1918 – Historiography. 2. World War,
1914–1918 – Study and teaching – Great Britain – History – 20th century. 3.
Edmonds, J. E. (James Edward), Sir, 1861–1956. 4. History of the Great
War based on official documents by direction of the Historical Section
of the Committee of Imperial Defence. I. Title. II. Series.
 D522.42.G75 2003
 940.4'07'2041–dc21

2003043983

Typeset in Classical Garamond 10.5/12pt by Servis Filmsetting Ltd, Manchester
Printed in Great Britain by MPG Books Ltd, Bodmin, Cornwall

To Catherine, Alex and Nicky

Contents

Illustrations

All prints reproduced by courtesy of the Liddell Hart Centre for Military Archives, King's College London, Edmonds Papers.

Series Editor's Preface

The 19 volumes of the Official History of British military operations edited by Brigadier-General Sir James Edmonds and published between 1922 and 1948 – the last of which appeared when its author and the series editor had reached the age of 87 – are simultaneously a monument to sustained scholarship and a quarry that is still mined for the rich ores it contains. Such is their commanding presence that they are simply works that no serious historian of the First World War can ignore.

However, despite their many historical merits, they have not stood above the battles that have been, and continue to be, waged about that most affecting of wars. In his *Memoirs*, Captain Sir Basil Liddell Hart accused Edmonds – quite wrongly, as will become apparent to the reader of the pages which follow – of growing more inclined to whitewash the errors of the High Command as he grew older, and it has even been claimed that acquaintance with Edmonds and the other official historians did much to sour Liddell Hart's view of the British Army. Historians have not been much kinder to Edmonds over the years. He has been accused of writing 'technical history' in 'featureless prose' – charges that are repeatedly rebutted in what follows – and of managing to write an account of a great tragedy without any display of emotion whatsoever. A kindred charge is that he fails as an official historian because he did not educate the public in the 'realities of war'. If that is indeed one of the tasks of the official historian, which may be questioned, then it can certainly be said that few authors, if any, have ever achieved it. Perhaps the most extreme and unfair attack upon Edmonds and his work has been to allege that he wrote to a pre-determined story line, that his consultations of many senior and not so senior officers in an attempt to improve the accuracy and authenticity of his narrative were a sham, and that the resulting account of the Western Front is fraudulent.

Andrew Green's careful and authoritative account of how the Official Histories were produced under Edmonds's direction, and his scrupulous weighing of the accuracy of some of the key volumes, gives the lie to all these charges. From the account of the bureaucracy that necessarily surrounded the process, we learn of the constraints under which he and his team had to operate, not least the unavoidable requirement to run what Sir Maurice Hankey called 'the gauntlet of departmental criticism'. Such fundamental matters as costs and funding affect Official Histories, and we do well to acknowledge this fact. So, more importantly, does the task laid on their authors to inform and to educate the public. Here, Dr Green lays bare for the first time the historical method that was at the root of Edmonds's work and was a direct reflection of Clausewitz's remarks on the proper writing of military history and of the German 'applicatory method' that derived from it, with which Edmonds was acquainted. The core of this was the injunction not to be 'wise after the event' and introduce knowledge that contemporaries did not have at the time when trying to understand why they acted as they did. It is not an injunction that many contemporary historians would accept, and both Edmonds and his colleague Aspinall-Oglander, the author of the two exceptional volumes on the Gallipoli campaign, escaped from its shackles at times. But it explains a great deal about why the volumes are written in ways which have mistakenly been labelled as bloodless and uncritical.

Readers of this book will appreciate, and perhaps admire, the dedication and effort that Edmonds put into compiling his own volumes and editing those of fellow authors, a dedication epitomised by the statistic that 1,500 narrative drafts of his account of March 1918 were circulated for comment and reaction. They will note – as some have not – that he introduced direct but not *ad personam* criticisms of Haig and many of his subordinates into his later as well as his earlier writings, and will be able to identify the disguised arguments he artfully inserted into his works to challenge received opinions and popular misconceptions. They will also recognise that fundamental criticisms could as effectively be levelled unobtrusively – as when Edmonds called attention to the lack of a coordinated command structure in March 1918 by chronicling the unhappy consequences for directionless troops – as by obtrusive or strident charges and accusations. The result, presented here, is a major redefinition of Edmonds's reputation as an official historian able to chart a skilful route through the special reefs and shoals that face such men, and as a scholar whose writings combine a scrupulous attention to evidence and a subtlety of prose with a tireless quest for truth.

John Gooch
Series Co-Editor

Preface

I began researching the writing of the Official Histories of the First World War for my doctoral thesis at Leeds University. I had in mind that I might uncover some degree of conspiracy on the part of the government, who commissioned the works, or the military establishment, who provided its authors, to manipulate the course of history. Predisposed by the views of those few writers who had touched on the Official Histories in their work, I embarked upon my research expecting to find many instances of attempts to suppress the truth, the glossing over of unpalatable conclusions, the deliberate falsification of facts or simply slovenly historical writing. One is naturally sceptical about an author's freedom of expression in any work labelled 'official' particularly when its content has had to be submitted for approval before publication to the War Office, Foreign Office and a number of other interested government departments. With all original government and military documentation closed to public scrutiny for 50 years, these 'official' authors would have had few who could have argued authoritatively with their findings. If one adds to this the fact that these authors were army officers who had served in the war and were, in many cases, personal friends of those in high command of whom they wrote, one has all the ingredients for a potential cover-up.

When I began my research I found to my surprise (and in some ways relief, for it has made, to my mind, a more interesting story) that my anticipated view was completely incorrect. I looked first at the private papers of the official historian of the Gallipoli campaign, Cecil Aspinall-Oglander. Not only did this official historian approach his task with immense diligence but he steadfastly refused to bow to any attempts from any quarter to influence the findings of his work. In spite of attempts by the War Office, Foreign Office, Australian government and a number of high-ranking military officers to influence the content and tone of his work, Aspinall-Oglander succeeded in publishing an Official History not just of great academic integrity but of great literary interest.

However, within Aspinall-Oglander's private papers there did appear evidence that James Edmonds, the director of the Official History series and author of some of its most important volumes, had attempted to manipulate Aspinall-Oglander's work in deference to political and military sensitivities. Whilst very little indeed has been written on Aspinall-Oglander, a number of historians have focused on Edmonds' role in producing the Official History series. Just as the reputation of Douglas Haig and of his generals underwent considerable revision during the 1960s and 1970s, so the Official Histories, which were seen as generally defensive of the high command during the war, have been tarnished as unreliable and historically distorted works. Edmonds has been regarded as having taken at best a cavalier and at worst a deliberately negligent approach to historical accuracy.

In researching Edmonds' writings I turned first to his private papers, and these contain a considerable amount of correspondence with his friend and fellow historian Basil Liddell Hart. Liddell Hart was a frequent critic of the Official History volumes. However, it became apparent from this correspondence that Edmonds in fact took his historical responsibilities extremely seriously and was determined to publish a true and accurate account of the operations of which he wrote. He was not blindly supportive of Haig and where he did see shortcomings he was prepared to detail these in his official works. As director of the series, Edmonds operated under considerably greater constraints than Aspinall-Oglander, but in his own unique way he was skilfully able to retain his literary integrity.

In researching the vast amount of documentation and correspondence held at the Public Record Office concerning the writing of the Official Histories, much of which was used by Edmonds at the time to write his volumes, it also became clear to me that these works were in fact highly informed. Edmonds and his fellow official historians alone had access to this wealth of first-hand evidence. They alone had access to the personal recollections of thousands of participants from high command to company command. Indeed a number of them had themselves served at senior staff level in the theatres of which they wrote. Their evidence was painstakingly researched and was judiciously assessed. The resultant works are credible, reliable and extremely comprehensive. Indeed, notwithstanding the criticism of the official historians' motives and methods, the historical value of these works has stood the test of time. Not only have a considerable number of First World War histories relied extensively on the official volumes but even those recent works which offer new insights into the war have highlighted features which, in some cases, were already revealed in the Official Histories 70 or so years ago.

Over the course of my research, as I built up a picture of how Edmonds, in particular, approached the task of completing his vast enterprise, both professionally and personally, I built up too a respect for his tireless energy and scrupulous dedication to producing a reliable and accurate account. Moreover, Edmonds' task was made considerably more challenging by having, at the same time, to satisfy the conflicting demands upon him of those who sought to influence his writing. To cast aspersions on Edmonds' academic integrity is therefore to do him an immense disservice as well as to ignore the considerable amount of evidence to the contrary. Just as historians are beginning to re-revise the view of Haig in a more positive light, I feel it is appropriate to reveal to modern readers the true, and perhaps hitherto unrecognised, historical and literary value of the Official Military Histories of the First World War.

Acknowledgements

I would like to thank the following for granting me access to manuscript collections of which they are the owners or custodians and for permission to quote from documents whose copyright they control: the Trustees of the Imperial War Museum, the Trustees of the Liddell Hart Centre for Military Archives, King's College, London; the Public Record Office, the Newport Record Office, Isle of Wight, Mrs Oglander and Mr Rupert Dawnay. I would also like to thank Professor John Gooch, Professor of International History at the University of Leeds for his valuable guidance and kind support in supervising my doctoral thesis on which this work is based. I am grateful to Professor Keith Jeffery of Belfast University who provided me with some balance to Edmonds' own opinions on his relationship with Sir Henry Wilson. I am also grateful to Andrew Whitmarsh of Portsmouth City Museum for shedding further light on the pre-war manoeuvres of 1912 in which Edmonds and Haig were involved. I would also like to thank Stuart Moore, History Master at Haberdashers' Aske's School, Elstree, and William Thomas, Tutor of Modern History at Christ Church, Oxford. Their inspirational influence was far greater than they might perhaps have realised and without it I might never have returned to academic history in the midst of a business career. Finally, I would like to thank my wife, Catherine, and children, Alexander and Nicholas, for their support and for having graciously accepted my devotion to historical research in addition to my full-time career.

Abbreviations

APM	Assistant Provost Marshal
ASC	Army Service Corps
BEF	British Expeditionary Force
Brig.-Gen.	Brigadier-General
Capt.	Captain
C.-in-C.	Commander-in-Chief
CID	Committee of Imperial Defence
CIGS	Chief of the Imperial General Staff
Col.	Colonel
DMO	Director of Military Operations
Gen.	General
GHQ	General Headquarters
GOC	General Officer Commanding
GS	General Staff
GSO1	General Staff Officer 1
GSO2	General Staff Officer 2
IWM	Imperial War Museum
KCL	King's College, London
LI	Light Infantry
Lt-Col.	Lieutenant-Colonel
Lt-Gen.	Lieutenant-General
Maj.-Gen.	Major-General
MEF	Mediterranean Expeditionary Force
MO5	Military Operations 5
Newport RO	Newport Record Office, Isle of Wight
PRO	Public Record Office, Kew
QMG	Quartermaster-General
RMLI	Royal Marine Light Infantry

Introduction

In 1915, within months of the largest land force Britain had ever mobilised finding itself rooted on continental soil, work began on an historical venture which in its scale and complexity was as unprecedented as the army whose actions it sought to document and describe. The process of compiling and producing the Official Military Histories of the Great War was to take 33 years to complete. Another great war had come and gone before the final official volume was published in 1948. The entire undertaking, which resulted in 29 volumes of Official Military History, was vast. It involved the collection, sorting, recording and analysing of over 25 million documents. Every order, communication, unit diary and a number of personal diaries were studied by the official historians in preparing their works. This mass of information was supplemented by enemy and Allied accounts and the written evidence of several thousand participants, from Earl Haig to battalion commanders. There can be few academic works which have been based upon such a volume of research.

This work was undertaken by the Historical Section of the Committee of Imperial Defence which employed no more than a handful of official historians at any one time. Initially these were civilian authors or academics but for various reasons they proved unsuccessful and were eventually replaced by retired servicemen and staff officers. These historians worked under the directorship and supervision of Brigadier-General Sir James Edmonds, one of Haig's former staff officers and a former head of MO5. In addition to supervising the entire process, Edmonds wrote nearly half of the total volumes and three-quarters of those dealing with the Western Front. His work covered some of the most important battles of the war including the Somme, Third Ypres and the German offensive of March 1918. Having retired from the army in 1918, Edmonds was to direct the Historical Section for 30 years. He completed his final volume in 1948 at the age of 87.

These volumes represent a substantial body of work within the historiography of the First World War and have undoubtedly left their mark on the enormous numbers of historical writings that have followed them even, it will be seen, to this day. When the first official volumes began to appear in the 1920s they were eagerly greeted by the public for the promise they held of shedding some real light on the Great War. It is scarcely surprising that there should exist such a thirst for knowledge in the wake of such a catastrophic event. The unanticipated and attritional nature of the war, the scale of human suffering and national loss that it inflicted, and the social and political changes that followed it have left such deep impressions on Britain's collective psychology that it is fair to say that close to a century later we bear the marks to this day. Popular and academic interest remains as compelling now as in the immediate aftermath of war. Until the Official Histories were published the public had had to rely for its information on the contemporaneous despatches of journalists from the front or such early accounts as Buchan's *Nelson's History of the War 1915–1919* and Conan Doyle's *The British Campaign in France and Flanders 1916–1920*.[1]

By the 1920s and 1930s the Official Histories were no longer alone in offering some insight into the events of 1914–18. The accounts of both witnesses (Gibbs' *Realities of War*, Repington's *The First World War*) and participants direct and indirect (Sherriff's *Journey's End*, Remarque's *All Quiet on the Western Front* and Brittain's *Testament of Youth*) began the process of defining the Great War from a different perspective in terms of the personal suffering of the individual. Wider historical works, too, such as Masterman's *England after the War* and Liddell Hart's *The Real War*, helped to reinforce the great cultural mythology of the war as having wasted an entire generation of British manhood. There were also the personal accounts of more senior participants such as French's *1914*, Churchill's *The World Crisis* and Lloyd George's *Memoirs*, which dealt with the larger issues of strategy and politics. Motivated in the main by self-justification, these works advanced, through their accusation and acrimony, this sense of large-scale loss and waste and blame.

Amongst these publications the official volumes occupied a unique place in that their authors alone had had access to the official documentation and personal first-hand evidence of participants *en masse*. Senior politicians and soldiers might be able to draw upon their own memories or such documents as passed into their possession but none enjoyed the scale of vision available to the official historian. He alone could witness operations and affairs from the trench, from GHQ or from the Cabinet Office. Indeed, through correspondence with his opposite numbers in Germany, he was even able to experience the view from the other side of the battlefield.

It has been argued that as a result of this the official historians had an equally unique responsibility to lay the facts of this conflict truthfully and accurately before both the general public and, more importantly, future generations of military strategists.[2] This is undoubtedly the starting point for all assessments of the official works, not least this one. One of the main objectives of this work will be to assess the accuracy and historical merit of the Official Military Histories. It will examine whether these works took the opportunity available to highlight the vital lessons of the conflict. Of course, the process of drawing lessons from the Great War continues to this day as new research and new evidence throw up different perspectives. In order to assess the real value of the official works, their lessons and conclusions will also be considered alongside the most current academic views.

Whilst little research has been carried out into the writing of these official volumes, their critics have been far from scarce. Inevitably, because they were labelled 'official' and covered such contentious events, the Official Histories had numerous critics from the moment of publication. Captain Basil Liddell Hart frequently accused Edmonds of a partisan approach that sought to protect his military colleagues and concealed the vital lessons of the war.[3] Lloyd George accused Edmonds of perpetrating a great deal of nonsense in order to preserve the reputation of Sir Douglas Haig and to mislead the public and future generations as to the scale of military incompetence that dogged British participation in that struggle.[4] Recent writers, too, in assessing the evolution of British tactical methods, as in the case of Tim Travers, or in considering the historiography of the war, as in the case of David French, have accused Edmonds of ignoring facts and lessons in order to show Haig in a more favourable light.[5] One writer, Denis Winter, has gone so far as to suggest that Edmonds represented part of a wider conspiracy on the part of Haig and the post-war government to cover up the true facts of military incompetence by deliberate falsification and destruction of evidence.[6]

Broadly this criticism falls into three major categories. Firstly, according to their critics, the Official Histories were biased accounts in which Edmonds not only sought to protect and defend primarily the Commander-in-Chief but ultimately all senior officers. A number of critics hold that Edmonds deliberately eschewed overtly blaming any of the senior military participants and chose instead to apportion blame only to external factors, such as politicians, Britain's allies, the weather and the pre-1914 neglect of the army. Secondly, the charge is levelled that, by avoiding apportioning blame and shirking from direct criticism, Edmonds in particular and the Official Histories in general ignored vital lessons that needed to be learnt. Finally a number of critics have passed into popular mythology the view that the Official Histories were bland and unemotional – complex narratives of unit dispositions which have little literary interest.[7] Given that the principal reason behind the government's decision to publish the official works was to provide both a readable account for the general public and a staff textbook from which future officers might receive valuable instruction, these final charges are serious indeed. Another objective of this study, then, will be an assessment of this criticism and its validity.

This work will judge the Official Histories not only in relation to their critics' charges but also in relation to the expectations and motivations of those who set in motion the process of producing them. Established as a subcommittee of the CID, the Historical Section continued its activities under the auspices of the Board of Education. Given the nature of its work, however, it remained prey to the attentions and influences of the War Office, the Foreign Office and the Admiralty. Less spectacularly, although of no less influence, the work of the Historical Section was also constantly a matter for concern at the Treasury. The first chapter will show how and why the government decided to write a series of official works on the Great War. It will consider, too, what influence the government, once decided upon its action, was able to continue to exercise over both the process and the content of official work.

Subsequent chapters will consider extensively the process of writing official history. This will include an assessment of the selection, and indeed dismissal, of official historians and what this revealed about the motivations of the architects of the venture. The character and attributes of James Edmonds will also form a central part of this study, which will naturally consider not only his supervision of the Historical Section and its historians but also his method of writing. A full understanding of the nature and value of the Official Histories is only possible when one identifies Edmonds' precise motivations and analyses his methods and his particular literary techniques. Without such a thorough knowledge it is too easy to be misled by an out-of-context or mischievous Edmonds remark. It can also be difficult to penetrate beneath the surface of his narrative to the work that actually lies within.

An assessment of the process of writing official history will include the manner in which the narrative was pieced together from documents and diaries. This will demonstrate the influence of the vast amount of first-hand accounts submitted by participants to official historians. The enormous volume of this correspondence, which emanated from all ranks from field marshal down to colonel, was influential in shaping the content and tone of the official volumes to differing, and in a number of cases surprising, degrees. In determining the historical validity of these works, the extent to which this influence was beneficial or malevolent will be of considerable importance.

In order to consider these issues, this work will focus on four volumes covering the major and more contentious battles of the war. These are *Gallipoli*, written by Brigadier-General Aspinall-Oglander,[8] and *The Somme*, *Third Ypres* and *March 1918*, written by Edmonds. A study of these four works will not only reveal the purpose, process and method of writing the Official Histories but will allow detailed consideration of their critics' charges, their historical, academic and literary merit and the sturdiness or otherwise of their conclusions.

1

The Origins, Purpose and Workings of the Historical Section

I

The roots of the organisation which was to produce the Official Histories began in September 1906. Lord Esher proposed the establishment of an Historical Section, as a subcommittee to the Committee of Imperial Defence, in the aftermath of the South African and Russo-Japanese Wars. His aim was to provide a single department to control the nation's collection of military and naval archives and to ensure that the lessons of these conflicts were made available to military strategists. At that time histories were being prepared of three different campaigns in three different departments of the War Office and a further work was being compiled by the Admiralty. The lessons of the South African conflict, Esher believed,

> could not be adequately appreciated unless the naval and military operations were treated as a whole together with the political considerations . . . [N]either the Admiralty nor the War Office were specially qualified to deal with history from this aspect.[1]

Accordingly, in January 1907 a subcommittee of the Committee of Imperial Defence was established under the chairmanship of Sir George Clarke with its first task to complete an Official History of the South African War. The desire to learn lessons would remain a central feature of the Historical Section's future activities. The original South African history was undertaken by a retired officer, General Sir George Henderson, and, since it 'reflected upon the Government', it was considered unsuitable for publication.[2] The subsequent work had needed a large staff to complete and therefore had cost substantially more than had been anticipated.[3] On publication it was received favourably but not enthusiastically by the press

5

and did not sell well. The experience of writing this work was to fore-shadow a number of concerns which were to affect the subsequent writing of the Official Histories of the Great War, in particular issues of cost and criticism. Interestingly financial and not political issues were to exercise the greater constraints.

When the Great War began in August 1914 the Historical Section was in the process of producing a history of the Russo-Japanese War. This was immediately suspended in order to allow the Section to concentrate on collecting and collating the material now coming from the front in France. In the same month the Historical Section appointed a full-time Secretary, Lt-Col. E.Y. Daniel. He was to remain in his post until retiring at the age of 74 in 1939. Despite an inclination on the part of the government to allow a suitable period to elapse before publishing the history of a major conflict, the experience of the South African history had shown that the task became impossible unless the collection of information began immediately.[4] In May 1915 Captain C.T. Atkinson was sent over to the Western Front and began collecting unit diaries. He reported back on the difficulties of compiling diaries during actions, such as the retreat from Mons, when few were kept and those that were contained large gaps. He also suggested to the Historical Section that the diaries alone would not show why things had happened. Nevertheless, he recommended that work should begin immediately on indexing the diaries so that they might be grouped by unit, subject and chronology. This would allow the later compilers who worked on the information to subject to critical scrutiny any discrepancies that arose as a result of such a grouping and comparison.[5]

Notwithstanding this early activity, the formal decision to undertake this work and to aim to publish it as soon as possible after the end of the war was not taken until August 1915. At a Cabinet meeting on 26 August, Hankey, the Secretary of the War Council, argued strongly for the compilation of an official series of histories for the war. The aims of such a work were to be essentially threefold: to provide a popular and authoritative account for the general reader; for the purposes of professional reference and education; and to provide 'an antidote to the usual unofficial histories which besides being generally inaccurate, habitually attribute all naval and military failures to the ineptitude of the Government'.[6] Kitchener, the Secretary of State for War, argued that, in view of the length of time such a series would take to complete, work should begin immediately on a single-volume popular history which could be published immediately the war had ended. This was in order to maintain public interest in the larger work and to be able to put the government's case contemporaneously with the large number of anticipated accounts by popular authors or participants.[7] Based on the experience of the South African Official History, the Treasury raised strong objections to the cost of an Official History series, but Hankey argued that it was inappropriate

> to measure [the Histories'] value by the test of receipts and that if such a test were applied to other scientific works it was probable that scientific research would come to an end. A History was essentially a work of education and reference.[8]

The Treasury eventually accepted this argument and agreement was reached to proceed with both the Official History series and two interim popular volumes, one naval and one military.[9] In order to make these interim volumes attractive to the general public, two civilian authors were chosen to write them. Sir John Fortescue was selected to compile the military history and Sir Julian Corbett to compile the naval history.

Work on the military histories, both the popular volume and the series, did not proceed smoothly. In his Progress Report of 1917, Daniel reported that Atkinson had worked for two years with a clerical assistant and had only examined 160 of the 1,100 unit diaries received.[10] Hankey, however, was unwilling during a time of war to sanction the huge increase in staff required to do the work thoroughly. Fortescue, too, had progressed in his interim history only as far as November 1914. Even that was not considered by the Historical Section to be sufficiently comprehensive as his work had been based on unit diaries alone. To be fully complete it would need to wait until the more confidential staff correspondence was available. This problem was compounded by the fact that the British army now had over one million men serving in France alone and, as it was no longer considered possible to work on every diary received, the compilers would have to rely on a judiciously selected sample. In February 1919 Brig.-Gen. Sir James Edmonds, a contemporary of Haig's from Staff College who had served on his Staff during the war, joined the Historical Section. On 1 April he was appointed its Director.

It was the progress of the naval history, however, which in the short term was to present a greater threat to the viability of the military histories. The entire wisdom of producing an official series of military histories was called into question as a result of a dispute which arose between Churchill and Corbett over his naval history. The debate which resulted is revealing of the concerns and motivations of the architects of this process and laid down the guidelines on which the official historians subsequently based their writings. In March 1919 Churchill was sent a copy of Corbett's work on the eve of its publication. He strongly objected to the treatment of certain episodes and insisted that the official documentation be published alongside the work so that the public might judge for themselves. According to Hankey, 'every effort was made to meet [Churchill's] objections' but this did not 'prove practicable'.[11] As he wrote to Daniel:

> I do not see that we can do any more. We were instructed to produce a history; we engaged the best man we could, he produced the best history he could. The decision is now with the War Cabinet. I see no harm in the simultaneous production of documents provided the Admiralty agrees. I feel great sympathy with Corbett.[12]

Hankey prepared a memorandum for the Cabinet in which he acknowledged that the whole series of Official Histories was called into question by this issue. Was it feasible, he asked, to write an Official History of events which had only just occurred? An inevitable problem of doing so was that any writer, however discreet or sparing of personal opinions, especially in relation to unsuccessful operations, was bound to 'reflect on one leader or another'. Was it therefore fair to publish the narrative when the events were so recent that these principal actors were still 'on the stage of public life'? Julian Corbett was a discreet and experienced naval historian but his work had now caused concern. The military volumes would be likely to cover far more controversial ground.

Hankey conceded that there were powerful arguments against publishing Official History: it was liable to public and parliamentary criticism; its publication over a number of years would subject each work to individual scrutiny; and it did not pay. Furthermore the experience of this first work had revealed that administratively it would be a constant source of friction in which every history produced would 'have to run the gauntlet of departmental criticism which [was] apt to emasculate the work and deprive it of half its interest'. These arguments were, however, far outweighed by the benefits, indeed necessity, of completing an Official History series. Firstly, very little was known of the early part of the war, and the government had the monopoly of the 'mass of information which the public are entitled to receive in a readable form'. Secondly, Official History was not only for the enlightenment of the public but 'perhaps even more importantly for the education of the professional officer'. Where was he to go for information, asked Hankey, 'if there is no Official History'?

> It is by the standard of their value for professional education purposes that the Official Histories must be judged. It is doubtful if they will ever pay and it is to be feared that they will always be the subject of parliamentary and public criticism.

Finally, Hankey argued again that an Official History was a valuable antidote to 'unofficial histories which [were] apt to blame the Government or individual officers'. Far from shrinking from controversial issues and offending individual sensibilities, the Official Histories were to be educational and informative both to the general reader and to the military student. The government had a duty both to allow its monopoly of information to be disseminated to a wider public and to protect itself from ill-informed speculation and criticism. Hankey offered the Cabinet two alternatives: to announce that 'owing to the nearness of events and the delicate international and personal difficulties raised . . . the experiment had not proved a success' or to go ahead and publish.[13] As in 1915, Hankey's arguments once more carried the field and the government agreed to let publication proceed. It confirmed also that work should continue on the military histories although these were now to be submitted to the War Office and then the Cabinet before publication. The government remained concerned, however, that they should not be bound to continue publication of the official series if Corbett's volume had an unfavourable reception or led to acrimony and controversy.[14] In the end, Corbett's naval history was published in 1920 and was received extremely well in the press.

II

Progress on the interim and military histories throughout 1919 continued to be bedevilled by lack of resources and, until Edmonds took control, lack of direction. The interim history on which Fortescue had been working had originally been intended to deal with the entire war. By the time Edmonds took over as Director in April 1919 progress had been so slow that it had been decided to let Fortescue complete his work with the events at the end of May 1915 and then that it should not include any theatres other than France. Captain G.S. Gordon had been taken on in January 1919 to cover events thereafter and up to December 1915 and to include the Dardanelles campaign but he had departed for Gallipoli in June and made no progress whatsoever. Edmonds was also concerned by the state of the documents, which had been left in untidy, uncatalogued bundles, from which maps and sheets were missing where historians had worked on them and not replaced them. He felt the staff was entirely inadequate for the gigantic task of arranging the papers.[15]

More importantly, Edmonds began to harbour serious doubts about the content of Fortescue's work. These concerns are of interest because they reflect the seriousness with which Edmonds viewed the Historical Section's responsibility to publish both an accurate and a readable account. In February 1919, Edmonds' first opinions of Fortescue's work were that he was entirely ignorant of the modern army. He believed that Fortescue's comments 'seem based on a knowledge of warfare of 200 or so years ago and require revision'. Furthermore, Fortescue made no reference to dates or times and used archaic military vocabulary, referring to 'cannons' and 'tumbrils'.[16] Edmonds raised these objections with Fortescue and he agreed to revise his account. However, when Edmonds received Fortescue's revised draft he appeared to have ignored all Edmonds' recommendations. The account remained a 'confused story with hardly any clue to the general situation and practically nothing about the enemy'. Sir John French had been ridiculed, Sir Douglas Haig belittled, and the government was represented as having failed to stop the war when it could. In addition, the operations of the French prior to the arrival of the British were 'slurred over in less than one typewritten page'. Edmonds' main complaints, though, were twofold. Firstly, he believed that 'from a lack of interest and energy [Fortescue] ha[d] not troubled to read and study what has been available' (he refused to use any of the German information which Edmonds had sent him). Secondly, on a matter of literary style, Fortescue had 'squandered the opportunity to write a thrilling story of the old B.E.F. and . . . has produced a mere patchwork of summaries of battalions' own diaries'.[17] By the end of 1919 Edmonds had decided to rewrite Fortescue's work himself, as Fortescue continued to refuse to correct the 'absurd military mistakes' which Edmonds had pointed out to him and which he had in fact previously agreed to correct. In reconstructing Fortescue's narrative, Edmonds found it to be 'grossly inaccurate and misleading' with reference to the original documents upon which it was based.[18] Edmonds felt so strongly about such negligence that he suggested that, in the interests of the public, Fortescue should be called upon to refund the salary he had received.[19] At the end of 1919 Fortescue was removed.

This episode was of considerable importance because it altered Edmonds' own view as to the type of history which the Historical Section should produce. Until that point Edmonds had believed that the histories should be constructed by merely publishing the despatches of various units involved. Indeed on joining the Historical Section in February 1919 his guidelines to Gordon had been that:

> in a work issued so soon after the war it seems essential that the general line adopted in the despatches should as far as possible be followed and that it is unnecessary except in the case of special incidents to go much beyond the movements of divisions.[20]

After his experience of Fortescue's draft, Edmonds now realised that for a number of reasons such a narrative would be unacceptable. In an appreciation to Daniel written at the end of 1919, Edmonds noted that:

> [t]he necessity for an account founded on official documents, elaborated by statements and private records of officers and German information has become more and more apparent. Many complaints have been heard and received with regard to the garbled

and misleading accounts given in their books by Sir Arthur Conan Doyle, John Buchan and others.

Edmonds now believed that the publication of despatches would no longer be sufficient to rebut these accounts. He had become convinced by publishers and authors with whom he had consulted that a book of such a type would not have a large number of readers amongst the general public. Furthermore he believed that '[f]or educational purposes a foundation [wa]s required on which to base teaching'.[21] Interestingly, these observations match fairly precisely the three main objectives of the Historical Section as expressed previously by Hankey: of providing a readable account which the general public would buy, of providing a work of educational value to the military student, and of rebutting the 'unofficial' and inaccurate accounts of civilian authors. It will be seen in subsequent chapters how Edmonds' concerns for these fundamental objectives remained central to his work throughout.

III

Three years later the issue of cost once more surfaced to threaten the Official History series. On 13 June 1922 the financial burden of producing the Official Histories was debated in the House of Commons. Oliver Locker-Lampson, who proposed the motion, argued that their production should be left to private enterprise. A number of MPs said that they had heard nothing of the histories either in preparation or already published. Given that by 1922 five volumes had already been published, and that all had received extremely good press, this was rather surprising. Two weeks later Colonel Daniel was called upon by the President of the Board of Education, H.A.L. Fisher, to 'give evidence before his committee as to the value of the official histories which are at present being prepared'.[22]

Daniel responded to the issue of private enterprise by stating that Official History would never yield 'a living wage . . . [i]t must always be a labour of love'. He argued that for reasons of national education the government must be prepared to subsidise it, although in terms of their *value* the histories were exceptionally good and represented a relatively small price to pay. The cost of producing the Official Histories of military, naval, seaborne, merchant and air operations for the six years from 1916 to 1922 had been just over £42,000. The military and naval histories accounted for the largest amounts within this at £16,800 and £11,800 respectively. This compared to the annual cost of producing *Hansard* at £44,000. Daniel had also received Treasury figures for the total cost of fighting the Great War which from 3 August 1914 to 31 March 1920 amounted to £11,196,927,000.[23] He had calculated that this equated to a cost of £3,500 per minute and this, he felt, provided a compelling argument in favour of continuing with the histories:

> When we consider the vast cost at which our experience was bought the amount which is being spent on making that experience available for sound educational purposes comes clearly within the limits of sound economy . . . in actual money values the cost of the war for four minutes exceeded the annual cost of making its lessons available by means of the historical section.[24]

These considerations were put before the next meeting of the Historical Section subcommittee on 31 July 1922 and it was agreed that work should continue.

IV

The dual purpose, then, of Official History, as argued consistently by those who conceived and produced it, was very clear. Firstly, it was to use the government's monopoly of confidential information to provide a readable account for the public which would at the same time act as an antidote to unofficial accounts which had sought to criticise the government or the army. Secondly, and of no less importance, it was to provide a work of educational value to future military officers and strategists. Crucially it was the Official History's value as a means of learning lessons from the recent conflict which was considered to be a fundamental *raison d'être* by its creators. Of course, these two demands are potentially conflicting because a popular account which was both readable by the layman and defended the political and military authorities against criticism was unlikely to provide an instructive assessment for the military student in which lessons and mistakes were highlighted. How these two conflicting requirements were reconciled is the absolute crux of any understanding of the Official Histories. Therein lies much of the explanation for Edmonds' particular style and method of writing and the reason why much of his work has been misinterpreted. Furthermore, to recognise that lesson learning *was* an essential tenet of these works is to help explain how the Official Histories were able to retain their academic integrity despite constant attempts by various interested parties and government departments to interfere, with their content and conclusions. In order to understand the process by which official historians were able to fend off attempted interference, it is necessary first to consider the executive accountability and then the functioning of the Historical Section. It will be seen that finance rather than any other imperative continued to exercise the greatest degree of control, if not of any literary or academic influence. Finally, the particular involvement of Edmonds himself in guiding the early direction of the Historical Section will be assessed.

The meeting in July 1922 was the first occasion on which the Historical Section subcommittee met to discuss the Official Histories. Under the chairmanship of H.A.L. Fisher it met a further six times in 1923. On the penultimate occasion, 9 August, Hankey was successful in receiving approval for his proposal, first made a year earlier, to establish a permanent Cabinet Subcommittee of Control of the Official Histories. This was to be chaired by the President of the Board of Education (it saw 12 different chairmen between 1924 and 1946) and consisted of representatives of the Treasury, War Office, Admiralty and Air Ministry and the Secretary to the Committee of Imperial Defence. The Secretary of the Historical Section, Daniel, and the Director, Edmonds, were usually present, and official historians or representatives from the Foreign, Colonial or India Offices were occasionally invited to answer specific questions. The Committee met annually from 1924 to 1939. Whilst this Committee therefore controlled the activities of Edmonds and the Historical Section, the ultimate executive authority for any decision on which the Committee failed to agree rested with the Cabinet itself.[25]

Edmonds submitted an annual progress report to the Committee, and other official historians appended summaries of their own specific activities. These generally dealt with such administrative matters as progress towards publication, staff and personnel, the publication of foreign Official Histories and other activities of the Section. The Committee meetings dealt principally with matters concerning the cost and progress of publication, the number of volumes, the scope and size of the works and employment. Only very occasionally was a decision required by the Committee on the content of the histories where there had been disagreement from a government department to which a volume had been submitted for comment. One such notable meeting, which will be considered in a later chapter, occurred in March 1928 and concerned strong objections by the War Office to the Gallipoli volume then being prepared by Aspinall-Oglander. However, whilst there were some serious objections raised by the War Office and Foreign Office to a number of draft volumes it remained a rare occurrence for disagreements to require arbitration by the Committee for Control. (As will be shown later, that should certainly not be taken as an indication that these disagreements had been settled outside the meetings to the satisfaction of the War or Foreign Offices.)

V

The greatest influence that the Committee for Control continued to exercise over the shape of the Official Histories was in respect of funds.

Whilst this was in no manner responsible for altering the content and conclusions of the works, it did have a considerable impact on the speed of progress, the ease with which Edmonds could carry out his work, the size and number of volumes and even the selection of historians. Dealing with this latter point first, whilst Edmonds preferred for his own reasons, which are considered later, to employ retired military personnel, the attraction to the Treasury of employing army officers was that their half-pay or retired pay at £500 a year was generally half what a civilian author might demand. In addition they were prepared to work longer hours and volunteer for services for which they were not paid. Furthermore the Treasury itself actually demanded and obtained the removal of an official historian whose progress and forecast publication date were not considered satisfactory. In view of the importance of the failed German offensive of March 1918 it had been proposed by the War Office in 1923 that the official volume of this battle should be written ahead of the chronological sequence then being followed. Since Edmonds was fully occupied on current volumes on 1915, Lieutenant-General L.E. Kiggell, Haig's Chief of Staff, had been selected to prepare and write the volume. By 1926, after two and a half years, he had not produced even a draft narrative for circulation to surviving participants and estimated that he was still four years away from completion. At the meeting of the Committee for Control in January 1926, James Rae on behalf of the Treasury recommended that on grounds of economy Kiggell should be replaced and the work suspended until another historian was free to write it. Edmonds, who had expressed his own reservations that Kiggell's work lacked 'colour and atmosphere', agreed to his dismissal.[26]

Cost considerations also had an impact on the size of the Official Histories. The price of the early volumes of Official History had been set at 21s with a further 21s for the accompanying maps. As this level was considered prohibitive for one of the very sections of the population for whom the works were intended, the professional officer, it was reduced in 1923 to 12s 6d. This had the effect, according to Edmonds, of leaving no margin for advertising and too little for booksellers who would not stock the volumes or display them in their windows.[27] More importantly for the content of the works, it forced the publishers to insist on a maximum number of pages per volume. This was a constraint which was taken seriously enough to require the Committee for Control to recommend an increase in price in 1924 to 15s.[28] In March 1933 Edmonds brought copies of the French, German and Austrian Official Histories into the annual meeting of the Committee for Control in order to show 'how elaborate and voluminous they were in comparison with our own which were more condensed'.[29]

If the size of volumes and their potential sales were dictated by financial necessity so too was the breadth of subject matter covered within the series. Various departments put forward proposals between 1922 and 1939 for the compilation of histories of actions outside the Western Front. These requests are of interest because they further reveal that those who promoted Official History did so as a vehicle for learning lessons. In March 1930, for example, both Edmonds and the War Office requested approval to write an Official History of the occupation of the Rhineland in order to counter the German version which had recently been published. The Treasury refused to pay as it was anxious to keep the estimates for the histories down and there were no more funds available.[30] It was eventually published after having been paid for directly by the War Office, although it remained 'confidential' and was only released to the public in 1987. In March 1931, the War Office requested the writing of an official volume of the East African campaign as it was considered to be of particular value in 'offering lessons for the future differing from those of other operations'. Again the Treasury refused to pay but suggested the War Office follow the precedent set by the West African volume and seek funds from the Colonial Office. A volume on East Africa was eventually published in 1941 and paid for by the Colonial Office. At the same meeting the Foreign Office stated that they were anxious for an Official History of the blockade and were prepared to pay for it themselves. They considered it of value for the study of lessons and useful to them for conferences in international law. As it would not be released for sale to the public and would be classified 'confidential', it could 'therefore be written very fully'.[31] What this meant for the official series as a whole was that because of lack of funds a number of volumes were produced under official auspices but were paid for directly by those departments that considered them of instructive value. Notwithstanding this, they were all written under the supervision of Edmonds and as such were subject to the same constraints which he imposed on all his volumes.

Where financial considerations had a larger impact on Edmonds was on the efficiency of his organisation and the speed with which he was able to progress. Edmonds' activities were constantly hampered by lack of sufficient funds, which impinged upon his premises, the ability of his historians to visit battle sites (the Treasury vetoed a proposed visit of Captain Falls to Mesopotamia at a cost of £200 in 1927 although they sanctioned a similar visit by Aspinall-Oglander to Gallipoli at a cost of £50)[32] and, most importantly, the size of his group of historians and administrators. Indeed in 1922 Edmonds threatened to resign unless he was given additional help. General Sir Cecil Romer at the War Office wrote to him that he

> should regard it as a great loss if you were to give up the Official Histories so I will do my best to get you assistance. But I never know whether we have to pay the piper. You know money is difficult to get.[33]

At any one time, though, the Historical Section consisted of no more than three or four full-time officers in addition to Daniel and Edmonds himself. These officers had between them not only to write the official volumes and prepare them for publication but maintain the library of documentation and maps, examine POW records and foreign official and non-official publications (usually in the original language), and assist the War Office, War Graves Commission, Staff College, educational establishments and other government departments with their enquiries. This was in addition to dealing annually with around 2,000 visitors to their small offices at 2 Cavendish Square. (They were moved out of these in 1922 because they cost £1,500 a year and were on a short-term lease. In the event the Office of Works located larger rooms on the third and fourth floor at the Audit Office on the Embankment, with storage space in the basement.)

In 1924 Edmonds' staff consisted of five people dealing with administrative matters and eight involved in writing histories. At about the same time the French and German Historical Sections numbered approximately 130 each.[34] Furthermore, along with Edmonds himself, the staff was not only overworked but underpaid. In 1924 Edmonds requested that the Committee for Control increase the salary of one of his assistants, Major A.F. Becke, from £500 a year. Edmonds argued that Becke frequently deputised for him in his absence and effectively saved employing another officer by allowing Edmonds to carry out his dual role as Chief Historian and Director of the Section. The Treasury refused although they did agree to raise Edmonds' own salary from £560 a year first to £800 and then, in December 1924, to £1,000 after the First Lord of the Admiralty, Leo Amery, had expressed surprise that Edmonds was earning less than Fortescue had done.[35] At this time not only was Edmonds writing the majority of the histories which the Section produced, but he was also running the entire operation and working hours that could not have been asked of, or expected from, a civilian employee. For much of his 29 years spent employed in this capacity Edmonds worked seven days a week for three months, after which he would take ten days' leave.[36] He expected his own writers to be conscientious although he monitored their output and not their hours in the office. On one occasion he had to instruct one of his historians, Lieutenant-Colonel Hyslop, whom he felt was working too hard, to take 'Wednesday half-day holidays and have alternate Saturdays off'.[37]

In terms of documentation and records, the largest land army Britain had ever put in the field had, by 1924, returned over 25 million documents. Edmonds estimated that it would take his staff nine years simply to sort them.[38] This process had not been helped by the way in which the documentation had been handled. When Edmonds had joined the Historical Section in 1919 he had arrived at the office, then in Chancery

Lane, to find records, diaries and documents 'piled in untidy heaps on the floor'.[39] (Edmonds claimed that he summarily dismissed the Chief Clerk, who refused to climb a ladder to pull some parcels down for him.[40]) His predecessor as Director of the Section, Atkinson, had, according to Edmonds, left most of the records in the bundles in which they were received and had allowed historians to take maps and documents without ensuring that they were returned to the correct place. It took until June 1923 before all records were correctly identified and organised.

Documentation received from the fighting, however, was by no means the limit of what the Historical Section had to handle. The first draft of an official volume was written by a 'narrator' who sorted through, read and analysed the vast amount of documentation available. This was revised by the 'historian' who, having read the documentation himself, added his comment and conclusion. This draft was then submitted to military participants (down to battalion commanders), senior military and political figures and various government departments for comment. As an example, the draft volume on the first day of the Somme was submitted to 1,000 officers and generated 600 replies in 1929, 770 in 1930 and 100 in 1931. Edmonds reported that comments on the first chapter alone, dealing with French and British plans for the Somme offensive, generated a pile of correspondence five feet high.[41] Edmonds complained that his staff was quite insufficient to deal with this, particularly as he had instructed them that 'every name, initial, rank and figure, beside fact must be carefully checked and the accounts of the German and French Sections compared'.[42] Edmonds' great concern, which was indicative of the seriousness with which he viewed his task, was not the burden which this placed upon himself or his staff. It was that his staff was simply inadequate for a 'great national work requiring infinite care, scrupulous accuracy and open to the criticisms of the whole military and literary world'.[43] It will be seen in a subsequent chapter that Edmonds did not allow these constraints to influence the care and thoroughness with which he approached the production of the Official Histories. However, this lack of human resource undoubtedly affected the speed with which the works could be completed. In 1922 Edmonds estimated that it would take his Section 20 years to produce ten volumes of Official History, a task which the French had been able to complete in three.[44] In the event, it took Edmonds and his staff 21 years (if one excludes the Second World War) to produce 14 Western Front volumes and 15 volumes of subsidiary operations.

VI

Financial considerations, therefore, were of considerable influence in the administration of the process of producing the Official Histories, but they had no great bearing on the literary or academic integrity of the work. Of far greater influence on the content of the work was Edmonds himself as Director of the Historical Section. Edmonds' particular methods of writing and his guidance on these methods to his historians will be considered in more detail in the next two chapters. These sections will deal, too, with the various attempts by the War Office, Foreign Office and other government departments to influence the content and conclusions of the Official Histories, largely without success. It has already been shown how none of these bodies exercised any real executive control over the production of Official History. It will be seen in due course how, contrary to the beliefs of a number of Edmonds' critics, they similarly failed to exercise any real moral control either. One example which is not dealt with in subsequent chapters will suffice to demonstrate this. In August 1927 the War Office returned to Edmonds the draft of the first eight chapters of his 1915 Volume II which had been submitted to them for comment. They passed comment on punctuation and the length of sentences, which they believed made the meaning of some passages unclear. Objecting to Edmonds' reference to 'meagre results', the War Office enquired whether it was not the case that at some stage all objectives were reported as having been gained. (Against this in the margin Edmonds had written 'No certainly not.') Finally, they stated that 'before giving approval to the publication of these chapters the Council would prefer that the present draft should be revised in the light of this memo[randum]'.[45] In response to these requests Edmonds suggested to Daniel that:

> the War Office might be thanked for the great care with which the transcript has been read and informed that the criticisms and suggestions will be dealt with in the revise. Whether the War Office should have another draft submitted to them appears to be a matter of principle for you to decide.[46]

In his Progress Report in November 1927 Edmonds referred to the need for the Committee to reach a decision as to whether the draft chapters of this volume should be revised in the light of the War Office comments. He contended that these comments dealt only with petty details and that no points were raised on training or his remarks on leadership 'for which alone they were submitted to the War Office'. Edmonds argued that it was a waste of time to redraft the chapters and have them sit at the War Office for many weeks awaiting approval. He proposed that the Historical Section acknowledge their request for revision with a note thanking the War Office for the 'trouble taken'. Reiterating the point he had made to Daniel in August, Edmonds instructed the Committee that he believed it to be a 'matter of principle for future consideration whether the War Office or the CID were the final authority on the official histories'.[47] This issue passed unnoticed at the next meeting of the Committee for Control, which took place in March 1928. This meeting was entirely taken up by War Office objections of a far more fundamental nature to the content, tone and findings of Aspinall-Oglander's Gallipoli volume. However, the debate at that meeting demonstrated quite clearly that the final arbiter of these matters would indeed be the Cabinet.[48] In fact, Edmonds' subsequent volume dealing with the first day of the Somme offensive generated similarly strenuous objections on the part of the War Office to what they considered to be highly emotive language and overly critical conclusions. It will be seen in the following chapter how little regard Edmonds felt obliged to take of these concerns.

VII

In 1939, as Daniel and Edmonds reached their 75th and 79th years respectively, the government considered calling an end to the Official History venture. The work of writing these histories had been proceeding for the past 20 years and the government had become concerned that the combined age of the Historical Section's most senior members of staff now exceeded 150 years.[49] The Secretary to the Cabinet, E.E. Bridges, communicated to Edmonds that whilst his work was 'most highly appreciated and valued' it was hoped that he might remain in place only so long as to complete the 1918 volume on which he was currently working. With regard to Col. Daniel, it was difficult to justify his retention beyond that summer.[50] Whether the government's concern was entirely for their age and health is not clear. However, the fact that Daniel was asked to submit an appreciation on the value of the Official Histories to the Treasury is perhaps an indication of the government's real concern. Once more the issue arose as to whether the operation should be transferred to private enterprise or postponed until suitable replacements for Edmonds and Daniel could be found. In his submission to the Treasury, Daniel reprised a number of the arguments which had been raised when the future of the Official History process had previously been called into question in 1919 and 1922. With regard to transferring the project to private enterprise, the experience of the previous 20 years had taught that only an accredited historian with a military background would be able to communicate directly with political leaders, senior officers and other participants. To postpone the work would mean the loss of valuable personal recollections and the abandonment of the government's duty to provide its confidential information to the public and to professional officers for the purposes of education. Official History volumes had been regularly set in army promotion examinations since 1927. Furthermore, to abandon the series with six Western Front volumes remaining, comprising three on 1917 from Arras to Cambrai and three on the last six months of the war, was to lose the opportunity to continue to refute the controversial and misleading mass of post-war literature. Daniel wrote that:

> it would be morally wrong to leave either the public or the services to such guidance; it is a matter of honour and common sense that the country's unprecedented efforts between 1914 and 1918 should be analysed and its effects made clear . . . It is the objective of the government to place before the public an absolutely reliable and impartial account of what occurred.[51]

Once again the government was persuaded both of the value of the Official Histories and of its moral obligation to produce them, and the process was allowed to continue. Daniel did retire in July 1939, but Edmonds continued to write and to direct the work of the Historical Section until it was concluded in 1948 with its publication of the final Western Front volume, *France and Belgium 1917*, Volume II: *Third Ypres*. (*Italy 1915–1919* was published in 1949.) Thus throughout its 33-year production of the series of Official Histories of the Great War, the Historical Section remained wedded to its three fundamental objectives: to produce a readable account for the general public of the military operations of that conflict, to provide a staff work of educational and instructive value to the professional soldier and to act as a reliable and impartial bulwark to the wave of literature that followed in the wake of the war. The degree to which these objectives were actually put into practice in the writing of four of the most important volumes of Official History is a different question, which will be considered in due course.

2

Sir James Edmonds

James Edward Edmonds was born in London in 1861. His family were from Fowey in Cornwall and could trace their ancestors back to Sir Thomas Edmonds, who had been French Secretary to Queen Elizabeth. As a boy Edmonds attended King's College School at Somerset House in the Strand. He learnt no Latin or Greek but studied science and geology. According to Edmonds his father taught him languages at the breakfast table and whilst still a schoolboy he became proficient in German, French, Italian and Russian.

At the age of eight Edmonds was taken to Paris and watched Napoleon III drive along the Rue de Rivoli. He returned two years later a few months after the end of the Franco-Prussian War. Having read of the bombardment of Paris and the fall of the Arc de Triomphe, he was struck by the sight of the great arch still intact and later claimed that his faith in the accuracy of war correspondents was thereafter shaken for life.[1] It was on this trip too that an event occurred which was perhaps decisive in determining Edmonds' eventual career in the army. At that time the Germans continued to occupy Amiens and, according to Edmonds, were 'strutting about with oak leaves round their helmets'. A Bavarian captain approached Edmonds and his father and asked if they were English. When his father replied that they were, the German said, 'Ve have beat de Franzman; you vil be de next.' According to Edmonds, his father was so impressed by the seriousness of this threat that he made sure both his sons spoke German and, as the sabre-rattling increased, determined to put both of them in the army.[2]

Edmonds was urged by his schoolmasters to study mathematics at Cambridge. However, when a friend of his passed third into the Royal Military Academy at Woolwich, Edmonds' father encouraged him to see if he could do better. In July 1879 he sat the examination and passed, obtaining first place in the process. Two years later, at his passing out examination, Edmonds once again achieved the highest marks of his year and was awarded the Pollock Gold Medal for distinguished proficiency

1. Edmonds (seated, second left) with Chatham colleagues, *c*. 1880/81.

as well as prizes for mathematics and mechanics, fortification and geometric drawing, military history, drills and exercises, and exemplary conduct. In passing out, this model pupil was singled out for praise by the then Commander-in-Chief, the Duke of Cambridge. With his mathematical mind and interest in science, mechanics and fortifications, Edmonds chose to join the Royal Engineers and on 26 July 1881 was given his commission as a lieutenant to the corps and was posted to their Brompton Barracks at Chatham.[3]

Edmonds clearly possessed a remarkable intellect and at Staff College 15 years later continued to achieve significantly higher marks than all of his peers, who then included some very notable individuals, two of whom went on to become field marshals and 16 of whom later became generals. Indeed, it was whilst at Staff College that Edmonds acquired from his peers the nickname 'Archimedes' which was to remain with him for the rest of his life. Edmonds himself, however, was never to achieve senior command in the army but instead progressed through the then embryonic field of military intelligence to divisional and ultimately army staff work. One might speculate on the potential loss to the army's higher command that one who was to surpass Haig, Allenby and Macdonough at Camberley should be consigned to an administrative role in the British army. However, there is more to high command than intellectual superiority. For one thing, when Edmonds was finally tested in combat at the beginning of the war he was unable to cope well with the physical strain, as will be seen later. For another, Edmonds lacked the necessary ambition required to secure a senior post in a relatively small Victorian army which took, in his case, over eight years to promote a newly commissioned lieutenant to the rank of captain. As Edmonds wrote to Swinton in 1934:

> you have ambitions and feel the ups and downs of life. I like things as they come and expect neither reward nor punishment; I function without fear of failure or hope of reward.[4]

In any case, the British army of the Victorian period, as Gerard DeGroot has pointed out, mirrored the stratified society of which it was a product:

> Technically-minded middle-class individuals who might have aided the Army's modernization either did not join or were not given much encouragement when they did. With individuality and imagination suppressed and cleverness deemed suspect, the institution remained safe and supreme.[5]

Indeed, Edmonds' only command came at the age of 24 when, following four years at Chatham and a year in Malta training on submarine mining, he was sent with two companies of engineers to garrison an undefended Hong Kong. On receiving the orders to go following Russian aggressive posturing in the Far East, the company commander reported sick and the subaltern claimed that his wife was expecting a child, so Edmonds was given command of the 50 men. His time in Hong Kong passed without incident and in 1888 Edmonds returned to Chatham after spending some time in Japan, America and Canada. At Chatham Edmonds was posted to the 38th Mining Company and was appointed Assistant Instructor in mining and electricity. The main duty of the Assistant Instructor, as Edmonds wrily recorded later, was to partner the Chief Instructor in a game of golf in the afternoon.[6] In 1890, on his promotion to captain, Edmonds decided to return to the Academy at Woolwich as an instructor. Five years later he competed for a place at Staff College and passed, once again in first place. In that year 24 candidates were admitted to Camberley by competition, or in other words by passing the examination; a further eight, who had failed it, were admitted by nomination. In that latter category in 1895 was the 34-year-old cavalry officer, Douglas Haig.

II

When Duff Cooper was writing his biography of Haig in 1935 he wrote to the War Office enquiring into the details of Haig's entry to Camberley. According to Edmonds, who was asked for information at the time, Haig had never let on to fellow students that he had failed the examination. His story was that he had qualified in 1894 but, for private reasons, had asked for a nomination in 1895 to join the college in January 1896. The War Office records in fact revealed that Captain D. Haig of 7th Hussars competed at the Staff College entrance examination in 1893 but failed to qualify as he only obtained 182 marks (instead of the required minimum of 200) out of 400 in mathematics, which was an obligatory subject. At that time Staff College regulations allowed for vacancies arising from insufficient officers competing or qualifying to be filled by nominations of the Commander-in-Chief. To be eligible for nomination vacancies, officers were nevertheless required to have obtained at least three-eighths of the marks allotted to each obligatory subject. In the case of Haig's mathematics examination this 'pass' mark for nomination eligibility was therefore 150. However, Haig had sat the examination in 1893 and eligibility for acceptance by nomination was supposed to allow candidates to gain their place only if vacancies arose in the following year. According to the War Office, it appeared that in allowing Haig's eligibility for nomination to be carried forward until a vacancy arose in 1896 the Commander-in-Chief made 'an exception [to this rule] in his favour'.[7] In taking his place in January 1896, Haig became an exact contemporary of Edmonds.

Edmonds' involvement with Haig at Staff College offers an insight into their subsequent relationship in later life, both when Edmonds served on Haig's staff during the war and, more importantly, when he came to write about Haig in his Official Histories. For one thing, Edmonds always retained a sense of superiority over those he believed to be less than his intellectual equals, of which he no doubt numbered Haig as one. In his memoirs, which he wrote late in life but never published, Edmonds recalled that none of his colleagues at Camberley, with the exception of George Macdonough, could master the mental gymnastics of some of the more intellectual pursuits, such as cipher decoding. He related how he was often assigned to work with Haig because he, Edmonds, was seen as a man of detail whereas Haig was considered to take too general a view. One might argue of course that the former traits well suited a staff officer and the latter one charged with command. Generally, though, Edmonds found Haig to be 'terribly slow on the uptake' and on one occasion, when Haig had asked whether he could ride with Edmonds on an exercise, Edmonds had ended up abandoning Haig as he 'could not afford to be handicapped' by his lack of progress.[8] One should be slightly wary that as the authority for these assertions was Edmonds himself they might be somewhat prone to exaggeration. However, on academic results Edmonds clearly was a more successful student than Haig. Moreover, Edmonds' experience of Haig at Staff College certainly underpinned his subsequent private statements to Liddell Hart about Haig's lack of intellectual clarity.[9] This knowledge no doubt also informed Edmonds' public pronouncements on Haig when he came to write about him in his official works.

Secondly, Edmonds began a tentative personal acquaintance with Haig at Camberley which was to develop during the war when he served on Haig's staff but particularly after the war when he began to write his Official Histories. The evidence for the depth of this relationship is largely one-sided as it comes from Edmonds' writings rather than Haig's. However, if one reads between the lines it is possible to discern a more accurate picture of the nature of their friendship than that apparent from Edmonds' words alone. Initially Edmonds, along with most of the others students, did not get on well with Haig whom they found 'abrupt and unsympathetic'.[10] Writing in his memoirs, Edmonds recorded that his fellow students were a cheery lot, with the exception of Haig who 'worked harder than everyone else, was seldom seen in the mess except for meals, kept himself to himself and had only one intimate, Arthur Blair KOSB'.[11] Colleagues of Haig's at Sandhurst had found him similarly taciturn and aloof and single-mindedly ambitious to the exclusion of all other activities.[12] Furthermore, again according to Edmonds, Haig outraged the feelings of his colleagues when he wrote in the Leave Book on his arrival at Camberley a request for three days' leave to 'shoot with the Prince of Wales'.[13]

25

Edmonds' decision to leave Haig behind on exercises, already referred to, did nothing to improve their relationship. Edmonds admitted that 'relations were strained for a time thereafter'.[14] According to Edmonds, matters were not improved by what happened when their paths again crossed some years later in 1912. Haig was then Commander-in-Chief at Aldershot and Edmonds GSO1 in 4th Division under General Snow. Haig's corps took part in manoeuvres against a corps of 4th and 3rd Division commanded by General Grierson and was defeated, although not perhaps as decisively as Edmonds later portrayed in his memoirs.[15] It is perhaps unlikely that Haig would have vented his frustration for such a defeat on a divisional staff officer with whom he was acquainted. However, if Edmonds is to be believed, Haig 'forgave' him sufficiently to appoint him to his staff at GHQ in 1915 where he remained for the rest of the war.[16] It was during the war that their friendship began to develop. Haig would ask Edmonds to dinner to 'talk of old times and forget the present'.[17] Again according to Edmonds, his long-standing acquaintance with Haig allowed him to tell the Commander-in-Chief many things about the feelings in the army and about 'events and personalities which hardly anyone else dared mention'.[18] However, this is slightly at variance with Edmonds' assertion elsewhere in his memoirs that he 'seldom made suggestions [to Haig] unless asked his views' as the responsibilities of the Commander-in-Chief were too great for an 'irresponsible critic without complete knowledge of all the factors'.[19] Edmonds recorded with some pride that Haig twice sent for him for advice and on one occasion, in March 1918, asked his Engineer-in-Chief, 'What does Edmonds think?'[20] So it would appear that, during the war, Haig appreciated Edmonds' company over dinner as a way of turning his mind from current preoccupations, that he was perhaps inclined to indulge in a little personal gossip but also that he only saw fit on two occasions from 1915 to 1918 to seek out Edmonds for professional military advice. This is not to understate Edmonds' role during the war, as clearly the Commander-in-Chief was not in the habit of soliciting the views of a wide range of relatively junior staff officers. However, it certainly tempers Edmonds' own assertion that he was an 'intimate' of Haig's during this time.[21]

It was also at Staff College that Edmonds took his first steps in his eventual career as an historian. A prolific reader of military strategy, he found his Staff College academic work sufficiently untaxing to write a history of the American Civil War. *The History of the Civil War in the United States 1861–1865* was eventually published in 1905 alongside a flurry of other works prompted by interest in the recently ended Russo-Japanese War. Written with his brother-in-law W. Birkbeck Wood, this work displayed many of the characteristics Edmonds later revealed as an historian in his official volumes. It was a work which, in the words of the *Times Literary Supplement* (*TLS*) reviewer, would attract both 'the soldier pure and simple and . . . the student of history'. It contained a mass of statistical information, was highly detailed (a feature which was criticised by the *TLS* reviewer, who considered Edmonds and Wood had attempted too much) and focused on the innovative aspects of the war, such as the use of cavalry, the battles of attrition and the ability to transform volunteers into disciplined soldiers. The book continued to sell for over 30 years. By 1936 it had been reprinted four times and was being used as a textbook at the US military academy at West Point.[22]

In 1899 Edmonds passed out of Camberley. He might have been one of the top pupils of his generation but it was Haig who, according to their instructor, Col. G.F.R. Henderson, would one day become Commander-in-Chief. Edmonds reminded Haig of this prophecy when Haig was appointed Commander-in-Chief at Aldershot in 1912, at which Haig scoffed that 'Henderson had been talking through his hat', and again in 1915, when the true meaning of the prophecy became reality.[23]

III

Within months of graduating from Camberley and ten days after the declaration of war against South Africa in October 1899, Edmonds was offered a job in the Intelligence Division. Between 1899 and 1910 Edmonds held a variety of intelligence posts, ultimately with the War Office as head of MO5, a subsection of the Directorate of Military Intelligence. He has rightly been credited with doing more than anyone else to establish the modern British secret service.[24] When Edmonds took over as head of the fledgling secret service in 1899, espionage and counter-espionage was very much in its infancy in Britain. For the next ten years this tiny department of the War Office employed no more than a handful of officers and agents and its work was characterised, to use the words of David French, by a spirit of 'amateur improvisation'.[25] Yet when Edmonds left it, he bequeathed his successors a security service, though at that stage not much larger, that was far more professional, tactically competent and strategically focused than anything hitherto. There has been some debate over the extent to which Edmonds fell prey to the exaggerated spy stories that swept Britain before the First World War fuelled by fears of invasion and the melodramatic scaremongering of writers like William Le Quex.[26] Edmonds was certainly taken in by these scare stories but, whether motivated by a false perception or not, his role in laying the foundations of the modern British secret service is not in doubt.

The Special Duties Section of the War Office, named Section H, of which Edmonds became head, was established in the early months of the South African War in 1899. It was responsible for cable censorship, surveillance of suspected persons, press correspondents and violations of the

Geneva Convention. Edmonds' staff consisted of one officer and a retired police detective and he had an annual budget of £200. As the war went on the section's functions extended to counter-intelligence and secret service work which involved sending a handful of officers to South Africa, one of whom was Baden-Powell, to study topography, communications and Boer troop movements. Messages and shipments of ammunition from Europe were also monitored by a temporarily established three-man section named Secret Section 13 (A).[27] When, in its first counter-espionage sting, the new secret service section intercepted some provocative Dutch correspondence to South Africa, it approached the captain of a well-known rugby team who offered to wreck the London offices of a particularly pro-Boer agent. According to Edmonds the offer had 'unfortunately' to be declined.[28]

At the end of the South African War, Sir William Nicholson, then Director-General of Mobilization and Military Intelligence, argued that the staff of Secret Section 13 (A) should be made permanent in order to 'train officers for intelligence work and [to] appoint and deal with our secret agents'. However, a committee of inquiry in 1903 chaired by Lord Hardwicke rejected this argument and concluded that these activities were needed *only in time of war*. As will be shown later, this was not the view taken by Britain's European neighbours and it was a principle which Edmonds was instrumental in overturning in due course. The officers were returned to their regiments and the activities of Section H, renamed Special Duties Section (MO3) in 1904, were allowed to die down.[29] Edmonds himself had been sent out to the Cape in 1900 as Lord Kitchener's escort and spent the next six years in a variety of intelligence postings in South Africa and the Far East.[30]

In 1906 Edmonds returned to head the Special Duties Section, MO3. Having seen its wartime activities disappear, the section was now chiefly involved in cryptography and the interception of telegraphic communications. Edmonds' predecessor, Colonel James Trotter, had devoted all his efforts towards producing a new secret code for the War Office and was committed to training new officers in the use of ciphers and code-breaking. Edmonds remained as head of MO3, which in 1907 became MO5, until 1910. In his memoirs he chose to emphasise his section's involvement in secret service and particularly counter-espionage work and tended to ignore his work in both intelligence gathering and cryptography. However, in both these areas Edmonds' work was of lasting value to Britain's intelligence capabilities.[31]

One of Edmonds' first tasks after his arrival was to devise a new code, called Double Playfair, for communication with the Japanese and for use by British forces in the field. He also assembled a list of experts in deciphering, and implemented the training of junior officers in cipher techniques in order to build up a reserve of potential intelligence officers in the event of a subsequent war.[32] In respect of intelligence gathering, as distinct from counter-intelligence, Edmonds was equally proactive. He set about putting British foreign intelligence on a comparable footing to that of its continental neighbours, France and Germany, which had been developing intelligence and counter-intelligence techniques and quietly gathering information about each other since before the Franco-Prussian war.[33] Edmonds recognised early on that the next war would require a very different intelligence approach from the last one. In 1908 he presented a lecture on tactical intelligence in which he contrasted the duties of a field officer in a small war with those of his counterparts in a European conflict. A European war, he argued, would require 'far greater vigilance, far closer watching of the enemy, far greater secrecy than [war] against the foes we have been accustomed to meet'. Once Britain had entered into a war against Germany, field officers would find it far harder to collect topographical information. By contrast with Britain's recent colonial wars, where this information could be gathered once a conflict had begun, a potential European war would require intelligence officers to gather information *in advance* during peacetime. Edmonds highlighted the lessons of the recent Russo-Japanese War where the Japanese superior tactical intelligence system with agents operating covertly in Russia before the war had been a significant factor in their success. Edmonds was convinced that clandestine intelligence operations in the field were vital to obtaining valuable tactical intelligence *before* the outbreak of a future war with Germany.[34]

In practice, though, Edmonds' attempts to realise these intelligence aims met with only limited success. This was no doubt a result of the limited personnel resources at his disposal but also due to the lack of experience of such matters which existed in the War Office at this time. Initially Edmonds attempted to recruit agents in Germany by asking friends of his who were visiting the country to enquire at local police stations for names of British residents on the pretext of finding witnesses for signatures for legal documents. This not surprisingly met with limited success and in any case, as the War Office acknowledged, there were too few British residents in Germany to expect to recruit any to work as secret agents.[35] In a further attempt, the managing director of Courage brewers was asked to put pressure on his representative in Hamburg to obtain information on naval matters and harbour works. However, the War Office subsequently came to realise that the representative was inventing information in order to satisfy his employer.[36]

It was in the area of counter-intelligence, however, where, judging by the space devoted to it in his memoirs, Edmonds concentrated most of his intelligence efforts. It was certainly true that it was in this field that he was most successful in changing the nature of Britain's security service, although the basis for his determination to achieve change may have rested on spurious and misplaced concerns. The worsening of Anglo-German relations in the early years of the new century provided a ready audience for the increasingly widespread stories of invasion threats and a network of German spies active on British soil. Chief amongst the campaigners against these generally imaginary invaders and spies was William Le Quex, who also happened to be a friend of Edmonds. Whilst there were undoubtedly some part-time German agents who attempted to feed back information from ports and dockyards, there was no coordinated network of German agents operating in Britain before the war. Faced with the prospect of war on two fronts, the German intelligence effort was concentrated almost exclusively on France and Russia. Gustav Steinhauer, the German naval intelligence officer responsible for pre-war espionage in Britain, ran an inefficient network, in Christopher Andrew's words, of 'poorly paid and clumsy part time agents'.[37] Le Quex however was convinced that the country was full of German spies who were working to lay the ground for a German invasion of the east coast. His book, *Invasion of 1910*, was written in collaboration with Lord Roberts, who saw it as a way of popularising his ideas for national service, and was serialised by Lord Northcliffe in the *Daily Mail* (after Le Quex had been instructed to amend the supposed invasion route to pass through major towns rather than the original small villages for maximum impact).[38] It subsequently appeared in 17 languages and sold over one million copies. In May 1907, the *Morning Post* carried a story that 90,000 German reservists and spies were resident in Britain and that a store of arms was held for them in every major city.

Such scare stories fuelled an invasion frenzy, which was further exacerbated in 1908 by the news that Germany was stepping up its dreadnought-building programme. Under pressure from a mounting press campaign led by Leo Maxse and supported by Lord Roberts and some of the Tory leadership, the government established a CID subcommittee in late 1907 to consider the threat of invasion. This subcommittee met 16 times between November 1907 and July 1908 before completing its report in October. Its conclusions were to demolish most of the invasion fears and to show that a surprise attack launched against the coast of Britain would be impossible. However, in the course of its deliberations Maj.-Gen. Ewart, Director of Military Operations, was forced to concede that the existing counter-intelligence machinery was far from effective and in 1908 he implemented a review to consider re-establishing a secret service bureau. A War Office memorandum prepared for Ewart in October 1908 recommended a new Official Secrets Act to allow arrest and search without warrant, the registration of aliens, the use of paid agents in Britain to identify foreign spies and, emulating the German system in existence since 1866, a police or private detective under direction of an intelligence officer to recruit and operate agents abroad. It concluded that unless a secret service system was prepared Britain would 'enter on a war fatally handicapped' and ominously warned that there was 'no doubt whatever that the same careful preparations which were made in France [by German agents] before [the Franco-Prussian War were] now being made in Eastern districts of England'.[39]

Edmonds was already suspicious of German activity in Britain as a number of his German friends had informed him that they had been approached by the German Admiralty to report on the movement of warships, work in dockyards and arsenals, and the building of aircraft and munitions factories. He claimed that he had actually recognised a German artillery captain who was working as the head waiter at the Burlington Hotel in Dover and that after Edmonds had spoken to him he had disappeared for good. In early 1909 Le Quex published a new book, *Spies of the Kaiser*, whose main theme was that London and the east coast were swarming with German barbers, waiters and tourists who were all employed as spies. Shortly after its publication, F.T. Jane, founder of Jane's defence journals and another friend of Edmonds', kidnapped a Portsmouth German and deposited him in the Duke of Bedford's animal park at Woburn to raise public awareness. Both of these elicited dozens of letters about suspicious German activity, such as early morning drives, curiosity about railway bridges, and enquiries about gas and water supplies, which were all handed over to Edmonds. He began classifying all German visitors to Britain in terms of those who were staying close to important engineering structures, those who regularly entertained parties of visiting countrymen, or tradesmen and photographers permanently established in dockyards and ports. Edmonds even claimed to have uncovered a German acting as a paymaster.[40]

Haldane, Secretary of State for War, and the Committee of Imperial Defence initially refused to accept that a network of German spies existed. Few in government seriously believed that Germany would attempt an invasion of the British Isles in a future war. Moltke himself had publicly stated that Germany might be able to land an invasion force but did not have the means to supply it or to extract it. Edmonds subsequently claimed in his memoirs that he also did not seriously believe that the Germans were capable of invading Britain but his contention had been that German espionage was designed, in addition to learning about the British Navy, to foster a *fear* of invasion, thereby frightening the government from sending troops out of England. He believed that a number of invasion schemes had been deliberately planted on agents so as to be discovered precisely for that purpose. However, this contention sounds rather too wise after the event, for it does not tally with what he told Captain Vernon Kell, the future head of MI5, in February 1909:

Day in day out the ceaseless work of getting information and throwing dust in the eyes of others goes on and the final result of it all as far as we are concerned is this: that a German general landing a force in East Anglia would know more about the country than any British general, more about any British town than its own British Mayor and would have his information so methodically arranged that he could, in a few minutes, give you any answer to any question you asked him about any town village or position in that area.[41]

Eventually, however, in early 1909, Haldane began to become persuaded of the German spy menace and set up a CID subcommittee to consider the 'nature and extent of foreign espionage that [was] taking place' within Britain.

By the time Edmonds was called upon to give evidence to this committee he appears to have been completely taken in by the Le Quex fantasy world of extensive German spy networks. Edmonds told the committee of the rapid rise in cases of alleged German espionage since late 1907. In 1908, 47 cases had been reported, and 24 had been reported in the first three months of 1909 alone. None of these cases, however, had come from the police but had all been reported by private individuals, almost all of which had been furnished to Edmonds by Le Quex. Half of these reported cases related to alleged reconnaissance work by Germans but in half of these cases the suspicious persons had not even been identified as German but were merely referred to as foreigners. Furthermore, much of the alleged reconnaissance had related to improbable military targets, such as reservoirs, railways, dykes and rivers. One of the reports had come from Le Quex himself who had nearly knocked down a cyclist who had been making notes on a map on a quiet country lane near the south coast and who had sworn at him in German! The other 12 cases related to suspicious activities and again included one reported case from Le Quex of a German barber in Southsea who was discovered to wear a wig over his normal thick head of hair and who showed much interest in naval gossip! From such flimsy evidence Edmonds inferred the existence of an extensive network of German spies. It seems he was already predisposed from his own circumstantial experience to accept this evidence without question or even the faintest degree of scepticism. Lord Esher, who was a member of the CID subcommittee, was unimpressed and described Edmonds as a 'silly witness from the War Office [who saw] rats . . . everywhere – behind every arras'. Nevertheless, Haldane had now become convinced along with Edmonds of an extensive network of German spies aimed at sabotage and invasion.[42] Whether their belief rested on naïve and fraudulent foundations or not is perhaps not as important as the fact that neither was wrong in recognising that the current intelligence apparatus was ill equipped either to determine the extent of German espionage or to do anything to counter it.

The conclusions of the subcommittee were published in April 1909. Its recommendations were that a secret service bureau should be established:

(a) To serve as a screen between the Admiralty and War Office and foreign spies who may have information they wish to sell to the Government.

(b) To send agents to various parts of Great Britain . . . with a view to ascertaining the nature and scope of foreign espionage that is being carried on by foreign agents.

(c) To act as an intermediate agent between the Admiralty and the War Office and a permanent foreign agent who should be established abroad with the view of obtaining information in foreign countries.[43]

In addition, it recommended that two ex-naval and military officers should be appointed to the bureau and that a member of the detective force should be attached to every important naval base in the United Kingdom. It envisaged the cost of establishing such a bureau to be in the region of £2,150.[44] In August 1909 the new bureau was set up within MO5. Edmonds appointed as its head his former right-hand man from Far East intelligence, Captain Vernon Kell, who began work in a small office on the first floor of the War Office assisted by a single clerk. Alongside the establishment of the secret service bureau, the government simultaneously introduced a system of controls to monitor and limit the freedom and movement of aliens and tightened the 1899 Official Secrets Act to give the police increased powers against spies. Having compared the legal powers used in states throughout Europe to control potential espionage, which were far more advanced and draconian than anything employed hitherto in Britain, Scotland Yard was given increased powers of arrest and search. Securing prosecution now relied only on evidence of suspicious activity; the onus of proof fell on the accused to demonstrate that he was not guilty.[45] On the declaration of war in 1914 all bar one of those identified by Edmonds and Kell as German agents were seized.

By the time Edmonds left MO5 in 1910 he had presided over an important transformation in Britain's military intelligence capability. He had been responsible for developing the embryonic secret service section from a piecemeal, ill-resourced and ill-coordinated handful of temporary, part-time, amateur field agents into the beginnings of a modern and effective intelligence-gathering and counter-intelligence organisation. He may have accepted too unquestioningly the fantastic claims of William Le Quex and exaggerated the nature and extent of the threat posed by German espionage in Britain but in so doing he bequeathed to Britain the foundations of what, within a few years, was to become what we know today as MI5 and MI6.

IV

By 1910 Edmonds had been in military intelligence for seven years and was anxious for an 'outside job'. He was prompted in his desire for a move by the appointment that year of Henry Wilson as Director of Military Operations and Intelligence. In his memoirs Edmonds claimed that he had clashed with Wilson over the value of teaching languages to officers when the latter had been head of the Directorate of Staff Duties. Edmonds, a strong advocate of the importance of knowledge of foreign languages, had been informed by Wilson that there was no reason for any officer to know any language other than his own and Wilson proudly boasted that he yielded to no one in his ignorance of French.[46] This seems improbable since Wilson spoke excellent French and must clearly have recognised the value of being able to communicate in it.[47] It is more likely that this is evidence of Wilson's sense of humour and that he was pulling Edmonds' leg. In any case, Edmonds held a low opinion of Wilson and this coloured his judgement of him when he came in his memoirs to describe the actions of GHQ during the retreat in August and September 1914.

Edmonds viewed Wilson as uneducated and ambitious, lacking in military judgement and a man who, having failed Woolwich and Sandhurst, entered the army through the 'back door of the Irish militia'. Indeed, on Wilson's appointment as DMO, Edmonds was advised by a fellow Royal Engineer, Sir William Nicholson, then Chief of the Imperial General Staff, to find another post as Wilson was 'not a man in whose hands any gentleman should leave his character'. The CIGS offered Edmonds the post of Commandant of the School of Military Engineering at Chatham or of GSO1 with 4th Division. Edmonds decided he would prefer a divisional staff post despite the advice of General Sir Herbert Miles, then QMG with 4th Division, who told him that if he wanted to get on in the army he should not go near troops. Edmonds' decision was to prove fortunate for his subsequent career as a military historian for, as he later admitted, he could not have written the Official History of the war had he not experienced the fighting at divisional level.[48]

This is a very interesting observation and one that is important in judging the relevance of Edmonds' personal experience in adding to his success as an historian. The selection criteria for historians for the official volumes have already been considered. It has been seen, and will be shown when considering the Gallipoli campaign, that participants were better able than those who had not participated to understand the nature

34

of the fighting from the available first-hand evidence. An important question then, if one is to select historians who have participated at first hand, is from what position they are best placed to have witnessed the events of which they are to write. It must be recognised that the First World War was unlike any previous conflict and therefore could not be written about accurately in the same way. Its actions involved the mobilisations of vast armies and support and communications infrastructures. The success of its battles and campaigns came to rely increasingly on integrated and sophisticated weapons systems and large-scale, carefully orchestrated troop and armament movements rather than, as previously, on the heroism and drive of local commanders supported by dashing and well-timed cavalry actions. In short, as Hew Strachan has suggested, 'the skills demanded in the leadership of mass armies in an industrialised age were more managerial than heroic'.[49] There can be no better perspective from which to judge this leadership and to understand what shaped and influenced the successes and failures of these mass armies than as a staff officer at divisional or army level. From this perspective, a participant could witness the integration of arms and troops, the logistical management of these vast forces, the qualities or failings of the commander and the performance of the men amidst the inevitable fog of war.

Many of the eventual official historians, including Edmonds, Aspinall and Falls, had been divisional or army staff officers and their writings were both better informed and, perhaps equally significantly, more dispassionate as a result. By contrast, the historical writings of those who had participated at more junior level tended to ignore the new order of mass mobilisation and mechanisation and concentrate instead on the old principles of command based on the personal will and example of the commander. This image of command was reinforced by their experience of warfare at platoon or company level. Liddell Hart, who ended the war as a company commander in the King's Own Yorkshire Light Infantry, was one such. His view of command tended to 'confirm the heroic model, not moderate it'.[50] By this view, Liddell Hart subsequently judged Haig wanting, in persisting with wasteful advances of attrition and in failing to create a war of movement and breakthrough as had Allenby or Lawrence. It is interesting, though, that this is not the view which Liddell Hart had originally come to on the basis of his own personal experience of warfare at company level. Liddell Hart's initial judgements on Haig, and indeed warfare, were quite different. From his hospital bed in September 1916 after being gassed at the Somme, Liddell Hart wrote:

Never has any military operation been so wonderfully and minutely organised or so brilliantly executed as [the Somme] offensive. The chief credit for this must go to Sir Douglas Haig who worked through all the winter and spring with his genius for efficiency, organising the resources of the army, making it an homogenous force, selecting and appointing young and efficient men quick to understand and practise the science of siege warfare as generals and staff officers. Every branch and department was overhauled and worked up to the highest pitch of efficiency until finally at the outset of the offensive Sir Douglas Haig, *the greatest general Britain has ever owned*, had created the finest fighting machine the world has ever known.[51]

Of the fighting itself, Liddell Hart wrote that war

has an awe-inspiring grandeur all its own, and it ennobles and brings out the highest in a man's character such as no other thing could . . . it is the finest forge of character and manliness ever invented when taken in small doses. The unfortunate thing is that this war has become an overdose. Still with all its faults and horrors it is above all a man's life in the fullest and deepest sense of the term.[52]

It is worth bearing both of these observations in mind when considering Liddell Hart's subsequent criticism of Edmonds' supposedly less than impartial perspective on both Haig and the fighting on the Somme.

Edmonds joined the staff of 4th Division on 1 March 1911. (He took three months' leave before taking up the post during which time he translated French and Russian treatises on the role of engineers in battle!) During the three years leading up to the outbreak of war, 4th Division were regularly involved in practising manoeuvres, including the full corps manoeuvres in 1912 already referred to in which 4th and 3rd Division defeated Haig's I Corps. Snow and Edmonds made a particular point of practising retreat manoeuvres despite the fact that to practise retreats was expressly prohibited by the War Office. This was to serve 4th Division well when it became involved in actual conflict.

When in August 1914 his troops were called upon to fight, Edmonds felt they were ready. He did fear however that they were woefully ill equipped in the essentials which he had seen employed to such good effect by the German army in their manoeuvres in 1908, such as machine-guns, light-ball pistols, trench mortars, and in other vital support equipment, such as ambulances, artillery telephones and mobile kitchens. At the outbreak of war Edmonds' division was stationed in Great Yarmouth and its first task was to clear the beach at Lowestoft of holidaymakers on report of a German transport fleet heading under escort for the East Anglian coast. While looking over the golf course for suitable battery positions, General Snow was just missed by a golf ball struck by a ladies' foursome. Furious, Snow approached the young women and informed them that the Germans were expected to land that very afternoon, adding 'Do you know what rape is?' Upon this the women gripped their 'long skirts and scuttled home'.[53]

By 23 August 4th Division had arrived at Le Havre and by 24 August was pitched straight into action supporting the retreating corps of Haig (I Corps) and Smith-Dorrien (II Corps) around Le Cateau. The division was ordered to secure the high ground south of Solesmes to assist II Corps in its retirement and then to move back on to Smith-Dorrien's left in the Le Cateau position. Heavy fighting was encounted by 4th Division and by the evening of 25 August, following a violent thunderstorm, they were only just arriving soaked, exhausted and starving at Le Cateau.[54] It was on the night of 25 August that Smith-Dorrien was forced to take his momentous decision, against his orders from Sir John French, to stand and fight. Smith-Dorrien had been informed at 2 a.m. by Allenby, whose cavalry was covering II Corps' flank, that the Germans were so close that unless he moved immediately he would be forced to engage in battle the following morning. To fight was contrary to Smith-Dorrien's orders from GHQ, which were to continue to retreat the following morning. To move immediately was impossible because men were still arriving and the roads behind were clogged with transport and refugees and had been turned into impassable quagmires by the storms. Unable to contact GHQ because no telephone line existed, Smith-Dorrien took the decision himself to engage in battle with the German forces opposite him, despite the fact that they outnumbered his forces by two and a half to one and despite the fact that this was contrary to the orders which he had been given.[55]

The decision, when it was communicated to GHQ, caused considerable consternation, particularly as Haig's I Corps was no longer supporting II Corps on the right. French felt that Smith-Dorrien's decision could jeopardise the entire BEF. He instructed Wilson to communicate to Smith-Dorrien that he was to retreat as soon as possible, for to remain was to risk another Sudan. Wilson managed to get through to Smith-Dorrien at 6.45 a.m. but Smith-Dorrien told him emphatically that he could not break away as the German guns were within earshot and that he was confident of delivering a crushing blow and slipping away at night. In response Wilson wished him luck and added that his was the first cheery voice he had heard for three days.[56] Interestingly Edmonds ignored this part of the communication when he related this episode in his memoirs. Instead of referring to the gloomy despondency into which Sir John French had been slipping over the previous two days (he had telegraphed Kitchener on 24 August to urge action to defend Le Havre), Edmonds chose to claim that it was Wilson who was gloomily forecasting disaster. He claimed too that it was Wilson who did everything to get Smith-Dorrien to change his mind when in fact Wilson had been acting on instructions from French and, despite this, had cheerfully accepted Smith-Dorrien's decision to fight.[57]

Snow and Edmonds, having practised retreat manoeuvres during peacetime, were also quite confident that they could extricate their division if necessary. Snow was of the opinion that they might never 'have such a good shooting match' again and did not, therefore, want to squander the opportunity.[58] They both therefore supported Smith-Dorrien's decision to fight. For Edmonds the subsequent two weeks were to be his only front-line, indeed only divisional, participation in the war; after the exhaustion and trauma of those 14 days he was unable to take any further similar active role again.[59]

The anniversary of the Battle of Crecy fell on 26 August, which, like that day in 1346, opened misty, damp and warm. Machine-gun fire began at 6 a.m. and, when riding with Snow shortly afterwards, Edmonds was nearly struck by shrapnel fire passing close above them. At 11 a.m. Noel Birch, commanding the Horse Artillery of Cavalry Division and a friend of Edmonds' from Camberley, rode up to inform Edmonds that they were 'for it' and should save the horses and artillery. At midday, with French believing his troops to be completely surrounded and the Germans to be in Amiens, GHQ fled from St Quentin 35 miles away to Noyon. Incredibly, they left without notifying II Corps of their move and it was only when Smith-Dorrien arrived in St Quentin to report later that night that he learnt of their new location. Throughout the day, on their 13-mile front from Le Cateau to Esnes, with 4th Division on the left, 3rd Division in the centre and 5th Division on the right, II Corps subjected an enemy more than twice its strength to a ferocious attack. Whilst its own casualties were heavy, at 8,000, II Corps inflicted losses on the Germans out of all proportion to its own and for the second time in four days succeeded in holding up the entire German army for a day. It then managed to slip away in broad daylight. Von Kluck, Commander of the German First Army, later admitted that he had been unable to outflank II Corps and that that failure had possibly cost Germany the war. As George Cassar has written, 'the stand of 4th Division and the II Corps in the delaying action at Le Cateau ranks as possibly the most brilliant exploit of the British Army during the whole of the war'.[60]

The night of 26/27 August was, according to Edmonds, the most miserable of his life. He was incredibly tired, hungry and thirsty, and it was raining. By Snow's order he was riding at the head of the column and was astride a tall, fidgety Irish horse. To check the route he had to haul his map from under his raincoat, put on his glasses and use his flashlight. If he had dismounted, which would have made the task considerably easier, he would have had trouble reaching the saddle again. His division stopped at midnight and men lay down where they were. They were up again and marching four hours later although there was still no sign of the enemy. The division continued like this for ten more days during which time Edmonds averaged no more than three hours of sleep per night. Food was running very low for everyone but Edmonds found that by the time he had finished his duties most of that left for the officers had been eaten by a large veterinary officer. Edmonds subsequently wrote that he did not believe that a man could be so tired and so hungry and still live. It must be remembered of course that in 1914 Edmonds was 53 years old and certainly not up to the rigours of campaigning without break in the field. However, he had been sustained by the feeling that he was merely repeating the previous manoeuvres they had practised in peace-time and by the expectation that the ordeal would soon end and the 'balloon would go up'. The order from GHQ, when it came on 5 September, to advance eastwards to attack was exactly what Edmonds and his comrades in 4th Division had been waiting for.

During the retreat a number of incidents occurred which served to reinforce Edmonds' low opinion of GHQ in general and of Henry Wilson in particular. On 28 August, Snow received a note from Wilson which Edmonds considered to be highly unworthy of a person of his position. 'Dear Snowball,' Wilson had written, 'throw overboard all your impedi-menta and trot along as fast as you can.' Apart from the irritating infor-mality and lack of detail of such an instruction, neither Snow nor Edmonds could see any reason for such panicked action. They neverthe-less conveyed to their brigadiers that they should burn or leave any super-fluous equipment. Edmonds wrily recorded later that one Irish battalion upon receiving this instruction had gleefully burnt their officers' kit. By the afternoon the formal order was then received that 'all ammunition on wagons not absolutely required and other impedimenta will be unloaded and officers and men carried to full capacity on all transport, both mechanical and horse'. Haig later told Edmonds that on receipt of the same message he had torn it up. Again, whilst there is evidence that Sir John French and his Chief of General Staff, Lt-Gen. Sir Archibald Murray, had descended into a state of mental defeat and despondency, it was somewhat inaccurate of Edmonds to single out Wilson for criticism in this respect. Wilson himself had written in his diary on 29 August that 'Sir John and Murray ought to be ashamed of themselves . . . Sir John has not once taken command.'[61]

In the same way the following episode which Edmonds related in his memoirs is of anecdotal interest and may well have been true of some at GHQ but once again Edmonds appears to have personalised the attack on Sir Henry Wilson. He related that when his division reached the vacated GHQ headquarters at Damartin on 3 September they found further evidence of panic and a hasty flight, with suitcases, tin boxes and papers lying on the pavements. An army car stood derelict and in the house used by GHQ for dinner the remains of an unfinished meal were left on the table. Edmonds was told that an ASC officer had brought a German prisoner into Damartin by car. The sight of a German was enough for GHQ, led by Wilson still holding a glass of wine in one hand and a plate of meat in the other, to 'tumble out of the chateau' at once. Despite the protestations of Macdonough, who shouted in vain that there was no German force within 30 miles, Wilson jumped into a car and ordered the driver to 'drive to Paris like hell'.[62]

The Battle of the Marne began on 6 September, and 4th Division now began to keep their war diary. They had been unable to do so during the retreat, and entries had to be written up subsequently. The same situation occurred during the retreat of March 1918, where entries were not only made later but often by officers who had not even been present. It was this first-hand experience in August 1914 which gave Edmonds a life-long distrust of war diaries and led him to rely solely on written orders and signal messages supported by the judiciously selected first-hand evidence of participants. On 9 September Snow was badly injured when his horse fell on him and shortly afterwards Edmonds broke down from the physical strain. He was transferred on medical advice to 'rest' at GHQ ten miles beyond the Marne at Fere en Tardenois.

Having spent two weeks during the retreat with very little sleep, Edmonds had then found that given the opportunity to sleep he could not do so. He suffered from severe aching in his jaw, could not concentrate when studying a map, and everything, according to Edmonds, seemed black or grey. He could remember every detail of that period precisely for the rest of his life but he experienced a curious sensation of *déjà vu* throughout the two-week period of the retreat as if, in his words, he had experienced the same ordeal in 'some earlier existence'. Edmonds, of course, was not alone in experiencing such curious, even supernatural, sensations during such a sustained period of severe mental stress and physical strain. He recorded how during the retreat there were constant rumours amongst the men of phantom columns marching in parallel to their own. The great length of the columns created sudden halts which would eventually clear with no apparent sign of any blockage, and this fuelled the sense that something 'out of the ordinary' was happening. It was eventually realised that these halts were caused by the artillery stopping to water their horses, and any modern motorway user will understand perfectly the phenomenon of being stopped by a blockage which has long since disappeared. Edmonds believed that these rumours of phantom columns eventually developed into the myth of the protecting Angel of Mons who followed alongside and guarded over the British troops as they retreated.

Recovering at GHQ, Edmonds was given light duties and was sent to assist Col. Swinton as an eye-witness charged with purveying information to the British public, since journalists had initially been banned from reporting directly on the action. Edmonds was sitting with Swinton one morning watching the infantry on the far side of the valley being shot at by machine-gun when Swinton said to him that 'something must be done to protect the naked bodies of our men'. Edmonds, remembering a picture he had seen in *Punch* of their 'Special Correspondent' careering over the battlefield in the Franco-Prussian War in a steel bathtub drawn by an armour-plated horse, made such a suggestion. Swinton told Edmonds not to be so frivolous and informed him that he had had an inspiration. Two weeks later Swinton presented his idea of a tank officially to the War Office.

By October 1914, GHQ was moved to new headquarters in St Omer. Having transferred to GHQ for a 'rest' Edmonds was eventually to serve out the rest of the war there, being finally appointed Deputy Engineer-in-Chief in 1918. In contrast to his first 14 days, the remaining four years of Edmonds' war service were uneventful. He chose to record relatively little of his personal experiences of that period in his memoirs. He had a few missions to the front line, was shot at a few times and, being billeted with Swinton and Lord Percy in the house next to the Commander-in-Chief in St Omer, he narrowly missed being blown up by a German bomb which destroyed the house opposite, killing its two civilian occupants. Edmonds found all at GHQ to be very sympathetic to his initial plight and when, in December 1915, Haig took over as Commander-in-Chief, Edmonds revelled in his association with old Staff College friends now in senior positions. The denizens of GHQ were, he believed, highly impressed by great personages such as Haig, Lawrence, Allenby and Macdonough addressing him casually as 'Archimedes'. 'I felt assured', Edmonds wrote, 'that I should not be sent home for age.' In March 1916 GHQ moved again, to Montreuil sur Mer. Life for Edmonds henceforth became 'very peaceful' and when he was not occupied in staff work he would bathe in the sea or search for wild flowers whilst touring the battlefields of Crecy and Agincourt.[63]

One might argue, as indeed David French has done, that the patronage extended to Edmonds in finding him a safe posting at GHQ when the stress of divisional staff work had overcome him would make him beholden to his friends and colleagues when he came to judge them in an official capacity. It was certainly the case as Edmonds wrote on a number of occasions that he did not want to be seen publicly to be 'crabbing' his contemporaries who were 'splendid fellows in a tight space'.[64] The extent to which this sense of duty and comradeship exercised any real influence on Edmonds' subsequent official writings will be considered in the next chapter. However, it is worth considering a point here with which we began. Edmonds was clearly the academic superior of Staff College colleagues like Haig, Allenby and Lawrence, and clearly was acutely conscious of the fact himself. However, these men went on to achieve far greater glory and recognition in the First World War than he did. Rather than assuming that he would naturally be predisposed to favour them in his historical treatment one might also consider whether such brotherly loyalty might not be somewhat tempered by a little professional jealousy at their success. Such a view would certainly put into context some of the remarks Edmonds subsequently made in private about Haig's intellect to Liddell Hart. However, if we are to believe Edmonds' own words already cited, written in 1934 long after the end of his military career, whilst others had ambition and felt the 'ups and downs of life', he took things as they came and expected neither 'reward nor punishment'.[65]

At the end of the war, Edmonds was mentioned in Haig's final despatch, as indeed he had been in French's first, possibly a unique achievement. His name, however, along with those of a few other officers who had incurred the dislike of Henry Wilson as CIGS, was cut out of the honours gazette. One might reasonably consider that this event could have had some influence on Edmonds' subsequent treatment of Wilson in his memoirs. Haig complained to the War Office on Edmonds' behalf but without success. Swinton had held the post of Director of the Historical Section before the outbreak of war but had no desire to return to it after the war and recommended Edmonds as his successor. Edmonds had the support of Haig and of Maurice Hankey, and on 1 February 1919 was duly appointed to the post which he was to occupy for another 29 years.

V

Edmonds' long career as the Director of the Historical Section and as an official historian lasting to the age of 87 is dealt with in the next chapter. On a personal level, Edmonds' life provides a fascinating biography of a time of great changes in our nation's history. He was born in the middle years of Queen Victoria's reign and when he died Queen Elizabeth II had been four years on the throne. He was brought up to regard the horse and bicycle as the only means of transport and yet by the end of his life had seen motor cars take over the nation's roads and satellites launched into space. Like many of his generation and class who lived through the momentous events of the First World War, Edmonds was born to that precious almost prelapsarian world as they saw it which disappeared before their very eyes amongst the brutal carnage of mechanised, industrial warfare. Edmonds saw the changes inflicted by the First World War in less cataclysmic terms. The memoirs he left to his grandchildren and great-grandchildren were certainly a 'story of the vanished world of yesterday' but he reflected this passing in more mundane everyday changes. 'If I had my choice', he wrote:

I would go back to age of 35 when we had acquired the bicycle and still had the horse but the motor car, aircraft and TV had not yet arrived. I should not like to start life in the present age of high prices . . . where men wear their hair long because it costs 1s 6d to have it cut . . . where a collar will not stand more than half a dozen washings . . . where shoe and pyjama strings are too short . . . where mustard does not make the eyes water and pepper does not make one sneeze.[66]

The fact that Edmonds chose to highlight these types of changes rather than any of the great political or social changes that took place during his life is indicative that, as he said, he took things as they came. Edmonds' experience of Flanders and the Great War, though arduous and no doubt traumatic, was not one of distress and disillusionment.[67] Edmonds was by nature a conservative. His education and military career allowed him to move in relatively exalted circles for someone of his middle-class back-ground.[68] He was, one might say, an archetypal establishment figure. How well such an establishment figure could write dispassionately and without bias of his military friends and colleagues amidst an atmosphere of public recrimination will be considered in the next chapter.

3

Edmonds' Method and Writing

Edmonds' first volume of Official History appeared in 1922 and was prefaced by the confident assurance that 'no deviation from the truth nor misrepresentation will be found in the official histories on which my name appeared'.[1] However, this assertion has been strongly challenged by a number of critics, both recent and contemporary. As a result of their endeavours the body of official work published between 1922 and 1948 has come to be almost universally regarded as at best a bland and sterile account of the military operations of the Great War and at worst a deliberately partial, misleading and self-justificatory account written in defence of the military establishment. John Keegan perpetuates the former view in his contention that:

> the compilers of the British Official History of the First World War have achieved the remarkable feat of writing an exhaustive account of one of the world's greatest tragedies without the display of any emotion at all.[2]

For a work whose purpose was as much to provide a readable account for the general public as to provide a Staff College textbook, this is a damning charge. Its validity will be considered in due course. However, the more serious and damaging criticism has come from those who dispute not merely the historical accuracy of the works but the good intentions of its authors. Sir Basil Liddell Hart, who was an ardent proponent of learning lessons from the conflict, claimed of Edmonds' volume on the March 1918 German offensive that it was not merely '"patriotic" history but parochial history'.[3] Norman Brook, one of Edmonds' own official historians, complained in 1945 that Edmonds could not be relied upon to revise the Somme volume because 'he ha[d] not been able in recent years to resist the temptation to introduce strong personal views into his historical work'.[4] These personal views have more recently been described by David French as a 'private purpose to conceal the truth about the high command in France from the lay public'. French has argued that Edmonds' official work became increasingly concerned with his own personal desire to counter claims by politicians and civilians that Haig in particular and the high command in general had shown incompetence in the face of crisis and wasted lives unnecessarily on futile offensives. Edmonds' work, like Victorian biographies, created heroes of his subjects and scrupulously avoided criticism of those of senior rank.[5] Travers has similarly accused Edmonds of avoiding direct criticism of his senior colleagues, of being obligated to Haig and thus overtly defensive of him in his narratives, and of manipulating facts and drawing false conclusions in three of his major works dealing with the Somme, Passchendaele and March 1918.

These charges must, however, be considered in the context both of the numerous constraints under which Edmonds operated and of the political climate in which he wrote. It has already been shown how the Historical Section's self-imposed terms of reference created a conflict for its writers in attempting to steer the difficult course between public interest, academic enlightenment, and military and political sensibilities. At the same time, those writers were placing confidential information in the public domain whilst attempting to protect the government and high command from what that information might reveal. Furthermore, an analysis of Edmonds' methods and intentions will reveal that he viewed the academic and indeed national importance of his work far more seriously than his critics would credit. This is an assessment which is borne out not merely by Edmonds' methods but by what he was actually able to publish. His works themselves stand as a measure both of Edmonds' genuine expertise as an academic historian and of his adherence to the principles under which the Official Histories were intended to be written. They contain within them sufficient evidence to challenge the critical view of Edmonds' writings, without recourse to explanations in mitigation. Indeed their conclusions and lessons drawn stand in comparison with the most recent academic views. This, and the following, chapter will consider the background against which Edmonds wrote, the various and often conflicting interests operating upon him and finally the historical and literary value of one of his completed works, *Military Operations: France and Belgium 1916*, Volume I: *Battle of the Somme*.

II

One cannot claim, as his critics have, that Edmonds' work was a travesty of historical writing without first considering its writing from an historical perspective. In judging Edmonds' work, one must recognise the numerous and quite serious constraints which acted upon him, both personally and professionally. One such was his position as both a soldier and

2. Edmonds (bottom row, second from right) with Staff College colleagues, including Allenby (second row from top, second from left) and Haig (third row from top, first from right), 1896.

a contemporary of Haig's. Like many officers schooled in the traditions of the Victorian army, Edmonds would have held a natural aversion to criticising publicly his superior officers. Indeed he was quite willing to accept Liddell Hart's charge of 'trade unionism' in his official writing, informing him in 1933 that he could not 'give away' people with whom he had lived and worked all his life. Edmonds admitted that although they were 'ignorant and did dishonest tricks [they] were good fellows in a tight place'.[6] Whilst Edmonds was keen to prove to the Committee for Control that he belonged to 'no party in the army', his list of friends would hardly suggest an independence of expression when it came to reflecting upon senior members of the military. He informed Daniel that his friends were 'such discordant elements as Haig and Allenby, Robertson and the late Henry Wilson, MacDonough, Smith-Dorrien, Archie Murray, Ian Hamilton in fact everyone of importance except the Lord Ypres, Lord Plumer and Lord Cavan'.[7] Edmonds confirmed on his appointment that he could be trusted to deal sensitively with issues of general strategy because all the Commanders-in-Chief, Haig, Allenby, Murray and Milne, were his personal friends. Daniel could therefore 'be sure that I shall try to see that justice is done to them'.[8]

It was undoubtedly the case that, when Edmonds began writing his Official Histories, Haig looked to him as a means of putting his case and that of his military colleagues before the uninformed public. At that time there was already a feeling amongst the military establishment that they had not been given due credit for having won the war. Popular revulsion at the high human cost of the struggle created for the British army in the inter-war period, in the words of Brian Bond, 'a depressing period more akin to the humiliation of defeat not victory'.[9] As Haig wrote in 1921 to J.H. Boraston, who was then in the process of completing *Haig's Command*, which was to be rushed to press ahead of the November 1922 election in the hope of damaging Lloyd George:

> There is a great need for enlightenment. Indeed the current esti-
> mate of the part played by the British Army in 1916–1918 is very
> incorrect and I hope your book will completely change it.[10]

One might divine from the specific dates cited that Haig's concerns were personal rather than general. Similarly, in another one of many deliberately unpublic complaints concerning his treatment by writers, Haig wrote to Edmonds in April 1927:

> It seems to me that so many inaccurate accounts have appeared of
> certain aspects of the war and the British Army has been criticised
> whilst the French is lauded to the skies that many of our country-
> men are inclined to speak apologetically of what our troops

accomplished. Really for the last 18 months of the struggle the British carried the Allies on their backs! So it seems to me time some reliable statement were made for the benefit of our countrymen at home and in the Dominions showing a little of what our Armies accomplished.[11]

Haig looked to Edmonds' official work as a means of providing just such a reliable statement.

Haig was certainly sent copies by Edmonds of all his draft volumes prior to publication, inviting comment and suggestions. One can conclude from the fact that so few drafts elicited any serious requests for amendment that Haig was generally satisfied with the content of Edmonds' official work. Haig pronounced Edmonds' Volume II on First Ypres 'very thorough' and confirmed that the German officers were 'pot-bellied beer swilling types' whom I Corps had beaten 'every time we met them'.[12] Commenting on Edmonds' next volume covering Loos, Haig pronounced it 'admirably written . . . a very true account'. He urged Edmonds not to 'cut it down in any way': 'Such an account will be invaluable for instructional purposes in the army as well as shewing [sic] the British public the price which *must* be paid for unpreparedness.'[13] Of course Haig was content to leave unchanged any frank appraisal of the 'terrible results of keeping the reserves too far back' and even added his own notes in support of what he termed his 'nightmare'-like recollections of this issue.[14] Haig placed particular importance on the way in which Edmonds was able to deal accurately and fully with events yet with tact and without recrimination. Returning the draft chapters on Neuve Chapelle, Haig congratulated Edmonds on the way in which he had told the story 'so accurately and yet without attaching blame to anyone'.[15] No doubt Edmonds found these comments of comfort, if not necessarily of any great assistance, for when Haig died in January 1928 Edmonds reported to the Historical Section that this would be a 'heavy loss' for his work.[16]

Whilst Haig's approval might have provided a measure of satisfaction to Edmonds, that is not to say that Haig had any great influence on the specific content of Edmonds' official writings. Privately, Edmonds was critical of Haig and it will be shown in due course that this criticism was at times quite openly incorporated into his official work. Whilst some critics have taken the fact that Edmonds and Haig were Staff College contemporaries to suggest a degree of comradeship, one can also see in this shared background some elements of Edmonds' poor opinion of Haig. Edmonds admitted in conversation with Liddell Hart that Haig had spent the first three days of examinations 'cribbing' from him.[17] He admitted to Liddell Hart in 1935 that Haig knew nothing of artillery matters and was dominated by a 'strong religious sense which made him feel he was called by God to lead the British Armies'.[18] During his writing of the first Somme volume, Edmonds informed Liddell Hart that: 'I have to write of Haig with my tongue in my cheek. One can't tell the truth. He really was above the average – or below the average – in stupidity.'[19]

What allowed Edmonds' private view of Haig to be expressed more openly in his official work was the fact that Haig had died in early 1928. It will be seen that Edmonds' volume on the Somme, published in 1933, was highly critical of the Commander-in-Chief. An illustration of this change in Edmonds' self-imposed restriction of expression was the treatment of an episode in his volume on the retreat from Mons. In his first edition of this volume published in 1922 Edmonds had, by his own admission to Liddell Hart, deliberately ignored the panic at Haig's II Corps. He had informed Liddell Hart: 'It was [Haig's] first test as a commander in war and he was rattled . . . He was standing on his doorstep, revolver in hand saying "We must sell our lives dearly."'[20] However, when Edmonds rewrote the revised edition which was published in 1933, he decided for the sake of historical accuracy that he should deal with this matter and added the observation that 'Haig momentarily lost his head'.[21]

III

One factor which did have some influence on the shape of Edmonds' work was the fact that the army faced real political dangers in the post-war period which might well have been aggravated by a frank exposition of military incompetence and weakness. Firstly, there remained after the unsatisfactory resolution of war by armistice and Versailles the possibility of future war with Germany in which Britain would again need to call civilians to arms in great numbers. In such circumstances it was important, as Maj.-Gen. Solly Flood wrote to Edmonds in October 1934, that revelations of mistakes did not play upon the 'minds of the uninformed public . . . which may be called upon in turn to undertake service on behalf of their King and Country'.[22] Secondly, after 1919 Britain faced a threat to its social and strategic stability on a number of fronts, a situation which would not be improved by questioning traditional institutions of authority such as the army. At home a large, demobilised civilian population facing a return to a country without work was prey to the strains of bolshevism spreading throughout Europe. In addition, Britain's imperial grandeur after 1918 with additional commitments in Mesopotamia, Palestine and Persia became through its overextension a source of great weakness and potential instability. Awareness of such overextension coming on top of a financially draining war fuelled an enhanced sense of national identity amongst Britain's dominion nations and an increasing wave of nationalism in India, Egypt and Ireland. Faced with such problems of strategic control, revelations of British military ineptitude and incompetence carried high political risks. The specific interventions of the War Office in certain passages in Edmonds' Somme volume are particularly illustrative of how seriously these matters were viewed by the authorities.

An already sensitive military establishment was galvanised into defence in 1933 in response to the publication of Lloyd George's *Memoirs*. In these volumes the former Prime Minister staunchly defended his reputation for having been responsible for victory in 1918 whilst denigrating the judgement and military competence of Haig and Robertson. The language of his account was subjective and highly critical. Haig was described as 'unequal to his task', ingenious in 'shifting blame to other shoulders than his own', 'preferring rather to gamble with men's lives than admit an error' and as having a mind like a primitive tank which 'only worked well when the objective was limited and within sight'.[23] Lloyd George was also strongly critical of Edmonds whom he accused of 'slovenly use of the documents at his disposal'. Of Edmonds' treatment of the German offensive in March 1918, for example, Lloyd George wrote:

> The Official History tries to persuade us that Haig was right in keeping his army as far away as possible from the area of impending battle. It seems to me a novel theory that the further reinforcements are away from the fight the more useful they are when they are needed.[24]

A number of former military participants urged Edmonds to use his Official History as a vehicle to respond to these charges. Maj.-Gen. Noel Birch, for example, wrote to Edmonds in 1938:

> After the vile attacks that have been made on Haig and his subordinates by people like Lloyd George, who only sat in a trench which was I think 10 miles from the front line, the world can see how disgracefully the British Army at that time and its leaders have been treated.[25]

Edmonds needed little prompting to take up the challenge on behalf of his colleagues and this reflected itself not just in private and personal attacks but in Edmonds' official work as well. Edmonds appeared to shape his Official History in direct response to Lloyd George's work, informing Liddell Hart in 1935 that 'what ammunition I will use will depend on what Ll.G says in his next volume'.[26] He also took every opportunity he could to defend himself and his colleagues in the press against all utterances of the former Prime Minister. An illustration of the levels to which this antipathy had risen is provided by Edmonds' letter to *The Times* in January 1939, in which he wrote:

> Mr Lloyd George's utterances are no longer perhaps a matter for serious comment. Certainly in a speech so [full] of contradictions and misstatements as that which he delivered last night it is impossible to refute his points one by one without devoting to it far more space than it deserves.[27]

In addition, Edmonds collected writings and comments which he used in further letters to service journals and the press. His papers contain a copy of a report by Frederick Palmer, an American war correspondent, comparing the straight, decisive look of Haig with the 'shifty look' of Lloyd George, and a note from an officer's diary of August 1915 in which a member of Lloyd George's Ammunition Committee had asked him whether 'we still used the round cannon ball'.[28] This last piece was used in a particularly vitriolic and defensive article by Edmonds published in the *Army, Navy and Air Force Gazette* in June 1933 entitled 'Mr Lloyd George and the Shell Shortage in 1914–1915'. In this article Edmonds accused Lloyd George of starving the War Office of armaments whilst he was Chancellor and of providing unreliable weapons and ammunition whilst Minister of Munitions. The main thrust of the piece, however, was to counter what Edmonds considered to be Lloyd George's attempts to manipulate the truth in his memoirs to produce a 'picture entirely favourable to himself and damning to the War Office and the Soldiers'.[29] Edmonds claimed that Lloyd George's facts could not be trusted because he had kept no diary during the war and 'has had to rely for his Memoirs on his memory and such reconstruction of the situation as his secretaries could manufacture for him'.[30] In a continuation of this theme, Edmonds recorded in his own memoirs that whereas:

> Mr Churchill commenting on Lord Macaulay's method of writing history said that this author left the room with the label 'Liar' pinned to his gentlemanly coat tails, in the Welshman's case it is not necessary to borrow the whole sentence.[31]

This display of personal bitterness inevitably spilt over into Edmonds' official work, and in his volume on the Somme the serious problems of faulty and insufficient ammunition made Lloyd George an easy target. The tone of Edmonds' condemnation of Lloyd George (employing the latter's own words) was starkly personal. He wrote:

> When, after the beginning of the Battles of the Somme, the wholesale and terrible defects of guns, ammunition and fuzes

were reported, the Minister of Munitions said 'The Garrison Artillery in France is entirely untrained, it cannot shoot, and it is quite unfitted to work the perfect weapons which I have provided.'[32]

To counter this view, Edmonds confirmed that 'General Rawlinson, when asked to express his opinion on this charge, at once repudiated it'.[33]

To consider only such evidence of potential bias is, however, to risk bringing the entire process of compiling the official histories under suspicion of deliberate malpractice. A consideration of Edmonds' motivations and methods will reveal that in fact he viewed as a matter of considerable seriousness both the compilation of an accurate account and indeed the revelation of mistakes. Furthermore, it will become apparent that the constraints detailed above exercised an influence not on what Edmonds actually wrote but merely how he wrote it.

IV

One might still argue with justification that an historical work is of no value regardless of the diligence of its preparation if it draws the wrong conclusions or fails to learn from the potential lessons. As Liddell Hart warned Edmonds in 1934, 'anyone who flatters the brasshats' self-delusion is preparing the country for a great disaster'.[34] 'There can be no hope of learning the lessons of the past', he wrote, 'unless one achieves a purely scientific enquiry and this is rationally impossible so long as any sentiment of comradeship and loyalty interferes with the impartiality of the view.'[35] However, it was far from Edmonds' intention to keep his knowledge of mistakes and shortcomings to himself. It is true that the public market for official history exercised an influence on what Edmonds was prepared to say. For example, he complained in 1928 of Churchill's insistence that the absence of a General Staff to determine strategy at the outset of war was a valuable lesson worthy of revelation by arguing that 'we should not rub it in. We do not want everyone to see the troubles we had and the mistakes we made.'[36] That is not to say that Edmonds wished to bury such lessons altogether. In his attempts to bring them to the attention of those who would benefit from them, military strategists and soldiers, he was enthusiastic and persistent. Edmonds argued strongly in favour of an Official History in 1919, as we have seen, precisely for educational purposes. In his view:

The British Army is singularly badly off in military literature and officers without a reading knowledge of French and German have little chance of improving themselves in the art of war.[37]

The key to understanding Edmonds' method of writing his Official History and his supervision of the work of the official historians is to acknowledge that he attempted to construct a complex narrative in which the lay person would have the facts merely placed in front of him without critical guidance, but from which the military experts could draw the right conclusions. As he told Liddell Hart, he 'could not tell the truth frankly in an official history but hoped that it would be evident to those who could *read between the lines*'.[38] This style explains why Edmonds' works have been criticised as sterile, and why so many critics have been misled as to their real value. Edmonds was certainly not in favour of denying future generations of soldiers and planners the benefit of past lessons. In 1932 he wrote: 'I want the young officers of the Army who are to occupy the high places later on to see the mistakes of their prede- cessors, yet without telling the public too much.'[39] From his days as head of military intelligence, Edmonds had been conscious of the value of lesson learning in the services. In an undated essay from the early 1900s entitled 'The Necessity of Collecting and Recording War Experiences', Edmonds had written that as there was

> no doubt that the lamentable failure in the Crimea was largely due to the experience of the Peninsula having entirely passed from knowledge, I think that an effort should be made to leave a record of our experiences for our successors.[40]

In this regard he wrote to Liddell Hart in 1928 of his volume of Official History then in preparation: 'I thought of cutting down *Loos* but the battle seemed to be an epitome of all the mistakes it is possible to make and worthy of full record.'[41] He was even prepared to use his knowledge and access to confidential sources to ensure that criticism of senior offi- cers where appropriate reached the public domain. For example, he assisted Liddell Hart during his preparation of his *The Real War*, sending him documents which revealed that the delay at the Aisne was not, as Haig had claimed, due to Smith-Dorrien's II Corps failing to keep up but due to Haig's 'usual Scots caution'. Edmonds wrote: 'You can use what I have enclosed provided you don't quote me.'[42]

Likewise, where Edmonds himself was not writing for his official work he was prepared to publish views in a direct language which he would no doubt have condemned had one of his historians sought to publish them in the official volumes. In the *Army and Navy Gazette* of 8 November 1930, for example, an article by Edmonds was published entitled 'Old Men at Suvla'. In this he argued that the lack of good generals available to command the Gallipoli offensive was due to a fault in the 'system which refused to maintain a sufficiently large army and to attract brains to it'. He warned that since the fate of the Empire depended upon the competence of such generals it was essential to secure the best possible men. Stopford, the corps commander of the crucial operations at Suvla, had been tried on manoeuvres and had, according to Edmonds, 'failed miserably' and would not have been given command in times of peace. Sir Ian Hamilton, who had the remedy to this particular failing of the system in his own hands, could either have gingered him up or removed him. 'He did neither. As C.-in-C. the blame for the failure must be his.'[43]

In Edmonds' Official History, on the other hand, he was more careful not necessarily about what he said but rather about the way in which he said it. In his notes on experiences gained in the writing of Official History, Edmonds revealed the guidelines he imposed for the writing of an official account. He stated that historians should 'avoid all but implied criticism and should be wary of being "wise after the event"'.[44] Discussions of enemy activities or forces should be restricted to small-type notes at the end of the chapter or a footnote because this knowledge created a 'wise after the event' impression which was implicitly critical of a commanding officer who did not have this knowledge at the time. A concluding chapter could be used for reflection or comment but 'not fault finding'.[45] For Edmonds, such a method of narrative construction was essential if the fine line were to be trodden between allowing the expert to read between the lines and placing the bare facts before a lay reader. That this method was widely practised under Edmonds' supervision is corroborated by Lt-Col. Horden, author of the East Africa volumes. His comments reflected precisely the approach of Edmonds himself. Horden wrote to the Historical Section that his predecessor Stacke appeared to have felt

> precluded from criticism and comment and obliged to gloss over (to put it mildly) mistakes and shortcomings to so great an extent as in my opinion to nullify the value of the work as history. Like him I have sedulously tried to avoid wounding any susceptibilities. But I have not shrunk from criticisms where they seemed necessary for the purpose either of impartial record or military study. In such cases . . . I have striven to say only enough to enable an intelligent reader to form his own judgement.[46]

This method of avoiding criticism derived from hindsight followed very closely the Clausewitzian guidelines of critical analysis with which Edmonds would have been familiar from his Staff College training. Clausewitz had asked: 'How far is the critic free or even duty bound to assess a single case in the light of his greater knowledge, including as it does knowledge of the outcome?'[47] He concluded that in ideal circumstances the critic must 'put himself exactly in the position of the commander, in other words he must assemble everything the commander knew and all the motives that affected his decision and ignore all that he could not or did not know'.[48] Clausewitz acknowledged that this ideal was difficult to achieve but warned that those who presumed to criticise a Bonaparte or a Frederick using full knowledge of all the circumstances could be suspected by the reader of arrogance and lacking critical judgement. The influence on Edmonds both of this positive ideal and of the risks to the historian of ignoring it is striking. Of the former, Edmonds informed Daniel in 1922 of his original work that 'I took the German official account of 1870–71 as my model.'[49] Of the latter, Edmonds became highly critical of his official historian of the Gallipoli volumes, Aspinall, when he flouted this convention. Edmonds accused him of bias and of writing 'without the cold judgement that an official historian should display'.[50] In 1928 Edmonds wrote on a draft of Aspinall's first volume:

> I have repeatedly told Aspinall that Turkish movements should be according to our practice a note at the end of the chapter. At present it is grossly unfair to the leaders of the troops who, of course, did not know what the enemy was about.[51]

When Aspinall refused to modify his work Edmonds accused him, exactly as Clausewitz had warned an intelligent reader might, of lacking critical judgement, of arrogant sarcasm and of producing a valueless work which he would one day come to regret. It is also worthy of note that Edmonds was no doubt further tempted to use such criticism by the fact that it was on a number of occasions levelled equally harshly at him. It will be seen later that a number of objections by the War Office and some senior participants like Montgomery-Massingberd and Luckock centred around Edmonds' own 'wise after the event' tone for precisely the same reasons.

In spite of these constraints, it is a measure of Edmonds' considerable skill that he was nevertheless able to write accurate and full accounts. Those who claim that his work shrank from apportioning blame or ignored vital facts are wrong. Liddell Hart, whose words are often cited out of context as highly critical of Edmonds, is in fact a revealing source of constructive comment which sheds valuable light on Edmonds' methods and motivations. His correspondence with Edmonds reveals that he held much of Edmonds' work in very high regard. His concerns were generally not that truth was manipulated but that in attempting to tread this careful path between the lines Edmonds risked devaluing his work in the eyes of future historians. Liddell Hart did not, for example, label Edmonds' work as 'official but not history', as David French has written, but warned that that was how future historians might view his work.[52] He wrote of Edmonds' volume on March 1918:

The facts necessary for judgement are given with few exceptions, but they are warped in interpretation – a subtle twist is given to them so that the average reader is likely to miss the natural conclusion and jump to a judgement which is contrary to the facts. There is scarcely a flicker of that penetrating insight which marks your reflections and admissions about the war in conversational discussions and by which you have illuminated for me not only the fundamental limitations of Haig, Robertson etc. but the causes that explain them.[53]

This idea that the average reader might miss the natural conclusion of the facts was undoubtedly Edmonds' deliberate intention, but the facts were nonetheless there for the informed reader to draw the right conclusions. Tucked away in the appendix, which along with footnotes Edmonds obviously considered unlikely territory for the member of the public, was Haig's letter of October 1917, which was inherently damning. Liddell Hart acknowledged that Edmonds provided a great service in printing this because it epitomised the defects of Haig's military mind in its 'false assumptions and illogical conclusions'. It was, according to Liddell Hart, simplistic, misguided over the confidence of the troops after Passchendaele, and hugely deluded that the enemy would have exhausted his reserves by the end of the year. It discredited the chance of the enemy transferring troops from Russia to the Western Front, displayed grotesque ignorance of military history by declaring that victory could never be won by divided forces, and suggested that '"Germany may collapse at any moment" and added with obvious doubt "even if they hold out until next year"'.[54] Edmonds' response to Liddell Hart's criticism of lack of focus was that 'many of your points passed through my mind but I had always space and the views of my comrades to consider'.[55] He had sufficient pride in his work, however, to hope that future historians would recognise the constraints which produced such a style and invited Liddell Hart to make this apparent:

I hope I have presented the relevant facts. The interpretation of them is that of a soldier and the public should have that interpretation. I shall be perfectly content if you make that clear in your review.[56]

V

That Edmonds took the compilation of a truthful account seriously cannot be doubted. In terms of Edmonds' method of evidence collection and compilation of the written account it can be argued that his primary motivation was to achieve for himself or his historians an accurate picture with which to work. For Edmonds, who personally wrote 11 volumes and prefaces to three, and supervised the entire process from 1919 to 1948, the scale, complexity and scope of this undertaking was vast. The untidy heap of documents that awaited him on his arrival at the record office in Chancery Lane in 1919 has been referred to in a previous chapter. Through the course of his writings Edmonds consulted, and required his historians to consult, 'every possible source . . . down to the smallest unit diaries which [were] often more accurate in detail than those of the higher formations'.[57] Over 7,000 unmarked and uncatalogued parcels of war records were handled, along with private diaries (compiled in contravention of War Office regulations and therefore noteworthy for their use in an official account), GHQ communications and Cabinet, General Staff and War and Colonial Office papers. Edmonds instructed the Historical Section in 1924 that 25 million sheets of documents received from the War Office would take nine years simply to sort.[58] The initial draft of each volume had to cover all aspects of the particular campaign including actual operations, medical services, supply, ammunition and other administrative arrangements. The second draft had then to include discussions of the higher aspects of war, strategy and politics. Edmonds himself was fluent in four other languages and consulted enemy official collections and records. He even advised his writers during the course of their work to consult, along with the Order of Battle, an almanac showing the type of moon, sunrise and events at sea and at home 'so that the influence of exterior events of importance may not be overlooked'.[59] This work was all undertaken by Edmonds and his Section, which never consisted of more than a dozen officers, whilst at the same time assisting governments, staff colleges, historians and graves commissions with their work. In addition, first narrative drafts were submitted to 'as many survivors as possible (down to battalion commanders)' and all replies acknowledged and responded to where necessary.[60] The Loos volume was circulated to 300 officers, the Somme to 1,000 and the March 1918 volume to 1,500. Edmonds noted that the remarks of 50 per cent of the responses to the latter were most valuable but had resulted in the rewriting of entire chapters.[61] He complained in 1929 that the 'revision of narratives in the light of criticisms required every name, initial, rank and figure, besides fact, to be carefully checked' and the accounts of the German and French sections compared.[62] To claim therefore, as Denis Winter has done, that 'it is sometimes assumed that the official historian canvassed veterans to enrich his narrative and make it truer to the facts. That was never the case' is simply untrue.[63]

This exhaustive method of data collection was deliberately enforced by Edmonds precisely to ensure that his accounts and those of his historians were based on accurate information. In February 1931 he wrote to the Historical Section rejecting suggestions by Sir Henry Newbolt that Official Histories should not be completed until 50 years after a war. He stated that after 50 years an official historian would find that his work lacked authority simply because there was 'no one to contradict him'. Equally the history should not be written immediately because the scale of the battle meant no one man could individually have a true picture of what occurred. It was only after all participants had been able to express a view that an accurate picture emerged. 'The only way to get a true picture of a land battle', wrote Edmonds, 'is to piece together the information obtained from a large number of participants.' He was fully aware of the criticism that surviving participants were liable to 're-paint the picture', but stressed that 'it was the duty of the historian to make head against these difficulties with the aid of documents and the evidence of other witnesses'. To assist in this process it was also important to consult enemy accounts, which provided a further requirement for a delay of a few years in writing the account.[64] This is not the attitude of a writer with a cavalier approach to historical accuracy, intent on ignoring the lessons of the past, the benefits of hindsight or the criticisms of participants.

Edmonds' instructions to official historians on 'Care of Records' and notes on 'Experiences Gained in Compiling Official Military Histories' show how seriously he took this aspect of his work. It is unfortunate that one critic has taken these instructions out of context in order to suggest that Edmonds deliberately wished to manipulate evidence to support his predetermined line. Thus Winter again states, supposedly verbatim, Edmonds' instruction, 'Don't ask officers for their version of events. Give them a narrative to chew on. There is great value after they have read it in chatting over lunch.'[65] 'In other words', Winter concludes, 'the more that got on to paper the greater the danger of leaks.'[66] Yet Edmonds actually instructed historians to avoid asking officers for their version first because recollections faded 'unless some unfortunate incident is written in their memory in letters of blood but give them a narrative to bite on and they can make important corrections'.[67] As for discussion over lunch, Edmonds was quite clear that notes of all interviews had to be kept and placed with the Chief Clerk for inclusion in the records. His suggestion concerning lunch was more in keeping with his advice to keep all dealings with senior officers as unofficial as possible in order that they might feel comfortable that their views were given in confidence and without prejudice. Winter's suggestion that Edmonds 'certainly never sent whole chapters or fragments of any length for comment' so as to avoid revealing the predetermined line has been dealt with above.[68] His correspondence is full of letters from officers from every level who had been sent a number of entire chapters and asked to comment as extensively as possible.

The extensive use of diaries from such small units as battalions is not evidence of restricting 'non-entity' historians to limited documentation, as Winter has suggested, but further evidence of Edmonds' attempts to build up the wider picture. Notably it reveals his scepticism of the accounts of more senior participants, who, by their very position of command, 'could not follow the fluctuations of the battle'.[69] Indeed, Edmonds remarked in his memoirs that the evidence from one such diary had allowed him to uncover the fact that an army diary had been destroyed and replaced by a 'mendacious narrative'.[70]

This attempt to 'suppress the truth' had been perpetrated by Sir Archibald Montgomery-Massingberd, then Chief of Staff to Sir Henry Rawlinson commanding Fourth Army, in the hope of concealing Rawlinson's reluctance to follow Haig's order for a quick breakthrough on the Somme on 1 July 1916.[71] Edmonds had uncovered this fraud by cross-checking the army diary against diaries from subordinate formations, which Montgomery-Massingberd had not bothered, or been able, to alter. Further, far from wanting to restrict access and prevent 'leaks', Edmonds constantly complained that his staff was inadequate for 'a great national work requiring infinite care, scrupulous accuracy and open to the criticisms of the whole military and literary world'.[72]

The seriousness with which Edmonds viewed the compilation of a truthful and accurate account cannot be doubted. His collection of evidence was painstaking and thorough and the manner of his writing influenced by training and convention. Influential too was the fact that Edmonds wrote both to satisfy a military establishment anxious to counter what it considered unjustified vilification by civilian participants and commentators and to satisfy his supervising authorities that his revelations would not undermine an increasingly delicate imperial stability. He did this through the medium of a vast work which was at the same time intended to inform the military expert and to interest the lay reader. In addition, Edmonds wrote, as a former military officer, of events involving his former senior commanders and political masters; even today this would have restricted his freedom explicitly to express serious criticism.

David French has written that 'there can be few if any modern professional historians who would condone the way in which [Edmonds] deliberately glossed over the professional defects of some of the senior officers of whom he wrote'.[73] Edmonds' work, however, cannot be judged in comparison with the standards of modern professional historians because Edmonds did not write as an historian in isolation from the official process. Yet even given the constraints and influences which acted upon him, Edmonds' volumes are remarkable for how directly critical they actually were of his former colleagues, including Haig. Once one has recognised the careful manner in which Edmonds chose to frame his observations, the true nature of his opinions and condemnation becomes clear. Indeed, at times, even the supposedly self-imposed conventions of avoiding outright criticism or knowledge gained in hindsight were blatantly disregarded. As such, a number of Edmonds' works can be judged on their own historical and literary merits without necessarily having regard to the background perspective in mitigation. Let us consider then how Edmonds' method of preparation, assessment of evidence and manner of writing were reflected in one such work, the history of the first day of the Battle of the Somme.

4

Military Operations: France and Belgium 1916, Volume I: 1 July: Battle of the Somme

I

Edmonds began work on the first Somme volume in 1929 and completed it in 1932. This volume covered preparations, planning and the events of the first day of the battle, 1 July 1916. In 1929 alone Edmonds circulated drafts to 800 officers who had participated in the battle. Not surprisingly, given the import and the tragedy of the events of that single day in British history, the drafts of the first volume attracted considerable comment. A number of senior figures, like Sir Archibald Montgomery-Massingberd, Chief of Staff Fourth Army, and his GS01, Maj.-Gen. Russel Luckock, objected to the tone of the volume and requested that key sections be toned down. Sir Launcelot Kiggell, Haig's Chief of Staff, expressed the same concerns and was anxious to seek omissions and amendments to sections which specifically reflected poorly on Haig himself. The War Office also intervened on a number of occasions for similar reasons. These interferences reflected not simply personal sensitivities but the grappling that was taking place in the late 1920s and early 1930s to shape the foundations on which the reputations of leading figures such as Haig, Lloyd George or Churchill were to be based.

The great debates and controversies of the war were being crafted and laid down in this period and a number of these centred around the Somme offensive. These variously viewed the Somme as a wasteful and misguided campaign in which the flower of British manhood was lost for nothing more than a few yards of ground, or as a part of a calculated and predetermined plan to wear down the German forces by a deliberate war of attrition which would take years to reach a successful fulfilment. A vital consideration in any assessment was whether, as a number of authors have claimed, the cost in terms of lives and casualties was far heavier on the part of the aggressor than it was on the part of the defender. Certainly,

3. Edmonds (standing on right) at the Geneva Convention Conference, 1906.

too the army and Haig had their defenders who wished to see their view prevail in the official version, and it was their involvement and influence which has been identified by Edmonds' critics as evidence of his partiality. However, there were others, not least a large number of senior participants, who expressed different views on failures and mistakes and were equally anxious to see these made clear. In such a climate it is of considerable importance to an assessment of the historical validity of the Official History to establish how exactly its author dealt with these consistent attempts to influence it and to determine how serious and lasting was its contribution to this debate.

Much of the criticism of Edmonds' work has revolved around the claim that he used his official work to defend the Haig 'viewpoint' and that he ignored or manipulated facts in response to pressure from Haig's supporters. However, a study of his Somme volume reveals that there were a number of instances where Edmonds actually hardened his tone and criticism in response to information from correspondents. His argument was a sound and balanced one built up judiciously from the details provided by participants, from records and from enemy official sources. Certainly, some sections were toned down in response to specific requests. Some information, too, was discreetly ignored in deference to personal or regimental sensibilities. However, far from failing to allocate blame, Edmonds identified a number of key factors responsible for failure, and it will be seen that the strength of their expression came directly from the criticisms Edmonds received from his correspondents. Some of this blame rested on the shoulders of the British government and on the French, but Edmonds' work was also particularly critical of Haig, Rawlinson and a number of senior officers on both a strategic and tactical level. Furthermore there were sections of the volume where the directness of the language in order to emphasise failure was as strong and emotive as it was in the more colourful works of Churchill or Lloyd George, or even of Brittain and Gibbs. Motivated by a desire to establish and then publish the true facts about the Somme offensive, what emerged was a remarkably frank and damning account. Its lessons and conclusions are a comprehensive record of failure which remains valid to this day.

II

Let us consider first the arguments of those who have shown that Edmonds responded to the criticisms of senior participants by altering the tone of his volume. There is certainly evidence that such revisions took place. One, in particular, came in response to a request by Kiggell to omit a potentially embarrassing charge that Haig pursued an attack against Beaumont Hamel in November 1916 for purely political reasons.

In the original draft, the Official History had suggested that both Kiggell and Haig had planned for an attack there on 13 November in order that Haig might attend the Chantilly Conference two days later having achieved some final success on the Somme. Initially Kiggell did not expressly draw attention to this claim, but rather chose to urge Edmonds to accentuate the positive tactical benefits of this attack. On 4 June 1938, he wrote that:

> the tactical advantages of the position gained on the Thiepval side overlooking the ground and German positions about Beaumont Hamel etc. were really what gave birth to the idea of an attack there and might, I think be brought out more prominently. They offered a good hope of a useful and reasonably cheap local success.[1]

A week later Kiggell wrote again, this time spelling out his concerns and asking Edmonds directly to omit the suggestion that Haig was motivated by anything other than tactical considerations. Kiggell explained that, after suggesting the attack to Haig, the General sent him to Gough for his opinion:

> At that time too I had heard rumours that L[loyd] G[eorge] meant to make trouble for DH over the Somme and the value of a good 'cheap' success from that point of view just before the conference came to me as an afterthought. Whether I mentioned this to Sir DH at first I don't remember and much doubt – at any rate the responsibility for it is entirely mine and if it is to stand at all I hope that Sir DH's mention of it to Gough at any rate will be omitted – as giving his enemies the opportunity of alleging that his decisions were influenced by such considerations.[2]

Edmonds agreed to comply with these requests and a few days later Kiggell wrote back with his 'many thanks for your decision to omit the bit about the influence of Gough's success on the forthcoming conference'.[3]

Travers, too, has commented on the objections by Luckock and Montgomery to the 'wise after the event' tone in Edmonds' first draft, and again there is evidence that Edmonds amended his account in response.[4] In August 1930 Montgomery wrote to Edmonds:

> If you will forgive my saying so, I don't like the tone in which this volume is written at all, and it compares most unfavourably with volumes I to IV; which to my mind were written exactly on the lines that an official account should be and were admirable. The

writer of this volume is much too wise after the event, which is so very easy . . . Instead of 'after the event' criticism, of which four of the chapters are full, I think the writer should try and point out the very great advance on previous attacks of the tactics employed on July 1st and how in the evolution up to 1917–1918 fighting the omissions of 1916 were eliminated.[5]

No doubt to strengthen the force of the message, Edmonds was faced by an attack on two fronts over this issue for these points were reiterated by Luckock. Indeed the argument is so precisely similar as to suggest that Luckock copied verbatim sections of Montgomery's letter. Luckock stated that he was in agreement with all 'Sir Archie's points' and had come to an identical opinion with regards to the tone.[6] He felt sure that the volume had not been written by Edmonds for not only was the 'tone entirely different' from the earlier volumes but the English was supposedly not of the same standard. He complained that:

the writer does not seem to realise that the organisation of the battle, though in the light of after events lacking in many respects, was a prodigious advance on anything that had been done before. A fair-minded author would emphasise this as one of the features of the battle, while pointing out how evolution during 1917–1918 led step by step to eliminating the omissions of 1916 . . . [Secondly] the writer constantly contradicts himself in his apparent effort to belittle the work of the Army Commander – he can't have it both ways – as a glaring example the writer wishes to have deep objectives and adequate artillery preparation which in the situation in 1916 is absurd.[7]

It was undoubtedly the case that Edmonds did alter his draft in response to these requests because in November Montgomery wrote to Edmonds:

I can honestly tell you that the two revises you have sent me are now I think an excellent and tremendous improvement. The captious spirit of which I am afraid I complained in the original has completely gone and any criticisms that there are in this is absolutely fair. If I may say so you have got back your old tone which made the earlier volumes so very pleasant to read.[8]

However, it is hard to reconcile this with what actually appeared in the volume. For whilst Edmonds appeared to have succumbed to pressure with regard to his tone, the content and indeed force of what he wrote scarcely altered. Furthermore, the specific requests of Montgomery and Luckock for inclusions were not met and the very tone of which they complained remained present albeit in *later* sections of the volume. If the intention of both senior officers was, as it appears to have been, to achieve some mitigation of the criticism of Fourth Army's tactical plan, then they clearly failed. Despite their request, there was no reference to any advance made at the Somme over the planning and tactics of previous years, and nor was there any suggestion that these continued to evolve over the next two years. On the contrary, Edmonds was particularly critical of Fourth Army and Rawlinson precisely for their tactical failings, which could not be justified by previous or subsequent events because sufficient information existed *at the time* to show that their plan was both too optimistic and too rigid. In essence Rawlinson ignored the lessons which he himself had previously learnt and accepted a plan of attack whose tactics ran contrary to his own better judgement and that of his subordinates.

This final point is particularly important, and it is interesting that Montgomery should have chosen to point out to Edmonds 'the very great advance' on previous tactics which was made at the Somme. A recent work by Prior and Wilson, *Command on the Western Front*, has traced, through an assessment of Rawlinson's career, the evolution of tactical success during the war. Their central argument is that the 'exercise of command on the Western Front was not a consistent process of learning'.[9] Rawlinson had learnt from experience at Neuve Chapelle that the appropriate level of heavy artillery bombardment coupled with a strictly limited advance, which did not go beyond the point at which the guns could protect the troops from counter-attack, was an essential feature of any successful attack. The objectives for the first day's advance must be strictly limited in order to allow sufficient time to bring heavy artillery forward. This resulted in the tactics of what Rawlinson termed 'bite and hold'. Yet in a process which was to become 'uncomfortably familiar', Rawlinson was to find that under the influence of Haig 'he managed by stages to cast off the wisdom of "bite and hold" and before long was endorsing the visionary proposals of his superiors'.[10] At the Somme, after considering the German defences, Rawlinson initially advocated a cautious step-by-step attack. He based the length and depth of his first day's objectives on a careful calculation (relating to the amount of heavy artillery available) learnt from his previous experience of successful advances. Yet he was ultimately to disregard these lessons following objections by Haig and effectively doubled the depth of the objectives for the first day in the full knowledge that he would not be able to achieve a corresponding increase in artillery support.

Edmonds had made precisely these points in his Official History and illustrated them with the benefit of knowledge which would have been available at the time. Dealing first with the planning of the battle he explained that Rawlinson had had in mind a limited objective, such as that carried out successfully at Messines the following year. He wanted to proceed by 'deliberate stages like siege warfare, slow and sure – as the Germans had done in the later stages of "Second Ypres" – making a belt of defences 2000 yards deep untenable by gun fire and then occupying it'. However Haig had 'more optimistically contemplated a break-through' and Rawlinson amended his plan to accommodate this. He did so in spite of fears by both his own staff and the artillery adviser at GHQ, Maj.-Gen. J.F.N. Birch, that it was stretching the men and artillery too far and despite his own private concerns that the new plan was 'too opti-mistic'.[11]

Dealing then with the tactical preparations for the battle, Edmonds stated that Rawlinson, in spite of his private misgivings, had told his corps commanders that 'nothing could exist at the conclusion of the bombard-ment' planned for 1 July across the entire 20-mile front. The 'infantry would only have to walk over to take possession'.[12] Edmonds then quipped that much the same had been said by the German Fifth Army Commander before the assault on Verdun. From this erroneous view grew one of the prime factors for failure at the Somme. Instead of viewing the assault across an impossibly wide no man's land (at places 4,000 yards wide) as a race to reach the opposing trenches before the enemy could leave his deep dug-outs and man the machine-gun parapets, the assault was considered something 'which could be done at leisure'.[13] Thus no mention was made in the Fourth Army Tactical Notes of the necessity of crossing no man's land at a good pace. Instead the infantrymen were so laden with equipment that they could move no faster than a slow walk. Edmonds detailed at length the contents of the infantryman's pack:

> steel helmet and entrenching tool . . . with rolled groundsheet, water bottle and haversack in place of the pack on the back. In the haversack were small things, mess tin, towel, shaving kit, extra socks, message book, 'the unconsumed portion of the day's ration', extra cheese, one preserved ration, and one iron ration. Two gas helmets and tear goggles were carried, also wire cutters, field dress-ing and iodine . . . Moving on from dump to dump the men picked up, besides 220 rounds of S.A.A., two sandbags and two Mills gre-nades . . . Each leading company also took 10 picks and 50 shovels and wire cutters were distributed to leading sections . . . The total weight carried per man was about 66 lbs., which made it difficult to get out of a trench, impossible to move much quicker than a slow walk.[14]

In respect of the tactics for the advance, far from suggesting an improvement over previous tactics, Edmonds stated that a better alterna-tive to that which was actually proposed was already known and proven at the time. This was the procedure of advancing by pushing forward patrols using local cover, which had already been tried with some success by the Germans at Verdun. However, Fourth Army commanders were definitely opposed to this and their plan instructed that 'the advance of isolated detachments . . . should be avoided'.[15] Instead the Fourth Army plan laid down that leading lines should advance no more than 100 yards apart and with the men in each line no more than two or three paces apart. Edmonds noted, somewhat ironically, that:

> The order that the 'four or more' successive lines were not to be more than 100 yards apart, where No Man's Land was several hundred yards wide, necessarily resulted in several successive lines being in the open together exposed to fire. Two or three waves should have sufficed to rush the trenches, if 'nothing could exist at the conclusion of the bombardment'. No number of waves, as it proved, were of any avail against the actual unshaken defence.[16]

Furthermore, because of fears at GHQ that the untrained men of the New Armies would be unable to exercise any initiative, a rigid and inflexible plan was formed based on precise orders. It was therefore instructed that 'troops once launched to the attack must push on at all costs till the final objective is reached'.[17] This attack was to be launched with equal vigour against the entire front, and the plan took no account of the need to halt an advance where it was held up by strong opposition or to reinforce an area where resistance was weak or non-existent. This was, according to Edmonds, 'the most serious omission'.[18]

The effect of all these failures resulted in a tragic waste of life suffered across the front as heavily laden men walked in thick formation across yards of no man's land into the unmolested fire of machine-guns. This was graphically illustrated by Edmonds as he dealt with the actions of each corps individually, as will be shown later. At this stage in the narrative, however, Edmonds felt his argument might be strengthened by a consideration of the instructions issued to the Austro-German army prior to the successful breakthrough at Gorlice-Tarnow on 2 May 1915 by way of comparison. Their plan was, by contrast, totally fluid, stating that the 'Army cannot assign to the attacking corps and divisions definite objectives for each day, lest by fixing them the possibility of further progress may be stopped'.[19] It was also made clear that it was not expected 'that the attack [would] make equal progress on the whole front', and so the necessity of being able to move troops away from areas where they met the toughest resistance was impressed upon the corps and divisional commanders. Equally those achieving greatest success were in danger of exposing themselves to envelopment, and so corps and divisions were instructed to keep up constant communication with neighbouring formations and with army headquarters.

It is difficult to portray such conclusions as attempting to avoid either allocating blame or condemning through the use of knowledge gained in hindsight. Even by Edmonds' own standards (as shown by the manner in which he later sought to judge his own official historians) this narrative was remarkably critical. Indeed there are further examples in this volume of the deliberate use of a 'wise after the event' tone; none perhaps more graphic than that employed in Edmonds' consideration of Rawlinson's failure to keep in touch with the battle once it had begun. This failure resulted in wasteful advances continuing to take place well into the evening when it should already have been clear that forward movement in those sectors was long since impossible. To illustrate this Edmonds juxtaposed Rawlinson's view on the spot (as recorded in his diary on the day) with the actual situation as known subsequently, which was recorded alongside in parentheses:

7.30 PM The VIII Corps have been pushed back into their own trenches at all points except the parallelogram (quadrilateral) . . . The III. Corps are in Contalmaison (There seems no authority for this in the bulletins) and I think Boisselle (No) but have failed to capture Ovillers. The XV. Corps have taken Mametz and established themselves behind it in touch with the XIII. Corps but are not in touch on their left with the III. (They were in touch at Scots Redoubt) . . . The XIII. Corps have done the best. They are in Montauban and have taken and are holding all the objectives allotted to them. The casualties to date are 16,000 (nearly 60,000).[20]

III

These examples not only provide evidence that Edmonds was quite prepared openly to criticise senior commanders where justified but they are also instructive of the mechanism by which Edmonds compiled his Official History. One might argue, with Travers, that the views expressed above satisfied Edmonds' ulterior motive that criticism of Rawlinson would deflect it from Haig. This will be considered in detail later. However, there is considerable evidence that all of the criticism expressed by Edmonds in his official work arose directly from the information and comments he received from a large number of correspondents. In fact, far from bending to the pressure of others to soften the tone of his account, it will be shown that in many cases Edmonds actually hardened his criticisms in response to the requests of former participants. Furthermore, where Edmonds received new information he went to considerable lengths to corroborate it by inviting comments from others. If supported, the argument or observations would be reflected in his work. Edmonds explained the influence of these personal views and experiences in the compilation of his account when he stated in his preface that '[t]he picture given . . . is a composite one, a mosaic one might say, and the most extraordinary thing about it is how neatly every piece, however strange it seemed at first, has fitted into place'.[21] Edmonds cited a military historian who had complained that there was nothing in the official account which did not contain anything which could not be verified 'chapter and verse', and he gratefully accepted the 'compliment'.[22] This was the case with all the key factors which Edmonds held as responsible for the failure of the offensive: the tactical flaws of the Fourth Army plan, the lack of tactical surprise, the reliability of ammunition and artillery and finally the failings of strategy.

With regard to the tactical flaws of the Fourth Army plan there is ample evidence that Edmonds' criticisms were influenced by the views of a number of his correspondents. One wrote:

> the plan was much too cut and dried and not sufficiently elastic. The Higher Commanders – Brigade, Divisional and Corps – could exercise little or no control and were unable to correct weaknesses in the original plan when these were disclosed. The main problem was that the plan looked too far ahead and depended on everything going right from the beginning.[23]

Another, Brig.-Gen. D.C. Rees (Commander of 94th Brigade in VIII Corps) informed Edmonds that the 'terrible document', 'Scheme for the Offensive', was received at Corps HQ two weeks before the attack. It was 76 pages long and contained for his division alone 365 supplementary instructions which took three days to reduce to brigade orders of eight pages. Rees wrote: 'The first principles of war were overwhelmed by a mass of detail which dispensed with individual initiative and any elasticity.'[24] Both correspondents' comments were directly echoed by Edmonds in his official version thus: 'In general the tactical plan of the battle was much too rigid . . . Principles were involved in a mass of detail which prevented elasticity and tended to destroy individual initiative.'[25] Rees also commented on the enormous weight the men had to carry into the attack as a result of officers attempting for months to legislate for everything. Another correspondent, G. Moberly, corroborated the effect of this. He informed Edmonds that he was watching from the high ground as the 1st Royal Inniskilling Fusiliers attacked on 1 July and was struck by the

> extreme slowness of the advance in the initial stages: it was carried out at a slow walking pace . . . After a time there were parties of Germans standing up on the parapet firing on the attackers in No

Man's Land at close range. Very few attackers on the sector which I could see appeared even to reach the German wire and I saw none get beyond the wire.[26]

Rees also commented on the total lack of surprise and requested that Edmonds remark more extensively on it. He stated that the first he heard of the postponement of the attack (from 29 June to 1 July) was 'hearing it shouted down our village street'.[27] In his official volume Edmonds wrote that '[n]ews of the postponement was shouted in many a village where troops were quartered regardless of what listening ears there might be'.[28]

This lack of surprise was another key feature which Edmonds highlighted in his work as having been responsible for the failure of the offensive. This too, like the faults of the Fourth Army plan, was a factor which was stressed by a great number of Edmonds' correspondents. S. Gillon wrote that the advertisement of the attack on his front was 'absurd'; paths were marked and cut through the wire days before and bridges were built over the trenches to allow the second and third waves to pass. 'Small wonder', he wrote, 'that the machine gun fire was directed with such fatal precision.'[29] A.C. Sparks informed Edmonds that the building of an 'exact facsimile, full size German trench system' opposite Gommecourt to prepare the attacking troops neutralised the effect of the eventual advance because it was spotted some days before by a German aeroplane.[30]

One further example is also interesting for the light it sheds on how Edmonds approached the information of correspondents in order to establish an accurate and truthful account. It reveals particularly that Edmonds did not rely simply on the views of a senior officer over a controversial matter but would canvass corroborating information from extremely junior officers and men as well. The issue related to the firing of the 40,000lb mine under Hawthorn Redoubt on the front of the 29th Division ten minutes before the attack, thus alerting the Germans to the imminent advance of British troops with, according to Edmonds, 'direful consequences'.[31] The original plan had been to fire this mine at zero hour but this was subsequently put back to zero minus ten. Edmonds wrote to the GOC VIII Corps, Lt-Gen. Hunter-Weston, requesting information on the reason for the change. Hunter-Weston confirmed that the mine was originally to be blown at zero but 'in consequence of representation of the Divisional Commander and of the Brigadier of the assaulting brigade it was changed to zero−10; their strongly urged view being that falling debris would do as much damage to the assaulting troops as to the Germans'.[32] Hunter-Weston stressed that this was merely his recollection and requested that Edmonds did not state it 'officially'.[33] Edmonds then circulated the draft of this section to at least two other, and considerably more junior, participants involved in the action and invited their comments. One, an infantry soldier in the 2nd Royal Fusiliers, thanked Edmonds for the honour of allowing him to offer criticism. His view was that it was

> indeed very unfortunate that such a long definite notice of the impending attack was notified to the enemy by the firing of the mine under Hawthorn Redoubt, as there is no doubt to my mind that had this been timed for firing almost simultaneously with the attack we should in the general confusion have been able to over run the Redoubt with little or no opposition, and thus stop the intense direct machine gun fire and permit following waves to get across No Man's Land.[34]

The other, F. Pursly, was a Royal Engineer in the 252nd Tunnelling Company. He informed Edmonds that when he had heard that VIII Corps were planning to fire the mine ten minutes before zero hour he complained to VIII Corps staff. They informed him that they would not fire it at zero hour because they 'feared the results on their men going across'.[35] Pursly then went to his senior officer, the Chief Engineer Maj.-Gen. Buckland. A member of VIII Corps staff informed the general that it was the 29th Division which would not agree to put the firing back to zero and the corps did not want to force 29th Division 'against their will'.[36] It was this view which Edmonds accepted. In his final published volume he stated that contrary to the opinion of the Inspector of Mines that the mine should be fired at zero hour, VIII Corps pushed this back ten minutes. 'It is said', wrote Edmonds, 'that some apprehension was felt in the 29th Division that if the mine were fired at zero the attacking infantry might be injured by falling fragments.'[37] In fact, Edmonds stated, all falling debris which might inflict injury comes down within 20 seconds. Furthermore, according to Edmonds, this fact was 'already well known in France from the experience of minor actions earlier in the year'.[38] The firing of the mine ten minutes before the assault 'undoubtedly prejudiced the chances of success', and Edmonds cited the German official account as confirming that 'this explosion was a signal for the infantry attack'.[39] Having already been warned of an impending attack by a daily bombardment at 5 a.m. throughout the previous week, the only question for the Germans was which day the assault was to take place:

> The mine announced not only the day but also the minute. Directly it was fired, without any appreciable pause the enemy machine gun fire became terrific; for the simultaneous lifting of the heavy gun barrage made it perfectly clear for the Germans to man their

defences. And the British creeping barrage moved on at zero, to the exasperation of the infantrymen, who were left to their fate.[40]

As a consequence, when the attack began the 1st Royal Inniskilling Fusiliers on the right suffered heavy casualties and all who made it through to the German trench were either killed or taken prisoner. On the left the 2nd South Wales Borderers were raked by machine-gun fire: 'By 7.35 a.m. nothing remained of the Borderers but some scattered individuals lying within a hundred yards of the German trench.'[41]

A further factor which Edmonds considered responsible for the failure of the Somme offensive was the reliability of the ammunition and of the artillery. Here again, the Official History was openly critical, and once more Edmonds took his lead from the views of his correspondents. Major V.A.C. Yate informed Edmonds that a number of casualties occurred in his battalion from faulty American shells which burst in the muzzle of the field guns.[42] I. Sandell also reported shells bursting in the bores of field howitzers and vast numbers of unexploded shells littering the German front.[43] Once more, Edmonds invited the views of specific participants. J.C. Mostyn, a gunner, returned Edmonds' draft chapters with the comments:

I can corroborate your opinion about faulty heavy ammunition – the safety arrangements were such that either the shell exploded in the bore ... or else buried itself so deep in the ground that its effect both material and morale was smothered.[44]

So, in his Official History Edmonds included a section on munitions which outlined the faults in every type of ammunition used at the front. He recorded that the fuses of the eight-inch shells often failed to ignite the charge and resulted in numerous duds, whereas the frequently premature explosions of the howitzer shells either in the bore or five yards from the muzzle resulted in their batteries being labelled 'suicide clubs'.[45]

Of even greater influence in Edmonds' account were the comments of Maj.-Gen. Noel Birch of the Royal Artillery. He informed Edmonds that the 'backward state of our artillery [needed] greater emphasis'.[46] He argued that after Neuve Chapelle the Germans had taken every precaution to strengthen the wire. This left the British army with miles of wire to cut whilst having no instantaneous fuses and no chance of concentrating on the areas of planned attack without destroying the element of surprise. Birch stated that these new problems of semi-siege warfare and the large concentration of guns necessary had never been studied by the General Staff in the way that the lessons of fortifications from the Russo-Japanese war had been taught at Chatham. He concluded:

If only the teaching of Chatham had been absorbed by the General Staff and they had at the same time understood the gunnery problem that the sapper had demonstrated had been absolutely necessary, thousands of lives would have been saved and the war shortened by years. I do not know what you will think of the above but I do feel something of the sort, very much toned down so as not to bludgeon the General Staff, would be worthy of the history and perhaps at the same time a good lesson for the future. There is no use in having brains in the army unless you use them.[47]

Birch's comments were incorporated almost verbatim into Edmonds' final work thus:

It must be admitted that the problems of semi-siege warfare and the large concentration of guns necessary for the attack of great field defences had never been studied in peace time by the General Staff . . . After Neuve Chapelle, however, the enemy had taken every precaution to strengthen his defences in depth, and particularly to improve his wire both in quantity and quality. There were acres and acres of wire to cut and, even had instantaneous fuzes been available in June 1916, its destruction in a certain area was to advertise where the assault would strike and 'give the show away'.[48]

IV

We have seen, then, how Edmonds developed his narrative from a great number of the views and experiences of participants of the offensive. Where an issue of interest or dispute arose, he specifically requested additional comment from a wider range of participants in support or corroboration. Having satisfied himself of the truth, Edmonds was not afraid to publish frank criticism where appropriate, even if that meant damning a senior officer. In many instances the criticisms of Edmonds' correspondents were incorporated directly into the text and certainly very little that Edmonds identified as a tactical or operational failing was unsupported by information he received from those who had taken part. However, what of the criticism that has been levelled at Edmonds himself that he used his work as a vehicle for the public defence of Douglas Haig? An exposition of the failings of the Fourth Army plan, of the tactics of the advance across no man's land and of the ammunition and artillery, frank though it was, could be seen in the context of deflecting responsibility for failure away from the Commander-in-Chief. Indeed, Travers has stated that:

> Edmonds seems to have followed a strategy in this volume of moderating the tone and removing specific criticism and of defending Haig and his GHQ. He allowed the blame for attrition warfare to fall on external factors such as the French, the battle of Verdun, the standard of training of the new officers and men, the equipment etc., while obliquely blaming Fourth Army staff for errors rather than GHQ . . . Actually this volume was a strong defence of Haig and GHQ particularly in regard to the casualty figures which Edmonds manipulated to show the battle in a better light.[49]

Let us consider first the issue of casualty figures. Travers has suggested that Liddell Hart and the official historian G.C. Wynne had calculated the German casualties to be 'considerably less than the British and French' at approximately 500,000 as against 624,000.[50] However, Travers accused Edmonds of having 'by various means' calculated the German casualties at 600,000.[51] Yet the issue of casualty figures was one which genuinely troubled Edmonds and, as has been shown with his compilation of other evidence, the diligence with which he investigated the matter belies the suggestion that he manipulated them for ulterior reasons. In his official volume Edmonds detailed the problems he encountered in trying to reconcile the various methods of calculating casualties employed by the British and German armies in order to produce a meaningful comparison. The British returns were a record of absentees from a roll call carried out on the day after an engagement. Only those definitely known to be dead or wounded were reported as such and a number of the 'missing' subsequently reappeared with their units. This method naturally produced an excessive amount of 'missing' personnel and relatively few dead.[52] In order to obtain more accurate figures it was decided to examine the Part II Battalion Orders, which 'sooner or later' accounted for every man.[53] To do this for 1 July alone took a member of the staff of the Historical Section nearly six months whereupon he was stopped for 'reasons of economy'.[54] However, the results of this exercise revealed that the original returns for 1 July were 7 per cent too high. The German methods, on the other hand, were based either on returns made in the field three times a month or based on casualty lists published for the entire army during the war (without, after June 1916, recording date and locality). The former method excluded those wounded dealt with in hospitals in the corps area and who would, under the British method, have been listed as missing. The latter, by contrast, included men so lightly wounded that they had not left their units. Edmonds concluded that to arrive at a sensible comparison with the British treatment of casualty figures one would need to add something to the first set of figures or deduct it from the second. This resulted in an indeterminate figure somewhere between 437,322 and 582,919. In the end, Edmonds concluded that at the Somme 'the Allies appear[ed] to have lost rather more than 600,000, the Germans rather less than that total'.[55] These figures are hardly very far away from the figures calculated by Liddell Hart and Wynne.

Further corroboration of the accuracy and diligence of Edmonds' calculations is provided by John Terraine. He stated that, following an argument about the Passchendaele casualty figures in the *Journal of the Royal United Service Institution* in November 1959, Liddell Hart accused the Official History of 'suppression and distortion'. Liddell Hart offered to show Terraine his files relating to the Somme figures, stating that if he had seen them he 'would hardly have been misled by the Official History'. Terraine wrote:

> Thanks to his hospitality, and with his assistance, I later examined the files which he considered to have a bearing upon this matter. I have to state that I found nothing in them which could stand as evidence in any serious, impartial historical examination.

Furthermore, Terraine stated that Sir Charles Oman, who spent two years examining German casualty lists, placed the German losses for the Somme at 560,000.[56]

Let us now consider the suggestion that this volume was a strong defence of Haig and GHQ. Both Haig's former Chief of Staff, Sir Launcelot Kiggell, and the War Office took issue with Edmonds' draft volume and sought alterations specifically in order to protect Haig's reputation. Kiggell was concerned about Edmonds' statement that Haig had been optimistic of a breakthrough and a decisive victory. He was particularly anxious to counter the arguments of Haig's enemies that the Somme offensive was intended as an operation which would break the German lines and strike out 'into the blue'.[57] The more charitable view that Haig's supporters wished to foster was that Haig intended the operation as part of a gradual wearing down of the enemy. In response to Edmonds' first draft Kiggell then wrote, 'What is the evidence of Sir DH's "optimistic . . . hope of decisive victory"? I never heard him express it.'[58] Again, later in the same month, Kiggell wrote to Edmonds requesting 'the possibility of finding some term to replace "breakthrough" which seems to convey to some critics (politicians among them!) the false conception of the ideas and hopes of the responsible soldiers'.[59] Kiggell argued that there was no reason to suppose that Haig felt the forces at his disposal were sufficient for anything more than to 'press the enemy back far enough to give us a good defensive position'.[60] 'Of course it was hoped',

Kiggell continued, 'to shake the enemy's power of resistance severely and according to Luddendorf's book even what was accomplished strained his power of resistance on the front of the attack to the utmost.'[61]

It is certainly true that the Somme offensive did create severe difficulties for the German army, and it can reasonably be argued, as have Edmonds and numerous others since, that the devastation wrought by the Allies in 1916 led to the German withdrawal to the Hindenburg line in 1917 and the eventual collapse in 1918. As Edmonds noted in his volume:

> the Somme battle destroyed most of what remained of the old German Army, so highly trained in peace time. From 1916, as his own writers admit, the enemy's fighting power, morale and discipline gradually but surely waned until the final disappearance of these qualities brought about the collapse of his war-worn legions.[62]

Edmonds included too, in support of this argument, the words of German divisional and army histories which concluded that the 'battle of attrition gnawed deeply into the marrow of the defenders' and caused the German army to suffer an immense psychological loss of morale and confidence from which it never recovered.[63]

However, the issue under consideration was not the ultimate effect of the battle but whether this was the deliberate and calculated intention of the British Commander-in-Chief. Notwithstanding Kiggell's protestations Edmonds' view as stated in the Official History *was* that Haig's plan was for a decisive breakthrough and, as such, was unrealistically ambitious and over-optimistic. Whilst exonerating Haig for the choice of time and location of the offensive, which was dictated by the French, Edmonds nevertheless was highly critical of the failure of Haig's plans to take account of the fact that his army was attacking the strongest part of the entire German front. The chalk surface allowed deep and secure dug-outs to be build by the defenders from which the artillery bombardment would be unable to dislodge them, and the valleys of the Ancre and the Somme provided 'a very serious military obstacle'.[64] Notwithstanding the strength of the enemy in this sector, Haig's plan was for a uniform effort by the limited forces and artillery at his disposal across the entire front at the same time. 'Put in the fewest possible words', wrote Edmonds, 'this meant a general advance of about a mile and a half on a 25,000 yards' front.'[65] At a number of points along the front the troops would be required to advance across an impossibly wide stretch of no man's land before reaching the German trenches. Of Haig's objectives for III Corps, for example, Edmonds wrote:

> The weakness of the plan lay in the great distance which the infantry north of the Ancre would have to advance – over 4000 yards

near Beaumont Hamel – in order to reach the 2nd position on the Miramount Spur.[66]

Far from obliquely attempting to shift responsibility from Haig to Rawlinson, Edmonds clearly stated in this volume that it was *Rawlinson* who expressed severe doubts to *Haig* about these objectives. According to Edmonds, Rawlinson privately believed them to be 'based on false premises, and on too great optimism, for there was no sign that German morale was in any way broken or weakening, and until that happened anything in the nature of a decisive success was out of the question'.[67] Furthermore his Fourth Army staff expressed their concern to Haig that his scheme would be 'asking too much of the forces at their disposal'.[68] Rawlinson had in mind a more limited offensive, 'like that carried out so successfully a year later at Messines by General Plumer', whereas Haig 'more optimistically . . . contemplated a complete break-through'.[69] Indeed, Edmonds even suggested that he himself had argued for a limited offensive rather than a breakthrough at the end of 1915 based on the evidence available to him at the time. He recorded in a footnote a conversation he had had with Sir William Robertson, who had asked him how he would 'move the Germans'. Edmonds had replied:

'If you will give me 20 divisions as a striking force, I will break the German lines: 5 divisions to break in, 5 on each side to expand the gap and 5 to complete the breakthrough and deal with the counter-attacks'. General Robertson merely said 'You can't have 20 divisions'. 'Well then' was the reply, 'there is nothing for it but steady siege warfare'.[70]

Rawlinson, like Edmonds, also wished to proceed 'by deliberate stages resembling siege warfare' as the Germans had done in the latter stages of 'Second Ypres'.[71] Haig, on the other hand, remembering the confusion of the enemy at the start of the advance at Loos, wished to take advantage of this confusion and push on far enough ahead in the first wave to take the second position and capture the enemy's heavy artillery before it could be withdrawn. Rawlinson pointed out that there was in fact little heavy artillery in front of the second position and, in addition, that the wire at this point could not feasibly be cut before the advance. He was also opposed to proceeding beyond the point at which his troops could be protected from counter-attack by his own guns. This reluctance, founded too on his experience at Loos, was shared by a number of Rawlinson's subordinate commanders and Haig acquiesced in their concerns. Furthermore, Edmonds commented that Haig's original condition that the corps must not attack until their commanders were satisfied that the enemy's defences had been sufficiently destroyed 'seems to have been dropped as time passed'.[72] He wrote:

> Departing from the old rule of siege warfare that a breach was not to be assaulted until reported 'practicable' . . . it was directed that the bombardment should become one of a fixed number of days, at the end of which the troops would assault.[73]

Edmonds was further critical of the faith Haig placed on the effect of this bombardment. He commented that Maj.-Gen. Birch, the artillery adviser at GHQ, had informed Haig 'that he was "stretching" his artillery too much', a view which Haig considered 'immaterial' and proceeded to ignore.[74] Edmonds concluded that Haig was thereby at fault 'in the expenditure on the 2nd position of ammunition badly wanted to demolish the 1st; and in the assumption that the Germans would be demoralised by the bombardment and yield to the British infantry'.[75] With some luxury of hindsight, Edmonds added that '[t]wo years had still to elapse before this stage was reached'.[76] In conclusion, Edmonds wrote:

> The British High Command had relied on the bombardment destroying the enemy's material defences and the morale of his troops. Confirmed in this belief . . . their plan was framed, its tactics settled, and the troops trained in the sure and certain hope that the infantry would only have to walk over No Man's Land and take possession.[77]

It is difficult to see how these direct criticisms of Haig and GHQ could be taken to be 'conciliatory' in tone, as Travers has contended.[78]

The War Office also intervened during Edmonds' compilation of this volume and their involvement is instructive both of the way in which the authorities sought to use the Official History to defend the public reputation of Haig and the degree to which they were able or not to achieve amendments to the work. As in previous examples, their requests for revisions to mitigate the unfavourable impression created of Haig were complied with by Edmonds to a degree. However, whilst suggested passages were grafted in, their desired impact was considerably undermined by sections elsewhere in the work which highlighted exactly those impressions which the War Office wished to dispel.

In November 1930 the War Office pointed out that to omit reference to the subsidiary operations prior to the Somme was to miss the opportunity to 'rebut the charge occasionally levelled that the British Army was doing nothing during the first half of 1916'.[79] To this Edmonds replied that he had reduced the treatment of subsidiary operations in order to leave more room for the actual Somme battles. Whilst he acceded to the request, the manner in which Edmonds chose to describe the effect of these subsidiary battles emphasised their futility and high human cost. He considered at length the strategic disadvantages facing the British in the area of the line taken over from the French in the spring of 1916, and suggested that it would in those circumstances have been appropriate 'for them to have kept as quiet as possible and not provoked the enemy to use his advantages'.[80] However, GHQ, on finding an unofficial truce prevailing in this area, decided to 'cultivate an aggressive spirit' to bring this state of affairs to an end.[81] As a result, Edmonds concluded that whilst these operations helped provide some experience of trench warfare, they 'cost the lives of many of the bravest subordinate leaders and soldiers'.[82]

Furthermore the War Office wished Edmonds to address the impression that the Somme offensive attacked the most heavily defended part of the line. They insisted that Edmonds take account of the decision-making process of high command in mitigation. They wrote:

> The subject of the responsibility of military commanders in decisions as to undertaking offensive operations is of such general importance that the [Army] Council considers that some reference to it should be made in the opening chapters.[83]

This reference was to be made in order to emphasise the reasons why a commander might have considered success possible. The power of the machine-gun in defence was already well known from the earliest days of 1915 but the War Office suggested that this might have been obscured to Haig by other factors, such as the breakdown of communications at Neuve Chapelle, the confusion of trench fighting at Festubert and the faulty handling of the reserves at Loos. In addition, the 'new' method of the creeping barrage offered prospects of mastering the machine-gun. Through reference to such considerations the War Office hoped to dispel the otherwise likely conclusion from Edmonds' draft that 'the acquiescence of military commanders in the offensive planned [could] not well be justified in the light of the results'.[84]

Edmonds did, again, include a section in his opening chapters highlighting exactly these suggested three factors as having resulted in the failure to recognise the machine-gun as responsible for previous difficulties. However, with regard to the choice of location Edmonds responded that it would be easy to add some paragraphs dealing critically with the decisions of the Allied high command to undertake an operation on the Somme. He informed the War Office that he had refrained from doing so because his 'original instruction [had been] to find the facts [and] make as little criticism as possible, leaving that to the General Staff'.[85] Thus the fact that the Somme was the strongest part of the entire front was emphasised on a number of occasions and in his conclusion Edmonds wrote: 'No attempt was made to select for attack a part of the enemy's front which had weak features: indeed the Somme sector may be said to have been the strongest part.'[86] In fact, once more perhaps mischievously using the enemy's words to emphasise his point, Edmonds argued that so unsuitable was this sector for an offensive that the Germans refused to believe it would be attempted, even when the front-line troops of their Second Army were definitely reporting that all signs pointed to an imminent attack. One might argue that the Allies were as much at fault in this regard as Haig. However, the objectives of the French high command were clearly different from those of the British. Edmonds had already shown that Joffre merely wanted a battle of attrition to attract German forces away from the French front and Verdun and in order to demonstrate the British commitment to the long-term struggle. He had also shown how Rawlinson had favoured a step-by-step advance based on limited objectives. It was Haig alone who wished to achieve the breakthrough; who anticipated a decisive victory against the strongest part of the German line. Not only was this misguided but, according to Edmonds, it was a fundamentally flawed strategy. As Edmonds wrote: 'A success such as Douglas Haig hoped would probably have created a salient vulnerable on both sides, as the German victories did in 1918, or an ulcer, as Ypres had proved to the British.'[87]

Later on Edmonds also contended that from the point of view of tactics it was indeed fortunate that the troops did not find themselves out in the open because none would have been prepared for a mobile offensive against a still powerful German army. 'Possibly it is as well', he wrote, 'that the breakthrough did not succeed, and leaders and troops were not tested against the Germans of 1916 in open warfare.'[88] This, more than anything, must strike a reader searching for the explanation of the strategy behind this episode as the ultimate irony of the operation. According to Edmonds, the strategy as envisaged by Haig alone was destined to failure one way or another.

It was exactly this point which continued to vex the War Office, who returned to the attack six months later. In May 1931, Widdows wrote of the chapters dealing with preparations for the offensive:

In considering these six chapters it must be remembered that they will be read by a public whose opinions have already been influenced by previous unofficial accounts of these operations; and they will be examined to see whether they bear out the opinions previously expressed. In particular one view voiced by several unofficial writers has been that in the Somme offensive the flower of the British New Army was wasted through the stupidity of our Higher Command who, without due consideration of alternative possible areas of attack committed troops blindly to an insufficiently pre-pared attack on the strongest part of the German line.[89]

The War Office accepted that Edmonds' draft, revised in the light of their previous comments, now made it clear that Joffre had selected the Somme and Haig had merely acquiesced in the decision. Nevertheless the impression remained that Haig 'tamely accepted the mistaken decision of the French leader without any independent consideration of the strategic problem'. The War Office suggested again that a wider discussion of the relative advantages of different fronts would mitigate this impression and that other positive factors, such as the good potential observation for artillery fire and the unbroken nature of the countryside (prior of course to the effect of this artillery fire), should be considered. Such would, in their opinion, do something to 'correct the misleading impression of unthinking stupidity in the British Higher Command conveyed by the picturesque phrases of Mr Churchill's in his *World Crisis*'. They also sug-gested that the subsequent effect of operations dealt with in a chapter on their preparations was out of place in the text and 'should be relegated to footnotes'.[90]

However, there is no evidence that Edmonds revised his draft in the light of these comments for the positive aspects of the terrain were not included. In addition, whilst Edmonds did make it clear that Haig had considered offensives in other areas, the impression clearly remained that Haig 'tamely' acquiesced in Joffre's decisions regarding both time and place of the offensive. Indeed Edmonds put the case for the prosecution fairly convincingly, introducing exactly the emotive phrase which the War Office was anxious to avoid:

> It would be easy to argue that in view of the short training in modern warfare of many of the new divisions and the prospect of receiving a number of tanks in a few weeks' time, that it would have been wiser if the British Commander-in-Chief had declined to send the flower of the nation into battle on the 1st July.[91]

For the defence, Edmonds stated rather more weakly that there were hints that the French army might not go on and that French officers did not believe the British army was pulling its weight and that thus the 'spirit of comradeship . . . definitely urged the necessity of giving some active assistance'.[92] The phrase 'active assistance' might be considered some-what ironic in view of the tragic events which unfolded on 1 July 1916. However, it is quite clear that Edmonds made no attempt to disguise the scale of this tragedy. His deliberate use of language and irony not only reinforced the strength of this message but sat alongside the 'picturesque phrases' of Churchill and others in mythologising the Somme offensive in exactly the way the War Office hoped it would not. Describing the scene that confronted the British troops taking over the Somme sector from the French, Edmonds wrote:

> After the dreary and depressing surroundings of Flanders, the new area, dry and bright, with No Man's Land a wide stretch of scarlet poppies, yellow mustard, red clover and blue cornflowers, was a pleasing contrast. The spirits of the troops rose accordingly, the ground seemed made for a successful battle.[93]

The mention of 'a wide stretch of scarlet poppies' contrasting with high hopes of a successful attack cannot help but strike a poignant chord in the reader's mind. Approaching zero hour, the sense of expectation contrasting with our knowledge of immense loss is further underlined:

> From 6.25 A.M. onwards there was an incessant roar of gun-fire with the screaming, whistling and bursting of shells above it. Eight minutes before zero the Stokes mortars joined in with a hurricane bombardment of 30 rounds a minute. At 7.30 A.M. the crisis came. Under a cloudless blue sky which gave full promise of the hot mid-summer day which was ahead, wave after wave of British infantry rose and, with bayonets glistening, moved forward into a blanket of smoke and mist as the barrage lifted from the enemy's front trench. Almost simultaneously the German gunners ceased their counter-battery work and concentrated their fire upon the assault.
>   No braver or more determined men ever faced an enemy than those sons of the British Empire who went 'over the top' on the 1st July 1916. Never before had the ranks of the British Army on the field of battle contained the finest of all classes of the nation in phy-sique, brains and education. And they were volunteers not con-scripts. If ever a decisive victory was to be won it was expected now.[94]

Yet those brave and determined sons of the British Empire, the flower of the British nation, were on their own not enough to guarantee deci-sive victory. They were attacking the strongest part of the front against an enemy well prepared for the attack and protected in deep dug-outs from the effects of bombardment. They crossed an immense belt of no man's land weighed down by their packs and constrained by the rigidity of their senior commanders' tactics to march in densely packed forma-tions and waves. Across the 20-mile front, almost without exception, these troops faced, in Edmonds' words, a 'murderous machine gun fire'.[95] For example, XV Corps lost 8,000 men 'due almost entirely to machine gun fire'.[96] The 34th Division of III Corps assaulting La Boisselle rose 'as one man' at zero and within ten minutes 80 per cent of the men in the leading battalions were casualties.[97] In X Corps, the 16th Northumberland Fusiliers followed a football drop-kicked by an eminent North Country player towards Thiepval. Edmonds wrote that '[w]hole lines of men were swept down dead or wounded at every attempt to get forward by rushes. It was said with some truth that only bullet-proof soldiers could have taken Thiepval on this day.'[98] In VIII Corps the 1st Newfoundland Regiment advanced over the open in an isolated and doomed attack. 'Dropping dead and wounded, as an artillery observer reported, at every yard, nevertheless the battalion pressed on never faltering . . . The battalion suffered 700 casualties and was literally annihilated, losing every one of its officers.'[99] The 1st Essex on its right was delayed by the 'complete congestion of the trenches with bodies of dead and dying, in places piled one on the other, through which it was attempting to move'.[100] The 31st Division started, according to Edmonds:

> in excellent order but gradually melted away. There was no wavering or attempting to come back, the men fell in their ranks, mostly before the first hundred yards of No Man's Land had been crossed. The magnificent gallantry, discipline and determination displayed by all ranks of this North country division were of no avail against the concentrated fire-effect of the enemy's unshaken infantry and artillery, whose barrage has been described as so consistent and severe that the cones of the explosions gave the impression of a thick belt of poplar trees.[101]

Finally VII Corps, whose sole purpose was as a diversion to direct against itself infantry and artillery which might otherwise be used against the left flank at Serre, attacked the enemy's salient at Gommecourt, 'a modern fortress'.[102] 'The attempt "to divert forces against itself"', wrote Edmonds, 'cost the VII Corps nearly seven thousand casualties.'[103]

Against these instances of bravery and sacrifice in the face of impossible odds must be set Edmonds' comments on the higher command, whose failings and misplaced optimism condemned this flower of the British nation to its fate. Edmonds' criticism of the part played by Haig, Rawlinson and the staff of GHQ and Fourth Army was unequivocal and direct. In the spirit of comradeship, Haig acquiesced in an operation which Joffre had always intended as an action of attrition and, notwithstanding the inherent difficulties of the terrain, he was confident of a decisive victory. Furthermore, the scale of the force and ammunition at his disposal could not possibly justify an attack of uniform strength against the entire 20-mile front and across a no man's land up to 4,000 yards wide. Yet no attempt was made to select weaker parts of the line, or to frame the plan to allow those forces held up to exploit the success of those facing little resistance. So optimistic was Haig of the success of the initial bombardment, despite the lack of ammunition and the evidence of artillery experts to the contrary, that there was no need to consider any threat to the slowly advancing, densely packed waves of men from the machine-guns of the enemy. Indeed despite the concerns of Rawlinson and his divisional commanders, Haig's plan continued to provide for a rapid breakthrough of the German lines. At 6 p.m., after the bloodiest day in British military history and unaware of the scale of the losses and setbacks, Haig was still pressing Fourth Army to continue the attack. Yet by this time, as Edmonds carefully detailed, 57,470 officers and men were either killed, wounded, missing or taken prisoner. In summary, wrote Edmonds: 'For this disastrous loss of the finest manhood of the United Kingdom and Ireland there was only a small gain of ground to show.'[104]

V

It can be seen, therefore, that Edmonds' work was founded primarily on thorough research and the careful sifting of first-hand evidence from a vast range of participants. If the personal and professional sensitivities of certain senior officers resulted in some changes to tone and style, their effect on the broad thrust of Edmonds' narrative was negligible. Well-founded criticisms, on the other hand, once Edmonds had established their justification, were included fully and directly in the text regardless of how junior the source whence they came. Working through the mass of correspondence generated in compiling the Somme volume, one obtains the distinct feeling that Edmonds treated the evidence of more junior participants with far more credibility than that of his senior colleagues. In a number of instances, this is borne out by the revisions Edmonds chose to make (or chose not to make) to his drafts. Where Edmonds felt that mistakes could more usefully be brought out he was prepared to use the benefit of hindsight, or of knowledge available at the time but ignored, in order better to highlight the shortcomings of the higher command. In addition, far from being the sterile account for which it has been condemned, Edmonds' Somme volume employed a language and tone which enlivened the strength of his message and little disguised the tragedy of the loss. The abiding impression left from a reading of this work is that Haig, Rawlinson, GHQ and Fourth Army staff made serious and fundamental errors of judgement and planning. These errors did not merely become apparent with the benefit of hindsight but might have been prevented had Haig and Rawlinson applied the lessons of their own experience, knowledge of which they possessed at the time. For this failing was the flower of the British nation destroyed on 1 July 1916.

5

Military Operations: Gallipoli, Part I

I

In the early hours of 25 April 1915, lighters packed with men of the Anzac Corps and 29th Division slipped silently across the darkened and still waters of the Mediterranean towards the Gallipoli peninsula. The military operation on which they were embarked represented a daring attempt to land an amphibious force on hostile territory with the aim of capturing the Turkish forts dominating the Narrows and of assisting the now aborted passage of the Royal Navy through the Dardanelles. In an attempt to break out from the deadlock of trench warfare which was crippling forward movement on the Western Front, and in order to provide a 'demonstration' to assist their Russian allies, following reverses in the Caucasus, the British government had approved a plan formulated principally by the First Lord of the Admiralty, Winston Churchill, to force a passage through the Dardanelles. This action, it was anticipated, would paralyse Constantinople into submission, thus forcing the Turks out of the war and opening up a new front against the Central powers. Upon these men of the Mediterranean Expeditionary Force, under the leadership of General Sir Ian Hamilton, rested grand hopes and expectations of striking a blow which would end the world war. This scene and its sense of anticipation was dramatically conveyed by the official historian, who was himself present to witness these events first-hand:

> Sunrise at the Dardanelles on that unforgettable Sunday morning – the first Anzac day – was due at a quarter-past five, and the first streak of dawn at five minutes past four. During the hour of inky darkness that preceded the dawn the faint night breeze died suddenly, and the surface of the Aegean grew smooth and still as glass. In the face of the coming drama, the very elements appeared to hold their breath.

At half-past three, when two and a half miles from the shore, now completely invisible, the three battleships again came to rest. The signal 'land armed parties' was made and the twelve tows moved slowly forward in line abreast . . . It is difficult to appreciate the intense strain of being towed in an open boat to a hostile beach that is likely to be defended by machine guns . . . For the Australians the ordeal was a particularly long one. It prefaced, moreover, not only their own but their army's baptism of fire. The loading of the boats had begun at 1.30 A.M. Thenceforward for three hours, till half-past four, the men sat motionless and silent, so tightly wedged together that they could scarcely move their limbs, heading towards the unknown. Whether the landing would be a surprise or whether an army was waiting for them, was a question none could answer. But to the men in the tows, as the dark mass of the shore drew ever nearer, the hope of a surprise was dwindling, for the throb of the steamboats' engines seemed loud enough to wake the dead. Every breathless second a roar of Turkish fire was expected. Yet, till the shore was reached, they must remain motionless and silent – a helpless mark for the enemy.[1]

It was the enormity of this expectation contrasted with the eventual and resounding failure which predominantly accounted for the great historical and literary interest surrounding the Gallipoli campaign. Furthermore this sense of contrast was made more acute if one subscribed to the interpretation that most historians and writers have placed on these events, that on numerous occasions the prospects of success were within easy grasp. As a result, the burdens placed upon the official history of Gallipoli by a public eager for explanation and by various interested 'official' parties anxious for vindication were great. The ability of the official historian to balance and satisfy these generally conflicting responsibilities and pressures provides a compelling insight into the process, purpose and control of the Official Histories as a whole.

Furthermore these demands were exacerbated by the controversy surrounding the viability of the campaign as a military operation. There existed during and after the Great War broadly two opposing views of the prospects and merits of the Gallipoli operation. These followed mainly, although not strictly, along the lines of the 'Easterner' and 'Westerner' arguments that raged in the Cabinet and services during the war. In order to assess any historical account of this campaign, not least the official one, these viewpoints need to be recognised. The 'Easterner' perspective viewed the operation as a bold, radical and viable initiative which ultimately foundered on the lack of vision, leadership or competence of the military and political personnel charged with carrying it through to a successful conclusion. By this view, chiefly proposed by Winston Churchill,

4. Edmonds (standing on left of the group of four with General Snow looking towards the camera) on 4th Division Manoeuvres, 1913.

the diversion to Gallipoli of a fraction of the resources jealously guarded by the 'Westerner' camp, for what were rapidly becoming wasteful and fruitless offensives in France and Belgium, would have secured a famous and relatively cheap victory. The opposing viewpoint, argued predominantly by Sir John French, Sir Henry Wilson and to a lesser degree Lord Kitchener, was that the war in fact offered no cheap victories. Real victory could only be achieved against the Germans in the West. Whilst a substantial amount of French soil remained under foreign occupation, not least that which was only a few days' march from the Channel ports, to divert any desperately needed resources from this theatre was hazardous and reckless. The part played by the French in maintaining pressure on their British allies to support the effort in the West, a part which ultimately precipitated evacuation from Gallipoli, is an important consideration in any analysis of the British actions and fortunes in the East.

Of course, to place all interpretations of Gallipoli into these two camps is an oversimplification. For example, there were a number of senior politicians and service chiefs like Lloyd George and Lord Fisher who, whilst advocating the need for an alternative theatre, regarded Gallipoli as an inappropriate place. The peninsula held strong natural advantages of defence which would make a naval or amphibious attack perilous enough, but in addition a naval bombardment of its outer defences in November 1914 ordered by Winston Churchill had given away all prospects of hiding Britain's intentions and therefore surprise. This resulted in a Turkish effort to fortify the peninsula, which a number of commentators and historians argued in retrospect turned a perilous enterprise into an impossible one. The controversy surrounding the strategic viability of the campaign and the reasons for its failure generated intense political and public interest. The more dubious strategy employed in the West of pushing men forward against entrenched and well-armed positions was defended by its architects, such as Douglas Haig, as being vindicated by eventual success. Offensives originally intended as breakthroughs to regain mobility were portrayed by Haig and his supporters after the war as part of a deliberate policy of attrition to wear down the will and resources of the German enemy. Whilst this controversy was no less acute than that surrounding Gallipoli, in this case the end was said to have justified the means. Failure, on the other hand, greatly intensified the glare of the investigative spotlight and the apportionment of blame. Unique in comparison with the operations in the West (although in common with the failed campaign in Mesopotamia), the events at Gallipoli resulted in the establishment of a parliamentary commission in the midst of ongoing conflict in order to investigate the reasons for the campaign's failure.

The commission's parliamentary members interviewed extensively both military and political participants and considered in detail the strategic viability and decision-making process along with the tactical soundness of the campaign's key actions. They reported their findings in 1917 and 1918, and although the evidence they heard was never published, their conclusions laid the first foundations in the historical interpretations of these events. The commission's findings were to a large degree endorsed by the conclusions in the Official History. They differed mainly in their respective opinions on whether the potential benefits of the campaign outweighed the cost of its failure. All war papers, diaries and records considered by the commission remained confidential after the war and access was granted only to official historians.

For this reason the Official History was the first potentially comprehensive and authoritative work to be placed in the public domain and was eagerly anticipated as such. Until that time the public had had to rely for information upon the sanitised and heavily self-censored press reports during the war or the heavily self-justificatory personal memoirs after it, of which Churchill's *World Crisis*, published in 1923, was a forceful example. (Amongst the relatively few other works on Gallipoli to appear before publication of the official volumes were Ian Hamilton's *Gallipoli Diary* (1920) and John Masefield's highly romanticised *Gallipoli* (1916).) As a result, the official account of the Gallipoli campaign offered the Historical Section an important opportunity to fulfil its central purpose, to provide a military textbook for staff use and a readable and impartial account to satisfy the public's desire for knowledge based on 'official' sources. The ultimate failure of an operation upon which enormous hopes had rested added considerably to the importance of these dual roles. If the Historical Section and its author, ultimately Cecil Aspinall, took this responsibility seriously their work would be of lasting value to military and civilian readers alike. It has already been shown that Edmonds' work on the Western Front was more scholarly and impartial and more adept at criticism and laying blame than has hitherto been accepted. However, it has also been shown that Edmonds' method of doing so was such that criticism was sometimes implied but not always explicitly stated. Whichever interpretation is taken of the Gallipoli campaign, a true and valuable account of its prospects and its failures would be compelled to find fault at a number of levels, whether political and strategic or operational and tactical. The degree to which its author followed Edmonds' own methods and guidelines in determining the truth and presenting criticism provides further insight into the compilation and publication of official works.

Of course, of potentially greater interest than its explanation of mere tactical failure was how far the official account would involve itself in wider discussions and controversies of the campaign in the context of Britain's war effort as a whole. Sectional histories of operations subsidiary to the Western Front were never intended by the Historical Section to stray beyond the confines of tactical movements and actions specific to that theatre. Yet it could be argued that an account of Gallipoli which was not set within the wider context of the allocation of resources and commitment, of grand strategy and political decision-making, of constraints imposed domestically and by Britain's allies, was an incomplete and largely valueless work. To what degree the various 'official' authorities who had influence in the shape of the official work would want to present these issues, and indeed how far they were successful in imposing their views, is further illustration of the real scope and nature of the Official Histories. Indeed, the official volumes of the Gallipoli campaign reveal to a greater degree than any other official work the motivations of these authorities, both political and military, in their involvement in the process and the degree to which an historian writing under official auspices was free or otherwise to dictate the nature of his own work. If the Gallipoli campaign was unique amongst the operations of the Great War, its Official History was, in comparison with the remaining volumes of the series, similarly exceptional.

II

Work began on the Official History of the Gallipoli campaign, simultaneously with the work on the Western Front, before the end of the war. Captain C.T. Atkinson collected material and diaries, questioned leading participants and made preliminary notes in relation to his investigations. By July 1917, with the help of a single clerical assistant, Atkinson had been able to examine and précis 160 unit diaries (there was one per division per month) of the 1,100 which had been accumulated by that date. Of these, 900 related to the Western Front and 200 to Gallipoli. Atkinson's notes on these diaries and his correspondence with participants reinforce the view that the remit of the official work at that point, in addition to building up a thorough operational picture, was to consider any valuable tactical and indeed wider lessons that might be discerned from a study of the various actions.

In 1919, for example, Atkinson wrote to Brig.-Gen. Downing (previously Lieutenant-Colonel commanding the Royal Dublin Fusiliers at Gallipoli) asking for clarification on the times and position of advances of his regiment following the landings at Suvla in August 1915. He was also interested in any remarks Downing had on the general lessons to be drawn from the fighting as well as on tactical and administrative matters, particularly concerning the training of troops. General Downing in his reply frankly expressed his own opinion of the reasons for mistakes and failure. Referring to Atkinson's request for lessons, Downing stated that, whilst he recognised the need to maintain secrecy with regard to the landing place, much confusion had been caused by the fact that brigade and battalion commanders had been given no idea of the plan of attack or of their objectives prior to being 'dumped down' on shore.[2] In addition insufficient attention had been paid to the critical necessity of adequate water, ammunition and machine-guns (of which there were only two per battalion). The want of these few items essential for success 'led to disaster and a useless loss of life'.[3] Excessive secrecy and inadequate ammunition and water were mentioned by many subsequent correspondents of the official historian and, not surprisingly, the significance of these factors was duly highlighted in the final published version of the Official History.

A further contention of Downing's, which was typical of a number of the views expressed to the official historian, was that his men had not been properly honoured for their part in the campaign. Downing's recommendations for distinctions had been ignored and this had created a 'very bad impression in Dublin, in fact in the whole of Ireland'.[4] Downing had tried to pursue the matter but 'could not penetrate the deep fog of silence that had settled on the Gallipoli adventure'.[5] This particular concern was echoed by Downing's divisional commander at Gallipoli, Brig.-Gen. F.F. Hill commanding the 10th (Irish) Division, who continued to pursue this point with Aspinall in 1932. Much of the correspondence from divisional, brigade or battalion commanders to the official historian was based upon similar requests. In most cases, where the historian could establish that these requests accorded with the facts, the narrative was altered to incorporate the requested amendments, as will be shown later.

In January 1919 a civilian academic, G.S. Gordon, was appointed as a full-time historian to take over from Atkinson the work on Gallipoli. His remit, as presented to him by the Section's new Director, Edmonds, illustrates the official requirements for this particular volume:

> In a work issued soon after the war it seems essential that the general line adopted in the despatches should as far as possible be followed and that it is unnecessary except in the case of special incidents to go much beyond the movement of divisions . . . [A]ll controversies should be avoided.[6]

No praise was to be given to individuals except that which had appeared in despatches. Enemy troop positions were to be shown on maps and not referred to in the text unless considered absolutely necessary. If they were mentioned they were to be in the form of footnotes, and the air reports were to be used to show what was actually known of these positions at the time. These comments are important in the light of disagreements Edmonds had subsequently with the ultimate author, Aspinall. Edmonds' motive was to avoid damning the senior commanders with the benefit of hindsight. By restricting information of enemy positions to maps and footnotes, whilst using air reports to reveal the extent of what was known at the time, Edmonds hoped to ensure that the reader would have a fairer understanding of the decisions and perspective of the commanders on the spot.

The avoidance of criticism derived from hindsight was central to Edmonds' approach to his own work and a further constant source of friction when Aspinall refused to follow this example.[7] Aspinall was also to clash with Edmonds on the wider issues of following the line adopted in despatches and avoiding controversy. Notwithstanding, then, Hankey's original objective in establishing the Historical Section, that it should reveal to military students the lessons of the war, and indeed notwithstanding the fact that Edmonds genuinely attempted to meet this objective in his own work, the Official History of Gallipoli was intended to be a dry, tactical account of troop movements and dispositions during the various actions which formed the campaign.

It cannot fairly be judged whether Gordon's work ever achieved these objectives because he made so little progress that he was eventually compelled to resign his post. Appointed on 7 January 1919, Gordon began a visit to the Gallipoli peninsula on 21 June 1919 and contracted a fever which prevented him from continuing his work for a number of months. By February 1923, after four years employed in this task, he had completed only three chapters. The secretary of the Historical Section, Colonel E. Daniel, reported this fact to the CID Committee for Control of the Official Histories, which met annually, and it was decided that Gordon must thenceforth report his progress directly to the Committee. However, having recently been elected to the Chair of English Language and Literature at Leeds University, Gordon decided he could not do justice to his official work and resigned. Edmonds' view, subsequently expressed in his memoirs, was somewhat less charitable: after two years' labour Gordon and his 'learned assistant' had reached no further than the conquest of Constantinople by the crusaders, which was 'beginning in the year one with a vengeance'.[8] This was not strictly true because Gordon's opening chapters were eventually incorporated to some degree into the Official History and dealt with events considerably more recent than the crusades. However, Edmonds' claim was typical of his forthright views on the conduct of his staff and of what, he admitted to Liddell Hart, was his impish sense of humour. He later quipped that Aspinall had intended to retain a *single phrase* from Gordon's three chapters in his work but that this had been regrettably struck out in the proof![9] An output of three chapters in four years was scarcely acceptable by any standard but particularly for a work that it was felt necessary to publish quickly. As with the dismissal of Fortescue in December 1919, Edmonds now came to the conclusion that the selection of an appropriate historian for the task should be made from the military and not the civilian academic field. The Historical Section turned to Lt-Gen. Sir Gerald Ellison KCB to continue the work, who, as a Major-General on the General Staff, had been Deputy Quartermaster-General to the MEF from August 1915.

III

Edmonds' preference for military participants was partly that soldiers were cheaper than civilians[10] but predominantly that they had such intimate knowledge of events that they would not need to spend months reading the documents.[11] They were also more likely than a civilian writer to eschew criticism of their military and political superiors. However, one must also question the likelihood of enlisting an impartial writer by this approach (and indeed whether this was what the Historical Section wanted). Whilst Ellison's experience in Gallipoli undoubtedly aided him in respect of his knowledge of events, his close involvement also predisposed him to a number of strongly held personal views on the campaign's conception and conduct. Inevitably, an individual involved at a senior level in a failed campaign would have felt more acutely the disappointment of that failure and would focus more keenly on attributing blame for its mistakes. It was also highly likely that he would approach the task of its study a decade later, after a considerable time of personal reflection, with well-established views.

In fact Ellison did hold entrenched opinions on the reasons for the campaign's failure. He undoubtedly welcomed his selection as official historian as an opportunity to present these views, which he held to be fundamental to avoiding similar tragedies in future, before a wider audience. Ellison's firm conviction was that the original conception of the campaign as one in which ships alone could force a passage through the Dardanelles was fundamentally flawed. He held Winston Churchill personally responsible for forcing this scheme on the Cabinet against the better judgement of the General Staff and the Secretary of State for War and for persuading Kitchener, when this strategy failed, to despatch ground troops before the necessary preparation for a highly hazardous operation had been made. Straying far beyond Edmonds' guidelines to concentrate on the purely tactical dispositions of the land battle and to avoid controversies, Ellison's initial work focused exclusively on the strategic and political issues surrounding the campaign's inception. He was no doubt aware of the difficult territory into which this took him because he asked the Committee for Control to whom he sent his work for approval to refrain from commenting on any factual errors in the text (as these would be picked up by later circulation and review) and to concentrate instead on his proposed method of dealing with what was 'clearly a difficult subject'.[12]

In a memorandum to this Committee in November 1923 concerning the scope of the official work, Ellison confirmed that he proposed to retain the original two chapters submitted by Gordon and then, in a third, to concentrate on the issue of the availability of troops in March and April 1915. Ellison wished to counter by this the assertion, made principally by Winston Churchill in his recently published *World Crisis*, that Kitchener was to blame for not providing troops to attack the Turks sooner. Even when troops were available in April, he believed they were comparatively raw and by no means a suitable force with which to embark upon a difficult enterprise. Ellison also intended to consider the political process by which the Cabinet had come to approve the plan as a viable military option when the General Staff study of 1906 had concluded that an attempt to force a passage through the Dardanelles was strongly to be deprecated. Ellison's support for the views of the General Staff was clear, as was the opportunity he saw to defend it against its critics. In March 1924 he informed Lt-Gen. Sir Charles Harington:

> I quite agree with all you say about the 1906 memorandum and I mean to give it as much publicity as possible. In the Australian official account there are some rather bitter remarks about the General Staff. I conceive it to be my duty to do all I can in this history to give the General Staff credit wherever it is possible.[13]

Furthermore, Ellison was convinced that the real lesson of the campaign was that an attack on what he considered a powerful fortress should not have been undertaken in such a haphazard way. He believed it to be essential for a proper understanding of the failure that this be clearly revealed in his work:

> The crux of the whole thing in my mind is whether with a force thrown ashore on open beaches without heavy artillery – which could not be landed on open beaches – and with the enormous difficulties of supply that the situation entailed, we could ever have undertaken, or at any rate been successful in real siege operations against what I call the fortress i.e. Kilid Bair and Achi Baba positions. Personally I think not.[14]

In developing the presentation of these two quite plausible arguments, Ellison sought to lay the exclusive responsibility at the door of Winston Churchill. In pursuing what developed into an almost personal crusade, Ellison risked both devaluing his work and encouraging the intervention of the authorities supervising its content. Whilst the public might undoubtedly have welcomed an official work of greater vision and discourse than the narrow tactical confines originally intended of the

Gallipoli volume, such a one-sided and personal view would contribute little to a reasoned and informed consideration. However, in much the same way as Edmonds later viewed his official work as a vehicle with which to counter the attacks against the army made by Lloyd George in his *Memoirs*, Ellison saw the opportunity to use his official account to rebut the self-justificatory analysis of Winston Churchill in his *World Crisis*. Defending the nature of his treatment of these matters to the Historical Section, Ellison wrote that, whilst he accepted it was not his duty to apportion blame or credit:

> at the same time an official historian, if he is to do his duty, cannot altogether ignore criticisms and assertions made possibly in ignorance of facts or from want of military knowledge which tend to give a wholly incorrect impression of individual's motives and events as they actually occurred ... The whole trend of Churchill's 'World Crisis' is to attribute the failure of the Gallipoli campaign to the vacillation and shortcomings on the part of Lord Kitchener, who is no longer alive to answer strictures on his conduct and to explain the motives for his actions.[15]

Ellison was supported in these views by the former military attaché at Constantinople, F.R. Maunsell. Maunsell informed Ellison that in 1906 he had reviewed the General Staff consideration of that year and concluded that the only prospects of a successful operation were to launch a combined naval and military attack with 20,000 men *in complete surprise*. This opportunity, however, was squandered by Churchill, who gave warning to the Turks of Britain's intentions by the naval bombardments of the Gallipoli forts in November 1914 and March 1915. The purpose of this exercise, according to Maunsell, was quite unnecessary because the size and range of all the fort guns were already well known. Without this warning a combined surprise attack could still have taken place as late as the beginning of 1915. Maunsell's own view was that:

> the impetuous ambition of a versatile politician who wished that all the credit for the success of the expedition should descend on his own shoulders and of the Navy which he directed was destined to upset all this.[16]

The controversy surrounding this view centred principally, as has been mentioned, around whether the campaign was a viable though undoubtedly difficult gamble with reasonable prospects of success or whether it was a reckless venture destined to failure for which the principal and persuasive architect must therefore take the blame. Ellison's views on the nature of the fortress which was to be attacked, and on the fact that the

General Staff had consistently shrunk from advocating any such action from 1906 to 1914, naturally inclined him to the latter. The manner in which he presented this opinion ultimately resulted in his removal from his post and his Official History was never published. However, Ellison went ahead and eventually published his own account entitled *The Perils of Amateur Strategy* and this illustrates the likely content and conclusions of his official work. Ellison's motivation for publishing this work was clear:

> A few months ago, standing amid the cemeteries of Gallipoli – the 32 great cemeteries which lie scattered from Suvla bay to Helles point – I resolved to tell the story of events which, step by step, led to a land attack being launched against the Dardanelles fortress. If that story was to be told at all it had to be told fully, fearlessly and impartially . . . Individuals pass, systems remain. A system which produced a Gallipoli campaign cannot go unchallenged. If now the nations of the Empire will face with courage and determination the great issues that Gallipoli raises, the dead will not have died in vain.[17]

'In the interests of historical truth', he wrote, 'so much has to be said.'[18] This involved publicly denouncing the 'system' (in which Ellison included the War Office, Admiralty and Cabinet) which had failed the nation at the time of greatest need. More specifically he launched an outspoken attack on Winston Churchill's professional and personal conduct during the Gallipoli campaign. Ellison reaffirmed his view that the operation was not viable and had been condemned as such by the General Staff. The warning given to the Turks of an intended operation in November 1914 imperilled fatally any prospects of surprise, and the subsequent disjointed action which resulted in troops being thrown piecemeal into battle proved their undoing. Churchill had ignored the expert opinion of his service chiefs, bullied the War Cabinet into accepting his plans and 'acted throughout as though the office of Lord High Admiral had been revived in his own person'.[19] In summary, Ellison concluded that politics and strategy were radically and fundamentally matters which should remain apart from one another. Consequently, Churchill, as a politician, was ill qualified to meddle in strategic matters and therein lay the perils of amateur strategy. In fact, so strongly did Ellison wish to challenge the system which allowed this amateur approach to hold sway at a moment of great national crisis that he urged the peoples of the whole Empire to agitate through the organs of the press for an enquiry and eventual reform: 'If the peoples of the Empire will it the problem of democracy producing a rational system for the conduct of war is not insoluble.'[20]

It is not difficult to imagine that the Historical Section and supervising authorities would take exception to such an overtly critical and political stance in an official work. It was true that the histories *were* in part seen by their creator, Hankey, as an opportunity to defend the military and political authorities against the unsubstantiated charges of unofficial writers and diarists, and Edmonds certainly viewed them as such. However, if the Official Histories were to be written solely as the military case against civilian attack and self-justification, they would fall a long way short of their principal responsibility to use the classified documents available to their authors alone to set an authoritative and instructive account before their readers. It was the injudicious and unbalanced manner in which Ellison wrote that made his work so unsuitable in this respect and it not surprisingly faced considerable official objection.

On 3 December 1924 Edmonds reported to the Committee for Control that Ellison had spent too much time considering matters which were not within his remit and the Committee restated its view that the military histories were to deal only with operations. Hankey, too, complained that Ellison was writing a very different book from the one he was asked to produce and suggested replacing him with Aspinall (whom Edmonds had instructed to assist Ellison) if he could not write along the specified lines. Underpinning these demands was the determination of the Committee, expressed by Hankey, to retain complete editorial control over the work of its historians. Ellison, in response, made it clear that he was not prepared to amend the chapters he had so far written. In Ellison's view unless he was allowed to consider the political initiation of the campaign 'fully and fearlessly . . . a lesson of first rate importance to the nation and to the naval and military services [was] in danger of becoming obscured'.[21] He submitted that:

> the whole of the nine chapters I have drafted are essential to a proper understanding of the Gallipoli tangle, first as giving a necessary survey of the events which led up to the army being employed and, secondly, because the subsequent operations were governed by the way the campaign was inaugurated. Any interference with these chapters would, I am convinced, destroy the balance of the volume as a whole and would vitiate the coherence of subsequent happenings with what went before.[22]

Ellison revealed to the Committee that his entire work was to be built around this central lesson: 'as I have conceived the book in my own mind the chapters are the foundation on which the whole structure is raised'.[23] The Committee, however, did not accept these chapters as appropriate for the tone and direction of the Official History and Ellison was asked to resign. Notwithstanding the issues of control and scope, Edmonds confirmed in his memoirs that the predominant reason for the Committee's displeasure with Ellison was that he 'was using official material to attack "amateur strategy" and in particular Mr Winston Churchill'.[24]

What is particularly interesting about this issue is not that these forthright views on the failure of strategy and specific individuals were unacceptable to the supervising authorities but that Ellison's successor, Aspinall, succeeded in publishing an equally forthright and critical account. Furthermore, when faced with similar demands to modify the tone and content of this account from the War Office, Foreign Office and Edmonds himself, he successfully refused to do so on almost exactly the same literary and academic grounds as had Ellison. Certainly, Aspinall's account was a more balanced consideration with a less overtly political agenda which avoided attempting to identify a single scapegoat for the misfortune and error of Gallipoli. Nevertheless, Hamilton and Stopford, along with their subordinates, suffered explicit criticism which was considerably damaging to their public and military reputations. In addition Kitchener and the government as a whole were openly rebuked for what Aspinall considered their part in the failure. The method of doing so was also fundamentally at variance with Edmonds' less openly candid stance. Where blame was to be attributed Aspinall stated his view plainly and bluntly. He regularly broke Edmonds' conventions on knowledge gained after the event by using that knowledge both to show the frustrating loss of opportunity and to emphasise the strategic failings of Hamilton and his corps and brigade commanders. Further, his use of language actually to reinforce these criticisms was skilful and, for an official work, extraordinary. At times this language was emotive, poetic and on one or two occasions even ironic, as will be shown.

Aspinall's work actively strengthened the images that have come to symbolise in modern minds the intellectual and cultural landscape of the Great War: the loss of the flower of British manhood, the courage and physical tenacity of the common troops, who 'played the game' to the last, and the elderly and often inept senior commanders for whose mistakes these men paid a terrible price. Furthermore, Aspinall broadened his treatment of the operation to encompass exactly those matters which the authorities considered to be beyond his remit. He used his account to consider the far wider issues of Britain's entire approach to the strategy, politics and military demands of fighting a total war on all fronts. In the interests of historical accuracy and of learning vital lessons Aspinall both outlined specific operational criticisms and considered issues of a more fundamental importance in terms of Britain's military preparedness and subsequent fitness for war, the soundness of its strategic decision-making and the stature and determination of its political and military leaders.

These views were inevitably strengthened by the fact that behind them lay a study of great diligence and authority in which Aspinall left no route uncharted in his attempt to establish historical truth. His conclusions were based on extensive and judicious research along with the first-hand experience afforded him from his unique vantage point, as a member of Hamilton's staff, from April 1915 to the final evacuations in January 1916. In this way Aspinall's analysis is difficult to challenge, even given a passage of 70 years and indeed given access to the written material on which these views were largely based. Judicious and scholarly though this work might have been, however, that did not on its own ensure compliance with the particular requirements that the various interested parties held for the Official History. The key to understanding how Aspinall was able to resist these official requirements in favour of his own is predominantly, although by no means exclusively, to be found in the support of Winston Churchill. Churchill's one major involvement in this work, and its author's subsequent literary freedom of expression in the face of Edmonds' impotence, reveals a great deal about where the real authority and power of control over the official volumes rested. His intervention was therefore to play a significant part in the shape and nature of this particular Official History and, by extension, of the Official History series as a whole.

IV

Brig.-Gen. C.F. Aspinall was appointed to succeed Ellison on 26 January 1925 on a salary of £800 a year. Like Ellison he had been a staff officer serving at Gallipoli, having departed with Hamilton and the rest of his staff 'under a sky serene and cloudless blue' in March 1915.[25] As Hamilton's GSO2, Aspinall was responsible for the drafting of orders and for assisting his chief in the drafting of situation appraisals to be sent back to England. As a result he witnessed first-hand the higher command of the campaign in all its aspects from his vantage point alongside Hamilton on *Arcadian* cruising offshore during the main offensive actions. When Hamilton was replaced in October Aspinall remained at Gallipoli and was widely recognised by those commanders on the spot as having been largely responsible for the planning of the highly successful evacuations from the peninsula. It was a feat which, although Aspinall did not state it explicitly in his own work, allowed Britain to salvage some crucial vestige of honour from the wreckage of their Eastern strategy in the eyes of their Moslem subjects. At the very least it avoided the potential humiliation and its attendant political consequences that would have followed an evacuation involving serious loss. Indeed, in recognition of Aspinall's part in this Kitchener's military secretary, Basil Buckley, suggested he should have been made a field marshal![26]

Having acknowledged that Edmonds preferred military authors over civilians because of their already established knowledge, one might question whether an ex-officer too closely associated with the events of which he wrote was completely suitable as a neutral commentator. The experience of Ellison had already shown the dangers inherent in such a selection policy. To what degree did Aspinall's specific experience make him a suitable choice for writing a comprehensive and impartial account?

Aspinall's far-ranging knowledge of many aspects of the campaign undoubtedly enlivened his ability to add a poignancy and authenticity to his style of writing which would have been denied an author who had not been present. Such a close involvement, however, did predispose Aspinall, like Ellison, to a number of strongly held opinions, as well as implicating him personally in a number of important events. This certainly influenced his treatment of key actions and of individuals with whom he worked closely and there is much evidence to suggest that these personal opinions were not necessarily toned down in his official work. This was particularly true of his relationship with his Commander-in-Chief, Ian Hamilton. Despite a personal goodwill that existed between the two men, Aspinall, with other key members of Hamilton's staff, Guy Dawnay and Orlo Williams, experienced an increasing exasperation at his chief's strategic flaws and his failure to present a true version of events to Kitchener. Following the failure of the Suvla offensive in August 1915, Williams, the Chief Cipher Officer, recorded in his diary that Aspinall had tried

> over and over again to get a proper version of events sent but it [had been] useless. So again for the I don't know how manieth time the shallow optimism of an obstinate man who thinks it unsoldierly to tell unpleasant truths and who is no strategist has made it impossible for the staff which contains three pretty clear sighted fellows to give a logical and accurate view of the situation.[27]

Because of this, relations between Hamilton and these three key members of his staff deteriorated to such a level that they undertook to send Aspinall to England to report the situation directly to Lord Kitchener. Dawnay hoped that in this way 'the true position would be realised by Lord Kitchener and others able to form a judgement of the actual facts'. Hamilton refused to allow Aspinall to go, believing him to be the least sanguine of the three, but he did agree to send Dawnay, instructing him to 'answer all questions truthfully but in no way pessimistically' (in private Dawnay informed Williams that 'a really strong man would go home and get them both [Hamilton and Braithwaite] stellenbosched'). Following Dawnay's frank revelations to both Kitchener and the King, Hamilton was indeed recalled from his command of the MEF. Of course this important episode could not have appeared in Aspinall's Official History. Instead Hamilton's removal was blamed on the representations made to the King by four high-ranking generals based upon a report written by Lt-Gen. Stopford on his return to England.[28]

Aspinall also held particularly strong views over Hamilton's conduct during the Second Battle of Krithia and he incorporated these into his official version. When the Foreign Office complained that his treatment of Hamilton's actions was unnecessarily harsh Aspinall justified it by stating that 'he was with Sir Ian himself when the third attack was launched and he . . . was dumbfounded'.[29] The forceful and compelling manner in which these views found expression in the Official History will be shown in due course. Aspinall was also personally involved in one of the most critical 'lost opportunities' of the campaign, what he termed the 'wasted day at Suvla'. Arriving on the fringes of the Suvla shore 24 hours after IX Corps should have advanced inland, he was convinced by the 'holiday atmosphere of the place, that the hills had at last been captured. The whole bay was at peace, and its shores fringed with bathers.'[30] He was therefore dismayed to discover that the leading troops of the 11th Division were only a few hundred yards ahead and that, although the Turks had apparently retired, no effort was being made to press forward. Aspinall's treatment of this episode in his official volume is similarly tinged with the bitterness of personal recrimination, as will be shown in due course.

A further factor which might affect the writing of a military participant, beyond his own personal experience of events, was his previous treatment by the army. Edmonds acknowledged this in his instructions and guidelines on selecting an official historian, in which he urged avoidance of those who had had to leave their former positions 'because of an inability to fit in, who have been under any sort of a cloud in their past careers or who are known to have marked or queer idiosyncrasies of character and temper'.[31] No such suggestion was ever made in relation to Aspinall and certainly his military career showed him to be a capable and well-respected individual. However, there was one feature of Aspinall's military service which is at least worthy of consideration. This was the lack of adequate recognition by the War Office to the degree expected by both Aspinall and his senior colleagues. After leaving Gallipoli in January 1916 Aspinall was transferred to Hunter-Weston's 8th Corps on the Western Front where he became Chief of Staff. He was awarded the CMG and eventually a brevet but was not promoted to GSO1 or brigadier-general (GS) as he had expected. After the Gallipoli campaign Hamilton expressed his concern in a letter to Birdwood that the War Office had 'treated Aspinall hardly in three times ignoring my recommendations on his behalf'.[32] Dawnay, in a similar vein, wrote to Aspinall on his failure to be promoted to brigadier-general: 'It makes me hot to think that the authorities have done you so badly after all you have done for them.'[33] This feeling was also apparently common amongst a number of Aspinall's colleagues. Mitchell informed Aspinall that the fact that his efforts 'were so inadequately recognised is one of those mysterious things which is difficult to explain',[34] and even Hankey wrote in support that 'only those who saw something of the inner history of that desperate campaign know how much responsibility fell on you in drafting the orders'.[35] How far this failure by the War Office adequately to recognise Aspinall's role at Gallipoli could be considered to have prejudiced his official writing is difficult to assess. There is no suggestion in Aspinall's writing or correspondence that he felt any personal grievance towards the War Office but it would be difficult to imagine that the sense of dismay felt by his colleagues and superiors at this lack of due reward was not equally keenly felt by Aspinall himself at the time. One might also surmise that, if nothing else, this would have sharpened his determination in subsequent disagreements over his official work with the War Office.

V

Notwithstanding this personal involvement, however, there is no doubt that Aspinall's approach to his task was highly professional and scholarly. His attempts to establish and record a truthful version of events were, like Edmonds', scrupulous and exhaustive. Aspinall informed Brig.-Gen. Hill, for example, that he had written his work with extreme care to give 'an absolutely truthful and unbiased account'[36] and Col. Downey that his 'one idea [was] to get at the truth and to give honour where honour [was] due'.[37] Aspinall's method of compiling his account reveals how seriously he took his responsibility for accuracy.

The narrative was, as usual, compiled from unit diaries, reports and other official sources by a narrator who was a permanent member of the Historical Section. In the case of Gallipoli this was Capt. W. Miles who also went on to write two Official Histories on the Western Front (*1916*, Vol. II, *2nd July to the End of the Battle of the Somme*, and *1917*, Vol. III, *The Battle of Cambrai*). From the narrative framework the writer prepared his own draft, adding comments and conclusions, and once he had completed the chapters these were circulated widely. The subject matter under consideration dictated the recipients of the drafts, and since the early part of Aspinall's work dealt with the political and diplomatic inception of the campaign his early chapters were circulated to the War Office, Foreign Office, Dominion governments and the Admiralty. These authorities continued to receive and consider for approval all further drafts of the work, but, when Aspinall moved to the military operations of the campaign, chapters were circulated for comment and correction to a vast number of officers from generals down to majors. This involved Aspinall in a substantial amount of correspondence and provided him with a record of the experiences of all units from army, corps and brigade down as far on some occasions as platoon. In May 1931, for example, J.H. Jelson wrote to Aspinall explaining that he had been carefully through the chapter he had been sent but added that his comments were made as a platoon commander in an operation in which 'senior officers knew little and platoon commanders practically nothing of what was intended'.[38] In his Progress Reports covering the three years from 1929 to 1931 Edmonds recorded that Aspinall had circulated drafts to over 600 officers. Some were returned with a few factual corrections; many others contained expansive drafts of the correspondent's experience or opinions. All requests for amendments or additions had to be checked carefully to ascertain the validity of the points made and often generated a substantial amount of further correspondence. For example, a series of some 20 letters between Aspinall and Lt-Gen. Birdwood on one point alone, concerning a telegram sent by the latter requesting evacuation on the first day of the Anzac landings, began in April 1926 and was not finally laid to rest (although not actually resolved) until three years later in April 1929.

Aspinall's method of circulation of accounts involved sending drafts first to senior officers known to have been involved in specific actions and then to any others whose names arose in the course of this correspondence as a potential source of further information or corroboration. Some comments came to the Section unsolicited from those who were aware that an Official History was to be produced. For example, in 1920 Lt-Col. Jourdain asked Edmonds to rectify in the Official History the mistake made by Ian Hamilton in his despatches of December 1915 in attributing the taking of the wells at Kabak Kuyu on 21 August 1915 to the Indian Brigade rather than to the 5th Battalion Connaught Rangers under his command.[39] This was duly done and the history recorded that the '5/Connaught Rangers opened its attack with great promise and the small Turkish post at Kabak Kuyu was captured with very little trouble'.[40] Where Aspinall required additional information concerning a particular action he canvassed opinions and personal accounts from participants by advertising in the national newspapers. The events surrounding the various actions at Suvla, for example, gave Aspinall some problems to disentangle, with their night advances, intermingled units and conflicting accounts by the leading participants. When Aspinall came to deal with this at the start of his second volume in 1929 he placed an advertisement in the *Morning Post* of 17 June requesting officers who took part in the early days to let him 'have any information concerning the landing which they may have in their possession'.[41]

This public request for assistance in the compilation of the official account demonstrates that Aspinall not only approached the gathering of information extremely seriously but that he was, in the interests of historical accuracy, prepared to field the views of an enormous range of individuals who wished to express a personal opinion. Some critics have suggested that the official historians wrote under War Office guidelines to a pre-arranged script without valid reference to the views of participants, but the amendments Aspinall made in deference to these views illustrates clearly that this suggestion is incorrect.[42] Indeed, the influence of individual participants over the content and nature of the Gallipoli Official History represented an important part of the process of its compilation. To a large degree that influence was more significant in shaping the work than was the involvement of the War Office, Foreign Office and Historical Section itself. The prime motivation in Aspinall's willingness to accept a requested amendment was the degree to which he felt the contribution to be truthful. In the case of all comments and criticisms requesting revisions Aspinall went to painstaking lengths to establish their accuracy and, having done so, to give fair recognition where it had not previously been given and to use the information where he could to enhance the value of his account. This was as true of his dealings with Birdwood, Hamilton, Braithwaite or even Edmonds as it was with far more junior participants.

Typical of the kind of request for revision received from individual soldiers was one from Mrs Leonore Churchill concerning her late husband, Captain A.P. Churchill, who had commanded a company of the 1st Essex Regiment. Having contacted Aspinall, following correspondence with Hunter-Weston and Ian Hamilton, she wrote in 1925 that she now had 'the chance to get a thing put right that I have been trying ever since 1915 to get done'.[43] Her husband's company had been ordered to attack what became known as Hunter-Weston Hill (or Hill 138) following the landings at Helles in April 1915. They succeeded, held it through the day of the 25th and handed it over to a company of the 4th Worcestershire Regiment in the evening. This company named the redoubt they had occupied the Worcester Redoubt and therefore took full credit for the capture of this objective in all subsequent accounts. In response to this request Aspinall confirmed that whilst the Worcestershires had the harder task, Mrs Churchill could 'be sure that full justice [would] be done to both the Essex and Worcestershire' regiments.[44] Aspinall's account accordingly gave credit to both companies.

Typical, by contrast, of the kind of request which received scant consideration was the insistence of Brig.-Gen. C. Cunliffe Owen, who had been military attaché at Constantinople before the war, that he had been misrepresented, although only anonymously, in recent publications on the campaign. He complained first to Aspinall and then directly to the War Office that these accounts had stressed the complete lack of information available to Hamilton on his departure for the peninsula and he wished the Official History to provide 'an authoritative statement that the lack alluded to was in no way due to remissness on [his] part'.[45] Cunliffe Owen further claimed that when he heard of the landing in 1915 he had indeed offered information to the War Office but was informed that the Expeditionary Force had 'quite enough experts already'![46] Aspinall saw no reason to alter his account to record this fact, particularly after the draft of these events had been sent to Cunliffe Owen and returned with the comments that it was a 'very interesting and accurate statement' and a 'very sound narrative of what had actually transpired'.[47] He was supported in this by the War Office, whose view was that 'since no one has connected [Cunliffe Owen] personally to Gallipoli intelligence or lack of it, if any, it [was] hard to understand why an apology [was] required'.[48]

A large number of requests came from correspondents who, like Mrs Churchill, urged Aspinall to give recognition to individual units or to correct incorrectly attributed success. Again where Aspinall was satisfied that the request was warranted he amended his account. On occasions he received conflicting claims over which he had to adjudicate. After due consideration he offered a reasoned judgement which usually gave two units the credit both claimed as theirs alone. By the end of the work Aspinall had studied the events of these nine months so extensively that he was better qualified accurately to judge these matters than were those who had witnessed them first-hand. As he wrote to one correspondent:

> I have such a good knowledge . . . now that I can invariably tell with comparative accuracy when a new piece of evidence can be accepted or not. Somehow only the truth fits into the tale. If a writer is inaccurate I can nearly always tell because some tiny scrap of absolutely unpalatable evidence will always be there to confirm or refute the possibility of the new tale.[49]

A good example of this was a lengthy series of correspondence involving Brig.-Gen. Hill commanding the 10th (Irish) Division and the capture of Chocolate Hill at Suvla. Hill complained that Aspinall's original draft reflected the incorrect information published by Hamilton in despatches which credited the Lincoln and Border battalions with its capture and not the Irish battalions of the Royal Iniskilling Fusiliers, Royal Irish Fusiliers and Royal Dublin Fusiliers. He wrote that his troops were 'naturally very sick and disappointed at the inaccurate and meagre recognition they received when the gazette was published – in justice to them I trust history will now give them credit for the spade work which they did in the capture of Chocolate Hill'.[50] Hill complained too that Aspinall's suggestion that his division was slow in pushing forward to its objectives ignored the great problem of the 'lack of water [which] alone preoccupied our being able to make a move on the 8th'.[51] The commanding officer of the Dublin Fusiliers, Col. Downing, also wrote to Aspinall (following his earlier pleas to Atkinson) requesting that credit be given to the Irish regiments, and suggesting that to give credit to two English regiments would be the 'last straw in a War in which [the Irish] got nothing but death and wounds!'[52] However, Aspinall also received evidence from an F. Spring, who had received a draft of the chapters dealing with this action and was 'quite frank about things which I gather is what you want'.[53] He wrote that Aspinall's draft gave the inaccurate impression that the Lincoln and Borders regiments carried the Irish with them to take Chocolate Hill when in fact the Irish 'weren't for the job' and had 'definitely failed to get on' even when the Lincolns passed through them.[54] Furthermore a number of Aspinall's correspondents disputed the lack of water at Suvla. One, Major R.H. Scott wrote that from the day he landed until the day he left he 'never saw any shortage of water', to which Aspinall commented in the margin: '*Important*. Contradicts Hill and Corke Collis and agrees with my personal knowledge.'[55] In Aspinall's final account, then, the capture of the hill was attributed to the efforts of both the English and Irish regiments. After describing the constant checks and reverses suffered by the Irish, who by the evening of 7 August finally occupied the foothills, Aspinall continued:

> soon after seven o'clock the fire of the defenders slackened, and the impetus so long required was now supplied by the arrival of the 6/Lincolnshire. Surging forward in short rushes, this battalion, supported by the Border Regiment, assaulted the western end of Chocolate Hill. The leading troops of the Irish battalions simultaneously attacked the eastern half and also Green Hill and, just as darkness set in, the whole position was at last in British hands . . . For a long time, with five battalions intermixed on the slopes of the twin hills, there was a great deal of confusion and this was increased by the darkness.[56]

After publication of this volume Aspinall informed Hill that the entire Suvla episode had been written with extreme care to give an accurate and unbiased account. He wrote:

> I had indeed experienced more trouble over the Chocolate Hill episode than over any other portion of the campaign owing to the contradictory accounts of survivors. After unravelling these I had written the final word.[57]

Hill for his part acknowledged in return that Aspinall had 'made a great and consistent effort to get at the truth throughout [their] correspondence'.[58]

Other requests proved less controversial and in the absence of contradictory evidence were generally incorporated. Col. E. Dixon wrote to Aspinall suggesting that it would be a 'great honour' if he could insert the name of the 'Manchesters' to his description of 'parties of the 127th Brigade' which penetrated enemy lines at the Third Battle of Krithia.[59] This was thus incorporated into the account:

> Parties of the 127th Brigade penetrated the enemy's line to a depth of at least 1000 yards; 217 prisoners were captured; the Turks were on the run; and the Manchester Territorials, fighting like veterans, were all in high fettle.[60]

Col. Brighton, commanding 162nd Brigade at Kidney Hill, Suvla, asked Aspinall to include the name of his second-in-command, Major G.F. Davis (1/11th London Regiment), who remained behind during a retreat to allow the remainder of his troops to retire and was 'shot and clubbed with a rifle whilst doing so'.[61] Aspinall included his name, although not the manner of his death, in a footnote.[62] Similarly, Col. R.H. Haining requested that the 'gallant attack of the 14th Sikhs . . . be given full credit by a more vivid description than the mere footnote'[63] and Aspinall obliged with a description in the text of the 14th Sikhs, who fought with 'distinguished bravery'.[64]

When a justified amendment came to Aspinall's attention either too close to publication or indeed after publication he made amendments either in footnotes or in later editions. For example, in 1931 J.H. Patterson, commanding the Zion Mule Corps during the actions on 27 and 28 April 1915, wrote to Aspinall concerning what he considered misleading and inaccurate statements in his first volume, published in 1929. He wrote that Aspinall's statement to the effect that:

> 'The Zion Mule Corps began to land on the evening of 27th but was not ready for duty till after the advance had begun on 28th' [gave] the impression that the troops were slack and failed to perform. Nothing is further from the truth and it is a pity that such an erroneous statement should have found its way into history. As a matter of fact if the ZMC had not *slaved all night long on the night of 27th* in taking ammunition to the firing line a very grave situation might have developed all along the front . . . work went on without a break of any kind all night long and for three successive strenuous days and nights neither man nor mule in the ZMC had time to scratch himself! The historian has done an injustice to both Zion men and mules (no doubt in error) but I trust his sense of fair play will cause him to make amends.[65]

Unable to alter his already published first volume, Aspinall gave particular credit to this unit in his second volume in relation to the actions on 4 and 5 June at Krithia:

> Special recognition is also due to the infantry transport personnel, the Indian mule cart drivers and the Zion Mule Corps for their untiring energy in this action – bringing up ammunition close to the forward positions, and carrying back the wounded under heavy fire.[66]

Aspinall was undoubtedly a willing recipient of these particular requests because they enhanced one of the principal themes of his work. His desire to give honour where honour was due was founded upon his willingness to publicise the courage and accomplishments of the troops. Within his work there were instances where the spirit of bravery was paraded and glorified. In some of these instances the language Aspinall used forcefully reinforced this theme and was quite at variance with the tone of other official volumes. Most of these descriptions were based on reported instances or, more powerfully, upon Aspinall's own personal experiences. An indication of Aspinall's attraction to this particular theme was his response to a letter from Lt-Col. Armstrong of 157th Brigade in which he related the actions of Lt-Col. Evelegh of the RMLI during the battles of 12 July. Armstrong recorded that at zero hour Evelegh

> leapt on to the parapet in advance of any of his men . . . and standing on the parapet under a hail of shrapnel which came down at once as if the Turks had seen the preparations for the attack he took off his cap and cheered the men out of the trenches as if he was cheering on a pack of hounds. He was a fine sight.[67]

Alongside these words Aspinall had written 'Try to mention' and accordingly incorporated into his history the following words:

> Many eyewitnesses speak of the inspiriting sight of Lt-Colonel E.G. Evelegh, R.M.L.I., standing, cap in hand, on a trench parapet, cheering his men forward like hounds into cover, and then dashing on himself. He was never seen alive again.[68]

On a number of other occasions too Aspinall employed to powerful effect what have become pervasive images of the Great War of sporting daring, the notion of the flower of British youth and its counter-image of old and inept generals. In his account of the Third Battle of Krithia, for example, Aspinall described 'a brilliant summer's day' in which:

The first wave of King's Own Scottish Borderers was practically blotted out, only a handful of men reaching the enemy's parapet . . . Not a man in the first wave faltered, and even after the majority of their comrades had fallen, individual survivors pressed gamely forward till they themselves were killed.[69]

In Aspinall's account of the three divisions of the First New Army arriving for the Suvla landings, he described the 'splendid fighting material' and a rank and file who were 'the flower of British Manhood'.[70] Of the men in whose charge they were placed Aspinall wrote:

Age and length of service had been the chief qualifications for command, with the result that most of the brigade and battalion commanders were men well over fifty years of age who had retired before the war . . . some were men who would never have attained command in times of peace, and they lacked the power of inspiring the well-educated and enthusiastic young civilians who had flocked to the Army at the first call to arms.[71]

A most graphic example of the waste of this flower of British manhood was given by Aspinall in his description of the Second Battle of Krithia, to which he was personally witness. The description of these events in his volume demonstrates both the direct criticism of his narrative and the powerful effect of his writing. In his account of this battle Aspinall described how even the Great War had furnished few such examples of offensive operations being undertaken by men so worn out from lack of rest and continual battle. On the first day of the campaign only 400 yards in the centre of the front had been gained with no more than Turkish covering troops in opposition. On the second day the British and the French had advanced again with only a short preliminary bombardment (due to lack of ammunition) and in the face of fierce machine-gun fire and had gained 300 yards. The Turks had not even been aware that a general attack was under way because so few of their troops had been involved. After two days of such failure Aspinall argued that a continuation was folly, particularly as relatively few casualties had resulted hitherto. Hamilton, however, ordered that an attack should proceed on the third day at the same time, following the same period of bombardment: a bayonet attack without artillery support against machine-guns in the full blaze of day.

Despite demanding an attack 'with utmost vigour', Hamilton's eventual plan called for an isolated advance by one brigade of the 29th Division and an attack by four battalions of the New Zealand infantry against a position of at least nine Turkish battalions. By midday the attack had collapsed, but so unthinkable was failure to Hamilton that he ordered the entire Allied line to fix bayonets and advance against the Turkish front. In doing so they were 'lashed and scourged by a hurricane of lead' from shore to shore of the peninsula.[72] In some places not a single yard of ground was gained and on Krithia Spur the Australians lost in half an hour 1,000 of the 2,000 men engaged. After nightfall troops from 1st Lancashire Fusiliers and Drake battalion crossed without casualty a belt of country as wide as that which had cost the lives of 1,000 Australians. In the three days of fighting the Allies had lost 6,500 men (a third of those engaged) and still the Turkish official account made no mention of a general attack until the last advance at ten past five on 8 May.

If the recording of these facts were not sufficient condemnation, Aspinall's description of the moments before the attack, through its evocative imagery and language, particularly the dramatic use of the present tense, powerfully reinforced his message of the unnecessary squandering of life:

Not a shot disturbed the serene silence of the morning and to those who at this moment of tension had any eyes for the lavish beauty of their surroundings, there was an added and almost unendurable poignancy in the approach of zero hour.

The scene that unfolded itself from the forward slopes of Hill 114 still lives in many memories. The grassy slopes that crown the cliffs are carpeted with flowers. The azure sky is cloudless; the air is fragrant with the scent of wild thyme. In front, beyond a smiling valley studded with cypress and olive and patches of young corn, the ground rises gently to the village of Krithia, standing amidst clumps of mulberry and oak; and thence more steeply to the frowning ridge beyond, its highest point like the hump of a camel's back. Away to the right, edged with a ribbon of silvery sand, lie the sapphire arc of Morto Bay, the glistening Dardanelles and the golden fields of Troy. On the left, a mile out in the Aegean, a few warships lie motionless, like giants asleep, their gaunt outlines mirrored in a satin sea; while behind them in the tender haze of the horizon, is the delicately pencilled outline of snow-capped Samothrace. As far as the eye can reach there is no sign of movement; the world seems bathed in sleep. Only high on the shoulder of Achi Baba – the goal of the British troops – a field of scarlet poppies intrudes a restless note. Yet in half an hour that peaceful landscape will again be overrun by waves of flashing bayonets; and these are the last moments of hundreds of precious lives.[73]

There was another occasion where Aspinall selected to use colourful language to glorify the performance of the troops. This is of particular interest because it represented a rare occasion concerning an issue of substance where Aspinall was prepared to amend his account in deference to specific sensibilities despite what he knew to be the truth. The chapter in question dealt with the amphibious landing at Anzac of 25 April and the attempts by the Allied forces to establish themselves on the peninsula over the subsequent two days. Aspinall circulated the drafts of these during the latter half of 1926 and the senior officers and authorities to whom they were sent responded positively and without complaint. The Foreign Office, for example, informed Aspinall that these chapters were 'with small exceptions . . . admirable in arrangement and style and [called] for no criticism from this department'.[74] Braithwaite, Hamilton's Chief of Staff, who was to become a more severe critic of Aspinall's work in due course, offered only minor factual corrections and commented that the points raised were 'justified from the point of view of doing better next time'.[75] As Aspinall himself recorded in a letter to the Historical Section:

> In my first draft I did my best to tell the truth about the landing without hurting any feelings; to write a readable story which could be of military value to the student as well as of general interest to the public. The entire draft except in one respect met with entire approval. Sir Ian Hamilton, Sir William Birdwood, General Sinclair MacLagan (who commanded the covering force), the War Office, the Admiralty, the New Zealand government all saw it and approved it without comment and even General Edmonds himself pronounced it excellent.[76]

Interestingly a number of these reviewers, on finding fault with subsequent chapters, returned to this account and found much to complain about here that they had previously approved unnoticed. In fact during the circulation of these drafts the only source of potential controversy, possibly the one referred to by Aspinall in his note, concerned the Birdwood telegram requesting re-embarkation from the peninsula.

From the responses Aspinall received from those who had witnessed the action from a lower vantage point, however, he managed to piece together the picture at ground level and his findings were both previously unknown and, in one quarter, unwelcome. As Aspinall later recorded:

> This chapter was a difficult one to write because the truth about the Australians had never been told and in its place a myth had sprung up that the Anzac troops did magnificently against the odds.[77]

In fact, the version of events that emerged was one of untried and inexperienced troops who, when faced with a landing in the wrong place and the early loss of commanding officers, were unable to push on against an almost negligible Turkish force ahead of them. Aspinall's correspondence with German officers had established that until 9.20 a.m. on the morning of 25 April, the Turkish forces around Anzac comprised no more than 500 men to defend against an Australian force of by that time 8,000. His correspondence with Major Temperley of the New Zealand Infantry revealed that this officer had had frequently to turn back stragglers returning from the firing line to the beach under the impression that an order for evacuation had been given.[78] Following lengthy correspondence with the corps and divisional commanders Birdwood, Godley and Bridges (as well as Admiral Thursby), Aspinall had established that by nightfall the situation had become so serious that Godley and Bridges had recommended evacuation. Aspinall's first draft therefore incorporated these facts and had it been published unamended it would have ended the popular myth of the Anzac spirit on that day. However, unlike the discreet requests by Aspinall's previous correspondents, the reaction of Australian officers to this draft led to a very public outcry and to a unique reversal on Aspinall's part.

When this draft was sent to participating officers in Australia it provoked what *The Times* referred to as 'a storm of protest' in that country.[79] On 7 October 1927 the newspaper carried a telegram from Australian officers which revealed that the Official History had described the Anzac Corps as an 'ill-trained, ill-led, disorganised rabble . . . skulking on the beach [who] allowed a few brave men to storm the heights'.[80] Generals Monash and Gelisbrand complained that the book was being written by an officer who had witnessed the campaign from the luxury of the *Aragon* and was typical of the English 'depreciation which appeared periodically of Australian soldiers'.[81] On the same day a crowd of journalists stormed Edmonds' office requesting a statement. In Aspinall's defence Edmonds stated that the draft contained 'nothing of the sort' and quoted the Australian official historian, Charles Bean, who had described Aspinall's work as a 'fine, frank and clear account'.[82] Bean himself wrote to *The Times* on 10 October stating that the British historian and British fairness had been grossly slandered and indeed Monash, in a letter published on 2 November, wrote that he had in fact 'found nothing to which the Australians could take exception'.[83] As a result Edmonds sought the assistance of the Australian premier, Bruce, in tracking the source of the leak and what appeared to be a deliberate misrepresentation.

Nevertheless, despite these denials the Australian High Commission did raise formal objections to this chapter and requested wide-scale revision. Aspinall acceded to this in full measure and 'largely redrafted [his account] out of deference to Australian sensibilities'.[84] As he informed the Historical Section, some of their requests had been fair and others had 'been at the expense of historical accuracy; but in the new draft every word that was objected to by the Australians [was] expunged'.[85] Thus, in place of his revelations concerning the weakness of the Turkish force in defence, Aspinall omitted to cite any figures of its size (he told Edmonds that 'the High Commission particularly objected to this'[86]) but instead commented that '[the] delaying power of well-armed . . . marksmen, favoured by perfect knowledge of the ground [was] undoubtedly very great'.[87] In mitigation of Temperley's revelations concerning stragglers Aspinall added that:

hardly any of these men were stragglers in the ordinary sense of the word. Some of them had come back to the only centre of authority they knew in search of fresh orders. Others had returned in consequence of rumours that an order had been given to retire. Many of them though desperately weak were in high spirits.[88]

This last assertion was of course at variance with Aspinall's use of and concurrence in Birdwood's telegram requesting evacuation, which by contrast described 'thoroughly demoralised' men.[89] In place of descriptions of ill-trained and ill-led men Aspinall asserted that '[t]aking all factors into consideration it may well be doubted whether even a division of veteran troops could have carried out a co-ordinated attack at Anzac on 25th April'.[90] When, at a later date, criticism of Aspinall's work became focused on his comments on the competence of the higher command, Edmonds revisited and objected to this statement on the grounds that it reflected badly on Hamilton's decisions concerning the disposition of troops at his disposal. Aspinall informed him that this 'was one of the amendments made at the instance of the Australian Government'.[91] Far from exploding the myth that the Anzac troops performed magnificently well against the odds Aspinall actually perpetuated it. He concluded his revised chapter:

The predominant feeling which that astounding battlefield must always arouse in the military student who visits it, will be a sense of unstinted admiration for those untried battalions who did so exceedingly well. The magnificent physique, the reckless daring and the fine enthusiasm of the Dominion troops on their first day of trial went far to counteract anything they lacked in training or war experience. The story of their landing will remain for all time amongst the proudest traditions of the Australian and New Zealand forces.[92]

This widespread revision raises the question as to why Aspinall was prepared to defer to the sensibilities of the Australian government at the expense of historical accuracy but not later to the persistent and quite forceful requests on the part of his own government. One explanation must lie in the unprecedentedly public nature of this particular controversy. Given the reports in a number of London newspapers in October 1927 and Edmonds' statement in denial, a large degree of Aspinall's literary freedom of action would have been taken out of his hands. However, in addition one must consider that in accepting the modifications requested by the Australians Aspinall enhanced his theme of the spirit and courage of the troops even if, on this particular occasion, this was at the expense of historical accuracy. Whilst this departure from what he knew to be the truth was untypical of Aspinall, this specific case in no way threatened the more general lessons he wished to convey. Most of the accounts over which Aspinall clashed with his own authorities related to wider issues which he considered critical to a thorough understanding of the failures of the campaign.

To what degree did the amendment of this episode compromise the strength of Aspinall's arguments and criticisms? Certainly an important lesson of this action, that inexperienced troops should not be sent into a critical battle zone, was thereby ignored. Aspinall concluded that the documents revealed that whilst the Staff had recognised the potential of the landings at Gaba Tepe to 'win the war', they had perceived the Helles beaches to present the stiffest and most critical challenge.[93] They had therefore assigned the more experienced troops of the 29th Division to this landing and had assumed (correctly in the first instance) that the troops at Anzac Beach would face an easier task. Given that the importance of employing experienced troops in this theatre was clear only with hindsight, the failure to reveal this lesson in the Official History is a relatively minor shortcoming.

Of greater significance was the conduct of the senior officers commanding these troops. As Dawnay informed Aspinall:

I have always believed myself that if Birdwood had been in a quite different frame of mind from what he was on 27th April (as you remember well) that his people might not only have reached the top of the ground but kept it.[94]

It was largely for this reason that Aspinall was not prepared to alter another significant part of his account of this landing despite persistent requests from Birdwood himself to do so. Once more Aspinall's thoroughness in establishing the truth was evident, on this occasion against the efforts of a senior and influential officer and, indeed, Edmonds, to seek revision of his work.

The passages to which Birdwood objected concerned his actions on the evening of the first day, 25 April 1915. Called to the peninsula at 9.15 p.m., Birdwood was informed by his divisional commanders, Godley and Bridges, that the situation was so serious that they did not expect the troops to withstand a heavy attack in the morning and that they should re-embark immediately. In fact prior to Birdwood's arrival Godley had already sent a message to the *Queen* stating that 'All available boats are required on shore.'[95] Initially Birdwood refused to entertain a withdrawal but he was eventually persuaded of the helplessness of the situation and agreed to put the position before his Commander-in-Chief. At his dictation Godley took down the following telegram which was to be despatched to Hamilton aboard the *Queen Elizabeth*:

> Both my divisional generals and brigadiers have represented to me that they fear their men are thoroughly demoralised by shrapnel fire to which they have been subjected all day after exhaustion and gallant work in the morning. Numbers have dribbled back from firing line and cannot be collected in this difficult country. Even the New Zealand Brigade which has only recently been engaged lost heavily and is to some extent demoralised. If troops are subjected to shell fire again tomorrow morning there is likely to be a fiasco, as I have no fresh troops with which to replace those in the firing line. I know my representation is most serious, but if we are to re-embark it must be at once.[96]

The problem surrounding this telegram was that in the hurry of its despatch it was not addressed to Hamilton as it was intended but simply addressed *Queen*. (Hamilton was at that point upon the *Queen Elizabeth*.) It was thus handed to Admiral Thursby aboard the *Queen*, who naturally thought it was intended for him and made preparations to lower all boats to send them to the beach. Thursby was on the point of going ashore to confer with Birdwood when Hamilton's flagship arrived and it was only therefore by chance that the message was conveyed to him. Given the information from Thursby that it would take two days fully to re-embark the force at Anzac, Hamilton immediately despatched a telegram to Birdwood in which he informed him that there was 'nothing for it but to dig yourselves right in and stick it out'.[97] He added, 'You have got through the difficult business. Now you have only to dig, dig, dig until you are safe.'[98] The effect of this telegram was, according to Aspinall, to have an electrifying effect on the commanders on the spot and thenceforth all talk of evacuation ceased. However, the request had been made and, depending upon the interpretations placed upon the motives in making it, a senior commanding officer had, at best, argued strenuously that an evacuation was inevitable and, at worst, sought to evacuate without the consent of his Commander-in-Chief.

In preparing what was a passage of no more than three pages Aspinall encountered considerable difficulty in satisfying himself of the true facts, to the point where he was forced to admit to Godley, 'I doubt whether I shall ever be able to resolve [the issue].'[99] Aspinall retained in his papers the original hand-written message, and it was indeed undated, untimed and unaddressed, and although it was signed 'Birdwood' it had not been written by him. He originally suspected therefore that the message had never been intended for Hamilton but was a direct request to Thursby to re-embark the force and he informed Godley of this on 3 March 1927.[100] However, Aspinall was persuaded by Godley that the message was definitely intended as a signal to be conveyed onwards to Hamilton and that they would rather have died on the beaches than evacuate without Hamilton's permission.[101]

The issue Aspinall found more difficult to resolve was the exact motive in sending the telegram. Godley saw it as a definite request to re-embark and asked Aspinall to make clear in his account that, after representation by himself and Bridges, Birdwood was also convinced that such a definite request should be made. He suggested a modification which was eventually to appear in the published version: 'After a long discussion [Birdwood] accepted the opinion of his divisional commanders that from a local point of view evacuation must be contemplated and was the best military course.'[102] This made it clear that the three senior commanders on the spot, Birdwood, Godley and Bridges, actively requested evacuation. Birdwood, by contrast, argued that he had merely wished to put the facts of the situation before Ian Hamilton and allow him to decide, and it was in order to acknowledge this that he asked Aspinall to amend his version. Birdwood's own account was that he had been surprised on his return to shore to find that Godley and Bridges had drastically changed their view from earlier in the day and were 'most definite and earnest that unless we evacuated we would be swept off the hills in the morning'.[103] Birdwood claimed that he would have refused to countenance any such request to Hamilton, but because he had heard about the poor situation at Helles, he agreed to send the message on the grounds that his information would allow Hamilton to decide whether to concentrate his forces in one of the two locations. He added that because Godley's handwriting was clearer than his, he dictated the message to him. He stated to his commanders that he would rather stay and die than vacate the position and he was therefore greatly relieved when the message came back to dig in. As this version was at variance with Godley's, Aspinall sought additional sources for corroboration. One source confirmed that Birdwood had informed his divisional commanders of his preference to die rather than evacuate.[104] More crucially, from the log of messages and reports transmitted that day, Aspinall could find no evidence that Birdwood could have known about the situation at Helles. Aspinall informed Birdwood frankly therefore that he could 'not go along with his suggestion that the telegram was sent to allow Ian Hamilton to concentrate his forces', and he suggested again that he believed it was intended for Thursby alone to evacuate them without

Hamilton's knowledge or consent.[105] Birdwood naturally remained dissatisfied with this explanation and continued to pursue his requests, first with Aspinall and then, a year later, with Edmonds (whom he asked not to inform Aspinall of their correspondence as he would 'naturally . . . resent this'[106]).

The nature of Birdwood's repetitive pleas and shifting explanations is such that one must conclude that Aspinall was fully justified in refusing to believe his version. In May 1927, for example, Birdwood had told Aspinall that he purposely did not reveal in his telegram the suggestion which had been his motive in sending it, namely that Hamilton might wish to concentrate his forces. This was because 'it would probably convey the impression that my report was half-hearted'.[107] Yet when writing to Edmonds of his concerns in November 1928 Birdwood said of this point:

> I purposely did not give [Hamilton] this reason . . . for I thought it was a fairness to him simply to place the situation before him as it had been represented to me and leave him entirely free to judge.[108]

In April 1929 Birdwood referred again to his desire simply to place the full facts before Hamilton without 'attempting to influence him or presuming to make suggestions to him'.[109] Notwithstanding this discrepancy, the words and tone of the telegram cannot be read in this light. In addition, whereas Birdwood told Aspinall he had asked Godley to write the telegram because his handwriting was better, he informed Edmonds that it was because his hands were very cold.[110] This particular discrepancy may be no more than a mistaken memory or indeed no discrepancy at all as the effect of the latter can result in the former. However, this stream of correspondence and different explanations repeated at some length led Aspinall to detect special pleading. He told Birdwood that he had in fact written an amended version that made clear that Birdwood did not *want* to evacuate, but merely wanted to place the option before Hamilton. However:

> it seemed to call such undue attention to the frame of mind which, after all everyone who knows you would expect of you, and looked like such a bit of special pleading that I decided it would be a terrible mistake and erased it.[111]

This was also the conclusion at which Edmonds was compelled to arrive after considerable correspondence with Birdwood. This was despite the fact that Edmonds clearly led Birdwood to believe that he could secure an amendment to his satisfaction. In December 1928 Birdwood wrote to Edmonds:

A line to thank you so much for . . . all the trouble you have so very kindly taken on my behalf regarding the official account of our landing at Gallipoli. I look forward to receiving the official account in due course and will go through it with much interest. As you have had the drafting of this I feel quite sure it will meet all I am so anxious should appear on the subject and, as I say, I am most grateful to you for it.[112]

Yet Edmonds' reply in March 1929 suggested, as Aspinall had done, that Birdwood's attitude to evacuation was clear enough without saying anything additional in his support and that to do so would cause the suspicion that 'qui s'excuse s'accuse'.[113] Edmonds also now informed him that it was, in any case, too late to make alterations before publication. Birdwood was left with his concerns that his motives would be misunderstood by the 'world in general' and that the Australians would react badly to the suggestion that an evacuation was contemplated on the first day.[114] The fact, though, that the pleas of a senior officer for special treatment had no influence over Aspinall's work in any way reflected the genuinely independent and academic approach he took in compiling his official account.

6

Military Operations: Gallipoli, Part II

I

Far more concerted attempts to compel Aspinall to alter his history came when he began work on a section dealing with the struggle of the Allied troops to retain their positions on the fringes of the peninsula from 27 April to 8 May 1915. The great hopes of a speedy advance had by that point been dashed and the campaign had settled quickly into the familiar one of entrenchment and deadlock. To Aspinall, approaching the end of his first volume, this point prompted reflection on a wider level of the reasons for such disappointing failure so far. His study of these early days following the landings, particularly the offensives of the Second Battle of Krithia, called into question both Hamilton's leadership and his military competence and brought into focus the entire military strategy of the British government in terms of its provision of resources and its commitments to the various theatres of operation it had created. These issues were of vital importance in the process of exposing failure and learning from mistakes; indeed, Aspinall termed them the 'crux of the whole situation'.[1] As a result, Aspinall was not prepared on these issues to sacrifice his literary freedom of opinion to the political requirements of his own government.

Three chapters at the end of Aspinall's first volume contained explicit and graphic criticism of those he held responsible for the failure of the Gallipoli expedition. Because of the nature of this criticism these three chapters (entitled 'Reinforcements', 'The Second Battle of Krithia' and 'The End of the First Phase') were responsible for the vast majority of all governmental complaints concerning both volumes. These complaints are an indication of the level of concern various government departments had both for the particular nature of Aspinall's analysis and for the content of Official Histories in general. They reveal, too, the very active manner in which these departments sought to impose their views, even to the point of suggesting entire passages to be written directly into the account.

However, the most remarkable fact about these episodes was that Aspinall was largely able to escape the censor's blue pencil and succeeded in publishing a frank and personal account despite the serious objections of the army, of the great departments of state and of Edmonds himself.

Aspinall's chapter dealing with the Second Battle of Krithia with its explicit and implicit criticism of Hamilton's military judgement has already been described. In 'Reinforcements', Aspinall continued this attack on Hamilton. Although he blamed Kitchener for providing insufficient troops for the task, with no reserve and no allowance for wastage, he criticised Hamilton's reluctance to ask Kitchener for the necessary reinforcements and for his naïve optimism. Hamilton continued to approach with confidence what, by 27 April, had become an impossible task as his 53 battalions faced an entrenched and reinforcing Turkish army of 75. Indeed, it was only through the information supplied by the French admiral Guepratte that Kitchener learnt of the necessity for additional troops; Hamilton himself had made no mention of this. Aspinall recorded that, in Hamilton's anxiety to 'spare the overburdened War Secretary by not anticipating troubles which might never arise, none of his messages at this time gave serious cause for uneasiness'.[2] However, Hamilton's shortcomings aside, Aspinall argued that the campaign was destined to failure because the government failed to invest in it the necessary resources to see it through to a successful conclusion. The coinciding of the campaign with the German gas attacks at Second Ypres and the fact that every person of military influence was or had been serving on the Western Front created a jealous resolve not to divert resources from that theatre. In contrast, Aspinall cited Tirpitz in July 1915 as having recognised that the loss of the Straits would have resulted in the ending of the war: 'The situation is obviously very critical. Should the Dardanelles fall the world war has been decided against us.'[3]

This theme was continued more forcefully in 'The Ending of the First Phase'. By 7 May, following the wasteful and unsuccessful Second Battle of Krithia, the campaign had entered the deadlock of trench warfare that Britain had sailed thousands of miles to outflank. Having ridiculed Hamilton's excuse to Kitchener that 'our troops can do all that can be achieved by flesh and blood against semi-permanent works' by drawing on Turkish evidence to show that their positions at this time could in 'no sense' be described as semi-permanent, Aspinall again turned his attention to the government's inadequate response to the campaign's requirements. The 'deplorable situation' at the beginning of May was due to two months' warning of an impending attack having been given by the unsuccessful naval attempts to force the passage unaided. Had a combined attack been carried out before 25 February, as the Turkish official account acknowledged, it would have been successful. The importance of success in this theatre might have been apparent to Tirpitz but it had not been

5. Edmonds (in centre) with batman, Austin (on right), and chauffeur, 1918.

recognised at home or at Gallipoli. After the fleet had failed to force a passage of the Straits unaided there was no careful review of the military situation and no consideration of what action should be taken if the force despatched was too weak. As a result no attempt was made to consider giving Hamilton prior claim to men and material from the Western Front. Aspinall concluded:

> Here undoubtedly was the crux of the whole situation . . . [T]here can be little question that, in view of the shortage of men and ammunition it was wrong to embark upon [military operations in Gallipoli], and to proclaim that they must be carried through, unless it was decided that they were of such importance that, till success was achieved, the peninsula must be regarded as the active theatre of war. This was the acid test. There could only be one decisive theatre . . . With barely enough ammunition for one theatre, an offensive campaign was sanctioned in two, and both ended in failure.[4]

To Aspinall a crucial example of this acid test was the campaign conducted at Aubers Ridge on 9 May. Here three divisions of Haig's First Army and eight additional brigades supported by 500 guns and 80,000 rounds of ammunition, most of which was expended in the 40-minute preliminary bombardment, attacked two sectors of the heavily wired and fortified German line. Of the 55,000 men engaged the British forces suffered 11,000 casualties and 'were unable to gain a yard of ground. They did not attract a single company from the German reserves to the British battle front; and at nightfall the attack was abandoned on the score that its continuance would be a useless waste of life.'[5] Aspinall's contention was that had these 80,000 rounds of ammunition and 20,000 of the men been diverted from the Western Front to Gallipoli, there could have been no material disadvantage to the unsuccessful Aubers Ridge offensive, but it might well have allowed Hamilton to break through to the high ground and thereby carried the Fleet to Constantinople. The government, however, was too preoccupied by the shell crisis, fears of invasion, and Russian reverses in Galicia, and ultimately collapsed.

The government objected to these views and began to request revisions from the moment Aspinall circulated the draft chapters in early 1927. The objections of the Foreign Office centred predominantly around Aspinall's treatment of Sir Ian Hamilton. Their concerns were motivated by diplomatic considerations, and in this case, as in all their previous and subsequent interventions, their motives had little to do with historical accuracy and much to do with using the Official Histories as a vehicle for their own political expediency. On 26 April 1927 a Foreign Office representative, W. Childs, wrote to the Historical Section:

> I wonder if General Aspinall absorbed in the writing of the history is fully aware of the impression his narrative is building up regarding General Sir Ian Hamilton. If the impression being created is intentional on the part of the author I have nothing to say beyond suggesting its development should be carefully watched.[6]

Childs expressed concern at the growing impression of an inept and futile Commander-in-Chief whose actions were described as not always subject to the control of reason. These concerns were passed on to Aspinall who agreed to tone down some statements and add some 'palliative remarks'.[7] Nevertheless, Daniel argued, the facts spoke for themselves and 'it was a sorry business'.[8] In addition Sir Ian himself had seen the draft and, with the exception of some suggested modifications to show he had been to a great extent a victim of circumstances, had fully approved the chapters. In support of Aspinall, Daniel added that 'to [his] mind it is difficult to see how loyalty to or fear of one's chief [Kitchener] can justify the senseless sacrifice of a number of lives'.[9] In reply the Foreign Office, admitting that it was going 'rather beyond criticism which could naturally come from the Foreign Office', nevertheless revealed something of its own agenda for the Official Histories.[10] Many French and Dominion troops had served, and no doubt perished, under Hamilton, and his representation as inept was therefore politically damaging. Accordingly:

> although Sir Ian may not be unduly sensitive as to how his military reputation appears in History there is a public side to the question as well as a private one . . . is it not therefore politic that the Official History of the campaign should, so far as is compatible with historical truth, endeavour to present the Commander-in-Chief in a favourable light?[11]

A further issue concerned the perceived role of the Official Histories as a defence against anticipated attacks by civilian writers and diarists. In the view of its correspondent, Stephen Gaselee:

> it does seem inevitable that much criticism will be directed against [Hamilton] in the future and the Official History should therefore do what is possible to record and explain his difficulties and decisions and thus reduce to their proper proportions some unfortunate implications that arise in the course of the narrative.[12]

Aspinall, however, was not prepared to alter the tone or impact of his remarks and so in August the Foreign Office wrote to him directly with more specific requests for amendments (such as the request to remove the word 'violently' from the description of Hamilton as 'violently optimistic') and with specific suggestions of passages in their own words for inclusion in the text. Childs explained that he made no pretence at military criticism (a fact which did not prevent him from suggesting revisions of passages dealing with exclusively military issues), but was specifically concerned with the 'presentation of political and other relevant facts'.[13] Childs was critical of Aspinall's suggestion that the Second Krithia attack had been an 'impossibility' and his description of a 'four deep array of causes of defeat each serious enough alone to bring about failure'. This gave the impression of 'damning the attack before it began' and would lead readers to speculate on the 'capacity of the Commander-in-Chief'.[14] Childs objected particularly to Aspinall's suggestion that inadequate time was allowed for the issue of brigade and battalion orders, which meant that 'attacks meant to be simultaneous were almost invariably delivered piecemeal'. Childs asked, 'is not a very serious reflection of the C.-in-C. implied in this bald presentation of fact?' Furthermore, he argued that Aspinall had given undue equality to minor failures in relation to the principal one: that 'an advance by daylight without adequate artillery support against unlocated, unreconnoitred machine gun positions was almost an impossibility'. With regard to this specific point Aspinall amended his account as suggested. Thus the 'four deep array of causes' was assigned the role suggested by the Foreign Office and in the final version became 'to a minor extent other causes . . . [which] all had their influence on the course of events'.[15] Similarly accommodating, Aspinall identified the principal reason for the failure of the offensive: 'that an advance by daylight without adequate artillery support, against unlocated machine gun positions, is nine cases out of ten a sheer impossibility'.[16] However, on the question of delayed orders and the 'serious reflection' on Hamilton that this implied the account was not altered. Nor did Aspinall accept Childs' suggestion that Hamilton's concern not to lose any time 'certainly might [have been] used with a great deal more emphasis'.[17]

More significantly, Childs had been particularly critical of Aspinall's use of Hamilton's 'semi-permanent works' telegram and his subsequent comment that these so-called semi-permanent works were in fact only a few detached lengths of unwired trenches held by no more than advanced troops. This, he stated, 'made unfortunate reading in the light of previous optimism'. Childs suggested that Aspinall mitigate this impression by stating that the lack of aerial reconnaissance had concealed this fact and 'imposed on the British Commander-in-Chief the belief that they were formally entrenched'. This would 'diminish the awkward contrast exhibited between the situation as it existed in the C.-in-C.'s imagination and the truth as subsequently established'.[18] However, no such amendment was made and one must conclude that this 'awkward contrast' was specifically what Aspinall wished to emphasise. On a similar issue Edmonds later accused him of failing to adhere to his guidelines whereby knowledge gained after the event, particularly in relation to troop dispositions, was included only in footnotes. This was in order to ensure that the reader was possessed only of those facts available to the commander at the time so that he might be judged fairly in the light of his limited knowledge. Aspinall's response to that, along with his motives in failing to accept these revisions of the Foreign Office, was that to do so 'would deprive [his] work of its usefulness and the greater part of its interest'.[19]

The Foreign Office also intervened on other occasions to seek revision to Aspinall's work, and, although these related to different subject matters, the political and diplomatic motivations were the same. One such occasion concerned Aspinall's early chapters on the beginnings of the conflict with the Turks and dealt with the loss of Turkey as a potential Entente ally, or at least a neutral. The Foreign Office was at pains to draw to Aspinall's attention the numerous and inevitable consequences of German actions in bringing Turkey into the war on its side in order to counter any suggestions that it was the failure of British diplomacy prior to October 1914 which pushed a traditional sympathiser towards the enemy's camp. Aspinall was informed by Childs that he had underestimated the influence of the German Ambassador at Constantinople, von Bieberstein, in winning over the Turks. In addition, the presence of the *Goeben* in Constantinople, combined with the arrival of the *Breslau*, had overawed all active opposition in Constantinople to war. Aspinall was instructed to include a reference to pan-Turkish hopes of realising their aspirations with German help. The key to understanding the policy of Enver, Talaat and their inner circle was, according to the Foreign Office, the fact that:

a bargain had been struck and embodied in a secret agreement under which Turkey, as an active ally of Germany, was to be given the Caucasia, North West Persia and Trans Caspian provinces . . . This was the influence which ensured Turkey's participation in the war on the side of Germany.[20]

Aspinall did mention the influence of von Bieberstein ('His giant stature, heavy build and scarred face were all turned to account'[21]), of the *Goeben* and *Breslau* and of the extravagant promises of expanded territory which were, he claimed, almost certainly embodied in a secret agreement. However, Aspinall also argued that, notwithstanding the strength of these enticements, Britain might still have deterred an alliance with Germany. Even as late as the summer of 1914, '[a] friendly gesture by Britain and France . . . coupled with a guarantee of Turkish independence and integrity, might perhaps have recalled Turkey to her old attitude and ensured a benevolent neutrality in the Dardanelles'.[22] But, '[t]hrough all the critical days of July and early August, the British Ambassador at Constantinople was absent on leave. By the time he returned on 18th August the die was already cast.'[23]

Of equal significance was Childs' argument that it was important to avoid attaching too much importance to the Greek offer made before the war that they would land a force of 75,000 men to take the Dardanelles at the same time as undertaking naval operations to force the Straits. The reluctance of the Greeks to enter the war until a likely victor had emerged meant that this offer was to be 'discounted in value'.[24] In addition, the likelihood of their success had been greatly overestimated. It was interesting that the Foreign Office should be anxious to devalue this offer, particularly in the light of information Aspinall received from a former military attaché at Athens that the Greek army and navy *could* have been used to good effect even from April to October 1915 but for the 'stupid and unjust way the Foreign Office dealt with the Greek offer'.[25] As a result Aspinall not only mentioned the Greek offer but described in detail its plans for forcing the Dardanelles, whilst discounting Childs' suggestion that these did not offer a reasonable prospect of success. He noted that Britain had been unable to embrace the offer because it would have frustrated her ambition at that time to maintain Turkish neutrality and to preserve a neutral bloc in the Balkans.

Two further Foreign Office interventions are worthy of consideration. The first concerned their attempt to use the work as a vehicle to promote advances they wished to make towards the Turks under the leadership of Kemal Ataturk. Kemal had served as a lieutenant-colonel at Gallipoli. In 1931 the Foreign Office determined 'on grounds of political expediency' to present Kemal with a bound copy of the history.[26] However, they also desired that the information contained within this official work should reflect as far as possible a favourable view of their intended recipient:

> That is one reason why we have been anxious that justice should be done to the Turkish Army and Turkish Generalship; and it is just possible that it may make you feel inclined to say something more about him in the epilogue. On pages 10–11 your fine eulogy of the Turkish Army and Marshall Liman Von Sanders omits the part of one who is, for our present purposes, the Hamlet of the play.[27]

Rather magnanimously, the request went on to suggest that although Kemal had been only a divisional commander, it was he who had 'flung us off Chunuk Bair' and had been decisive in 'robbing us of success'.[28] Aspinall was evidently prepared to accede because his epilogue contained the following words, which, in the light of this request, can scarcely be considered to have been his own, unsolicited opinion:

It would be impossible to appraise too highly the assistance which Liman Von Sanders received from that 'Man of Destiny' the present ruler of Turkey, who showed on the peninsula, at the head of an infantry division, an outstanding genius for command.[29]

Aspinall credited Kemal as being primarily responsible for the Anzac Corps' failure to gain its objective on the first day of landing in April, for the checks and defeats suffered by the IX Corps at Suvla and for his brilliant counter-attack at Chunuk Bair which left the Turks in undisputed possession of the Sari Bair ridge. As such, Aspinall concluded:

[s]eldom in history can the exertions of a single divisional commander have exercised, on three separate occasions, so profound an influence not only on the course of a battle, but perhaps on the fate of a campaign and even the destiny of a nation.[30]

Whatever the basis in fact for such acclaim, the exaggerated manner and language with which it was incorporated into the text was markedly at variance with the considered judgement of the vast majority of the work. Nevertheless the tribute fulfilled its intended purpose for in a letter to the British Ambassador in June 1932, reprinted in *The Times*, the Turkish Foreign Minister acknowledged Kemal's thanks for an act of courtesy, nobly inspired. He wrote that to 'recognise . . . the qualities displayed by an adversary in moments of strife is to obliterate its bitterness and open up the path to friendship between two nations'.[31]

By contrast, a second intervention by the Foreign Office involved not the acclamation of a prospective ally but the denigration of an earlier one. It has recently been argued that '[t]o a considerable extent the "myth" of French war-weariness was manufactured by French politicians, soldiers and public figures anxious to convince the British government to concentrate its expanding military resources on the Western Front' and that such threats were in part responsible for Kitchener's final decision to argue for abandonment of the Gallipoli expedition.[32] The Foreign Office were aware of the impact of these threats on British strategy and sought to ensure that this was made public in the Official History of the campaign. In October 1931 they informed Aspinall that they wished him in his final chapters to explore the question of Kitchener and 'HMG giving way over evacuation against a/background of threats by Joffre and the French of rupture in the alliance'.[33] After Suvla, Kitchener had wanted to use all the British forces available to ensure ultimate success and had been supported in this by the Cabinet. However, French attempts to use the threat of a breakdown of the alliance to secure support for an operation in Serbia had decided the end of the campaign. The Foreign Office argued that unless Aspinall could use this information his history would be incomplete:

Gallipoli has now passed into history as perhaps the greatest failure of British arms and it is surely time that the public should be informed of the inner causes of this great disaster . . . You will see thus that we *want* these disclosures to be made, if they properly can.[34]

In order to assist Aspinall, the Foreign Office supplied relevant Cabinet and conference proceedings which were still subject to the Official Secrets Act. It has been previously mentioned that Aspinall already endorsed the interpretation that the campaign might have succeeded but for lack of men and *matériel* at critical moments. Already predisposed to deprecate any vacillation that prevented the necessary force at the disposal of the Allied powers from being brought to bear at Gallipoli, Aspinall used the information provided to him to make clear the part played by the French in the decision to withdraw from the peninsula. Dealing with the conference in London on 29 October at which Joffre argued for the removal of all British forces at Gallipoli to support an expedition to Salonika, Aspinall wrote:

The French Commander-in-Chief urged that if England could not send 250,000 men to Salonika she should send 150,000; and expressed the hope that Serbia could be saved from destruction and Greece persuaded or coerced to come in on the side of the Allies. The British members of the conference were disinclined to agree, but Joffre finally led them to believe that a British refusal to co-operate might entail his resignation and even the rupture of the Entente. Next morning a written promise was given to Joffre that the British Government would co-operate energetically with the French . . . By this agreement the possibility of sending more troops to the Dardanelles was seriously prejudiced even before the arrival of Sir Charles Monro's report.[35]

Whilst the Foreign Office might have justifiably argued that the incorporation of such evidence provided for a more complete work, its motivation was undoubtedly political and not academic.

In much the same way the interventions of the War Office, which would have made the work more narrow and arguably less 'complete', were motivated by its own view of the volume's revelations of military and political failings and equivocation. Where these requests accorded with his own view or where their inclusion would not detract from his central argument, Aspinall was prepared to revise his work. However, where they would have fundamentally altered the nature of his work and its lessons, Aspinall was not prepared to accede.

In reviewing the three chapters concerning the Second Battle of Krithia and the issue of reinforcements at the end of Aspinall's first volume, the War Office and the General Staff raised a number of objections which, had they been respected, would have almost totally removed this portion of it and thereby devalued the work considerably. In 1927 the General Staff submitted a list of concerns to Aspinall, in response to which he responded by refusing to amend his account. As a result, they were then submitted to the CID Subcommittee for the Control of Official Histories. Of Aspinall's comparison with the Aubers Ridge offensive, the General Staff informed the Subcommittee that the 'weighing of the relative advantages of offensives in different theatres in a sectional history is inappropriate and should be left out'.[36] Aspinall's argument concerning the failure of the government to decide its strategic priorities and to provide sufficient resources to meet them was strongly opposed. The committee was advised that the 'General Staff wish the whole of the following passage to be omitted on the grounds that it is a discussion of the very controversial matter of the inception of the campaign by the Western School'.[37] They objected, too, to the 'tone which differ[ed] materially from that adopted in writing the histories of the other campaigns in the Great War in which the facts [were] stated and the reader left to form his own conclusions'.[38] In addition, they demanded the deletion of passages dealing with Sir John French's attempts to hold back resources for the Western Front, with *The Times* leader of 27 April 1915, which stated that Britain must not be deflected from this theatre, and with Tirpitz' opinion that a landing prior to 25 February would have been unopposed and would have ended the war. However, having already considered these issues to be 'the crux of the whole situation', Aspinall responded that he attached great importance to their retention:

> In the author's opinion if the lessons that undoubtedly may be learnt from a study of this unique campaign are to be usefully brought out these passages must be maintained in their present form without alteration.[39]

It was thus decided that these matters should be resolved at the annual meeting of the Committee for Control on 9 March 1928. The proceedings of this meeting reveal how Aspinall was able to retain the majority of his work unamended and indicate where the ultimate authority for the approval of the content of an official work lay. Furthermore, they illustrate both the strength of Aspinall's determination to publish a truthful and valuable account and the motivations of Edmonds and Hankey in seeking to temper this approach in the interests of the 'official' version of events.

The meeting was chaired, as was customary, by Lord Eustace Percy, President of the Board of Education. Edmonds, Hankey, Sir Henry Newbolt and representatives of the services also attended. The Treasury was represented, as it had been since 1926, by James Rae. The presence of Winston Churchill, then Chancellor of the Exchequer, can only be explained by his particular and personal interest in this matter. His involvement was to be critical to the outcome of the meeting. Edmonds had his own list of complaints concerning tone and 'little lapses of taste' which he took the opportunity to raise. However, on the question of the General Staff objections his view was that, whilst there were lessons to be learnt, the Official History 'should not rub it in. [He] did not want everyone to see the troubles we had and the mistakes we made.'[40] Hankey's view was that deference must be given to the views of the CIGS because the book was written 'for soldiers on information supplied almost exclusively by the War Office'.[41] In reply, Aspinall argued that he did not want it thought that his views were those of the General Staff. He was clear that 'the story was not written for the General Staff, it was not a General Staff publication'. Furthermore he 'could not see the value of history written in blinkers or read in blinkers'.[42]

Aspinall was forcefully supported in his argument by Churchill, who naturally saw in the publication of criticisms of the government and Kitchener an exoneration for his own part in the failure of the campaign. The passages which the General Staff now wanted to delete added considerable weight to Aspinall's contention that the Gallipoli plan had been a viable and visionary operation which had foundered on the paralysis and vacillation of those charged with its execution. Aspinall had already written in the introductory passages of his work that at the very moment when the Fleet was 'thundering a message of resolve' in the early months of 1915, politicians, 'Western influences' and Lord Kitchener were creating 'doubt and indecision'.[43] The passages now under review by the Committee clearly demonstrated that in the author's view it was not Churchill's concept which had been at fault but the manner in which the government had squandered the critical opportunities it offered. It was therefore not surprising that Churchill viewed the attempts of the General Staff to keep this from the public domain as 'an atrocious falsification of the true presentation of the case'.[44] Having entrusted the task of compiling the history to an officer of 'high distinction and great experience', the Committee could not cut out what this officer regarded as essential to a 'proper and intelligible presentation'.[45] Churchill stated that the

> whole ghastly error which lay at the root of this story and of our war conduct was the inability of the military and naval authorities to distinguish between the main and the decisive theatre . . . [T]o smudge over that lesson, written in blood and disaster, would be to render the greatest disservice to future students of the war.[46]

In typically robust fashion, Churchill threatened the Committee that an omission of the sort recommended by the War Office would undoubtedly become known and this would lead to the belief that the contents of these passages were much more important than they actually were. Offering a not particularly enticing alternative, he suggested that he would have no complaint if the Committee chose to uphold the view of the General Staff on condition that the offending passages were left blank in the text, reproduced in an appendix, and a footnote included advising readers that the blank section had been struck out 'in deference to the susceptibilities of the General Staff'.[47] Churchill also insisted that if this were to be done it must be made clear that this was in spite of the author's view that the original passages had been necessary for an integral and comprehensive treatment of the campaign. The War Office representative on the Committee, Buchanan, remained unmoved by these arguments and insisted that the Army Council stood by its view. The strength of Churchill's position, however, lay in the fact that the ultimate authority in this matter rested with the Cabinet and he 'would not agree in any circumstances to these passages being cut out without a Cabinet decision'.[48] At this the Committee concluded, through its Chairman, that Aspinall should retain most of these passages but should offer some mitigation for the government. Percy suggested that the difficulties it experienced in balancing its commitments could be explained 'if only in charity, even if not quite true'.[49]

Thus the freedom of a determined and conscientious author to express his informed though personal view in an official work was accorded, despite the attempts of a normally influential section of his government to prevent him. The fact that this literary integrity was guaranteed by a politician who saw in this work an opportunity for public exoneration should not detract from the value of what eventually emerged. Given that the ultimate authority of sanction or veto rested with the Cabinet, Churchill, alone of all the leading participants of the Great War, was in a position to exercise influence. Whilst this influence was unquestionably self-motivated, its implications for the nature of this particular official work were considerable and went beyond this issue alone.

II

Subsequent to this episode Aspinall was to enjoy considerable latitude in three significant areas. First, he was able to publish the much criticised chapters of his first volume with scarcely an amendment despite the fact that there was clearly agreement at the 1928 meeting that some specific sections would be omitted. Aspinall's copy of his original draft of these contentious chapters included his marginal notes showing the final agreement as to what was to be retained and what was to be censored.[50] However, a number of passages which Aspinall had marked as apparently 'blue-pencilled' in fact appeared in the published version. The portions explaining that the Gallipoli landings coincided with the German use of gas in Flanders and that Sir John French therefore resisted 'to the uttermost' the expenditure of any more strength in the East were published almost verbatim. The section dealing with the leading article in *The Times* of 27 April 1915 arguing against distractions in the East, with the 'Westerner' bias of all influential figures in the government and services, and with the acknowledgement by Tirpitz of the critical importance for Germany's entire war effort of retaining the Dardanelles, appeared in their original form (only in an earlier chapter). Finally, a section dealing with Kitchener's fear of invasion, which had been 'objected to on the ground that a discussion of the liability of England to invasion [was] out of proportion to the requirements of a history of the Dardanelles campaign' was retained with all but minor adjustments in the final published version.[51]

The consideration of these issues by the Committee for Control and Churchill's involvement marked a significant change in the relationship between Edmonds and Aspinall. Until this point Edmonds had had little to criticise in Aspinall's drafts. Indeed, at the end of 1926 Edmonds viewed Aspinall's work with sufficient regard to recommend him as an author for the potentially controversial and sensitive volume dealing with the near-triumphant German offensive of March 1918.[52] In March 1928, however, Edmonds' approach not only became highly critical but he began to look for fault and inappropriate content in drafts which he had previously approved without comment. Significantly, though, Aspinall was able to challenge these concerns and to publish an account of which Edmonds strongly disapproved.

At the 1928 meeting Edmonds complained about Aspinall's style and tone, which resulted in an impression which was 'too unkind to the various generals'.[53] In Edmonds' view 'they did not deserve much praise but in an official history he thought it sufficient to state the facts and not to rub them in'.[54] He objected too to the devotion of three pages to Birdwood, Godley and Bridges losing heart on the beach at Anzac when half a dozen lines would have sufficed, and insisted that the telegram requesting evacuation be omitted. In his defence Aspinall commented that Godley had gone through his narrative point by point and had been delighted with it. Concerning the Birdwood telegram Aspinall asserted that since every history on the subject had commented upon it he did not see how the Official History could 'burke what was the most discussed telegram of the whole campaign'.[55] Within days of this meeting, however, Edmonds passed on to Aspinall further criticism of his work from an 'eminent critic' whom Edmonds wished to remain anonymous. This objection centred around the same issues raised by the War Office and Foreign Office of the scope of the work and its explicit criticism. The author wrote:

If Gallipoli had only been written in the same spirit as were the first two volumes on France . . . all would have been well and it is all the more pity because the description of the fighting in Gallipoli is very graphically written and it is only the criticisms which are so, to my mind, wrongly conceived.[56]

It is possible that the author of this was Hamilton's Chief of Staff, Braithwaite. It resembled very closely the sentiments he had expressed directly to Aspinall some months before without effect. In April 1927 Braithwaite had written:

I am altogether opposed to your method of criticism . . . There is a tone of sarcasm running through many of the criticisms which I think is quite out of place in a book of this description . . . Writing with after the event knowledge you give a somewhat unfortunate impression which I personally should be sorry to see go down as the official view. In short I suggest you follow the lines of Volumes I and II of the Official History of the Campaign in France and Flanders.[57]

Aspinall confided to Liddell Hart in 1930 that he believed Braithwaite to be the chief factor in the War Office objections to his work, which had resulted in the dispute being brought before the meeting of the Committee for Control in 1928.[58]

Whether Braithwaite's or not, these opinions further crystallised Edmonds' objections to the nature of Aspinall's work, and the depth of his dissatisfaction was evident from the comments that accompanied this anonymous letter. He informed Aspinall:

There is a distortion in your glasses which prevents you seeing Gallipoli events without a certain bias; this is so obvious that most of the press critics will see it and I fear it will destroy the literary and historical value of your work. I am sure that in another ten years you will regret having written this book. It will carry no more weight than Harper's volume on Jutland.[59]

Aspinall however remained unmoved and within four days of this letter, and no more than a week after the Committee for Control meeting, he nevertheless pressed ahead with arrangements to release his drafts to the press. This prompted Edmonds to write on 6 April: 'Dixon tells me you want your chapters prepared for the press. Is that not a little premature? The Committee directed me to settle certain things with you; we have only considered one point.'[60] A further small insight into the way in which Aspinall viewed Edmonds' complaints is provided by the fact that Aspinall attached Edmonds' letter of 2 April, which threatened criticism in the press and inevitable regret, to the front of his scrapbook containing the universally favourable reviews of his book.[61]

Edmonds also now revisited the drafts of sections which he had previously approved and found in them a number of passages with which to reinforce the themes of the complaints raised by Braithwaite and the War Office. Towards the end of 1928 he forwarded his objections to Aspinall's chapters on the Anzac landings. Edmonds accused Aspinall of a bias in the narrative which had begun with a consideration of what was happening on the Turkish side prior to landing. This study of Turkish movements on the morning of 25 April inevitably emphasised the loss of opportunities. Edmonds wrote:

> I have repeatedly told Aspinall that Turkish movements should be, according to our practice, in a note at the end of the chapter. At present it is grossly unfair to the leaders of troops who, of course, did not know what the enemy was about.[62]

Aspinall, already having defended this section against criticism from the Australians and amended it in deference to their views, responded that to place such information in a footnote as General Edmonds had originally requested would have deprived the work of the greater part of its usefulness and interest.[63] Indeed the issue of footnotes had, according to Aspinall, been referred to the Historical Section, which had informed him that he could continue with his own practice of incorporating such information in the text:

> In no case where I have mentioned enemy dispositions has there been any suggestion that the British leaders or troops were to blame for not knowing as much in 1915 as we do in 1927; I have used such phrases as 'in the light of the knowledge which only comes after the event' and I am surprised that if General Edmonds thought I was being 'grossly unfair' he should have waited till this very late hour to say so.[64]

Aspinall concluded, in addition, that such criticisms were difficult to deal with because to agree them would have necessitated an entire revision not only of the chapter in question but of the whole book.

III

In Aspinall's second volume, excepting the already cited involvement of the Foreign Office in the matters of Kemal and the French threats, there were no further governmental attempts at interference. This inactivity

135

did not reflect any change in tone or emphasis on Aspinall's part. Indeed, he devoted considerable sections of this second volume to reiterating and strengthening exactly those points to which the General Staff and Foreign Office had objected in Volume I. In Volume II Aspinall's continued criticism of government strategy was uncompromising and his 'controversial' view of the damage caused by Westerner prejudice was once more used forcefully in support of his argument. His view was that on two occasions after June the fortunes of the force clinging to the fringes of the Gallipoli peninsula were squandered by a government which vacillated between its various commitments and was pushed off course by the conflicting influence of its allies and its own members. Aspinall reiterated the comparison with Aubers Ridge and included also the offensive at Festubert where 10,000 rounds of ammunition were expended and 17,000 casualties incurred. Had these resources been available at Gallipoli, Aspinall argued in familiar refrain, the British would have long before opened the Narrows. Churchill had calculated that between April and June 1915 300,000 Allied troops had been lost in the recovery of eight square miles of the 10,500 square miles of French and Belgian territory then under German occupation. It was only through his powerful advocacy that government policy in July 1915 veered back towards the Dardanelles and 'when the offer was too late to be of any value they offered [Hamilton] every man and gun he could use'.[65] Already committed to a further offensive, Hamilton could not afford to postpone his plans until these new troops arrived. Once more, in contrast to the German view of Gallipoli as vital to the entire outcome of the world war, Aspinall reflected that 'on the one hand singleness of purpose was carrying the Central Powers from strength to strength; on the other divided counsels were jeopardising the chances of the Entente'.[66] It would be difficult to imagine a more critical attack on the inactivity of one's own government at a moment of great national crisis.

When Aspinall considered the reaction of the government to Hamilton's position following the failure of the Suvla operations his conclusions were in fact more damning still. The contrast with the Western Front was once more powerfully advocated. The campaign at Loos had cost the Allies 50,000 lives, more than double the losses at Suvla and Anzac. Kitchener was persuaded of the need for offensive action by Joffre's threats of insurrection, although these concerns were not shared by 'responsible French statesmen'. As a result, Sir John French was 'compelled to undertake operations before he was ready, over ground that was at most unfavourable, against the better judgement of himself and General Haig . . . with no more than a quarter of the troops . . . that he considered necessary for a successful attack'.[67] In the course of these operations 250,000 men were vainly sacrificed on the Western Front when, again, the supporters of Gallipoli had claimed that half that number would have secured the opening of the Straits. The lessons of this failure were twofold. Firstly, Britain had paid dearly for the 'cardinal error' of denuding the War Office of its most trusted officers by sending them to France in August 1914. In an echo of Ellison's contention, Aspinall concluded that 'for lack of this advice, Britain's wavering war policy in the spring and summer of 1915 had violated every principle of sound strategy'.[68] Secondly, returning to the theme of Volume I, the crux of the situation lay in the government's inability to recognise and commit to the vital theatre of operations. The heart of Aspinall's argument, which dominated both his volumes, was contained within the following lines:

> Committed up to their eyes since the outbreak of war to land operations on the Western Front in France, the Government had drifted in April 1915, without the semblance of a plan, into a military campaign in Gallipoli. Without sufficient ammunition for one theatre, the country had found itself engaged in two. After the initial deadlock which followed the April landings, when modest reinforcements might well have led to victory, the invading army had been starved through protests from France that reinforcements for the Dardanelles were merely prolonging the war. But the Gallipoli operations, though ill-supported, had been allowed to drag on, while the main effort continued to be made in the Western theatre of war.
>
> The student of war might search in vain for a clearer instance of a distracted war policy and a consequent wasteful dissipation of force.[69]

As remarkable as the clarity of this criticism was the fact that no objections were raised to this passage from any quarter. Whereas its equivalent passage in Volume I had generated vigorous and acrimonious debate, neither the General Staff, Foreign Office nor Edmonds offered any comment with respect to these comments in Volume II.

On an operational level Aspinall was equally forthright in his views of the senior commanding officers, particularly in relation to the Suvla offensive. The Commander of IX Corps, Lt-Gen. Sir Frederick Stopford, was singled out for particular criticism. Stopford was 61 at the time of the campaign and in poor health. He had never commanded troops in battle, had no personal experience of actual fighting and had been living in retirement since 1909 until uprooted by the advent of war to accept a senior command. Although briefed by Kitchener before his departure for Gallipoli on the necessity of initiative and surprise, Stopford appeared from the outset to want to slow the pace and expectation of the coming offensive. On arriving on the peninsula at the end of July Stopford went through Hamilton's plan with Aspinall line by line and pronounced it a good one. However, after considering it in detail with his senior staff officer of IX Corps, Brig.-Gen. Reed, Stopford began to have second thoughts and requested significant revisions to the objectives which were to prove disastrous to the success of the operation. Reed informed Hamilton that 'the whole teaching of the campaign in France proves that troops cannot be expected to attack an organised system of trenches without the assistance of a large number of howitzers'.[70] Notwithstanding their belief that the positions to be attacked were scarcely defended at all, Hamilton and GHQ acquiesced in what was to prove a crucial change of emphasis in Stopford's objectives. Thus the original instruction to have captured Chocolate and W Hills 'by a *coup de main* before daylight' was watered down to gaining these hills at an early period of the attack 'if it is possible, without prejudice to the attainment of your primary objective'.[71] Even this objective, which was to push on to the heights of Tekke Tepe to assist the Anzac breakout to the south, became commuted to the establishment of Suvla as a base in the northern zone. Aspinall skilfully demonstrated in his narrative how this fatal phrase 'if possible' infected all orders now passed from GHQ to corps and from corps to division to the point where Hammersley instructed his brigade commanders that they were to capture the Chocolate Hills and *if possible* the W Hills. Hammersley was also unaware that the primary objective in capturing these hills was specifically to assist the Anzac breakout in the south, for his orders actually stated that the purpose of the *Anzac* attack was to distract attention from the landings of his 11th Division.

At this point in his narrative, with the scene set for the attack the following day, Aspinall employed once more the tools of language, anticipation and ironic contrast to enhance the drama of his history. He first described the character of the men of the 11th Division leaving Imbros on 6 August for the 15-mile trip to Suvla:

> At a quarter past seven the sun went down in a crimson blaze, and half an hour later the whole flotilla crept quietly out of the bay. This departure was marked by none of the gay enthusiasm of the original Expeditionary Force as it started out from Mudros on the 23rd April bound for the 'Great Adventure'. Three bitter months had passed since that day . . . Stripped of its veil of romance, the gaunt figure of war stood out in all its grim reality, yet the more serious demeanour of the New Army troops as they slowly filed on board left a good impression on all who watched them embark. Grave but determined, they bore the air of men whom their leaders could trust.[72]

Were those leaders in turn, however, men in whom their soldiers could trust? It cannot be without purpose that Aspinall then related an occurrence wherein a staff officer visiting GHQ that night was informed that Stopford wished to see him. Stopford was lying down on his valise spread out on the floor of his tent. Without rising he informed the staff officer that he should instruct Hamilton he would do his best but if the enemy held strong lines of continuous entrenchments he would need guns to dislodge him. '"All the teaching of the campaign in France" he added, falling into the exact phraseology used by his Chief of Staff eleven days earlier, "proves that continuous trenches cannot be attacked without the assistance of a large number of howitzers".'[73] By such a cautious and pessimistic approach was a critical attack condemned before it had even begun. It was over 36 hours later, following a successful and almost completely unopposed landing, that Aspinall was sent ashore to ascertain the reason for the uneasy silence from IX Corps. Whilst men bathed naked offshore, Stopford remained on *Jonquil* still under the misguided impression that his forces were facing deeply entrenched positions. In fact, Aspinall revealed, his 22 battalions were opposed by no more than 1,500 Turks, who had withdrawn all their guns for fear of capture. It was at this point that Stopford, 'in excellent spirits', informed Aspinall that it was impossible to move until the men had rested and more guns had been brought ashore.[74]

If Aspinall's treatment of Stopford might be considered deliberately harsh, he was no more sparing in his frank and critical assessment of Hamilton's conduct of this phase of the campaign. Certainly, too, any opinions which might have been considered by both the Foreign Office and War Office in Volume I to have been inappropriate were restated and indeed amplified in Volume II. Hamilton was once more shown as over-optimistic and strategically weak. His acquiescence in Stopford's crucial change of emphasis to the Suvla plan has already been mentioned. In addition, the plan that Hamilton framed was inherently flawed as a viable operation because the success of the whole venture depended entirely upon the success of the first phase. The exigencies of the situation 'did not allow of more than a very narrow margin for the inevitable accident and normal human error'.[75] Hamilton's only chance lay in surprise and the momentum generated by seizing immediately a winning opportunity before the enemy could concentrate his forces. This called for determination and energy from the leaders as soon as their troops were ashore. If Hamilton was hampered in this by the senior officers available for the task, he did not help himself by his obsession for secrecy. No officer, however senior, was to be told anything that it was not absolutely essential for him to know. Indeed 'so determined was Sir Ian Hamilton to keep the Suvla plan profoundly secret that even General Stopford, who was to be charged with carrying out, was allowed to know nothing about it till 22nd July'.[76] Furthermore, Hamilton remained timid in his requests to Kitchener, which were couched in the obsequious terms which had characterised his earlier communications. Although Kitchener had offered Hamilton additional men, for example, two of the promised divisions were to be sent from England without guns. On 13 July Hamilton therefore begged Kitchener for an additional 15,500 rounds of high explosive and asked for two batteries of 4.5-inch howitzers for the 10th and 11th Divisions. According to Aspinall the moderation of the demand made 'pitiful reading'.[77]

Having thus hampered the already difficult prospects for success of this vital action, Hamilton's further failure to react to the unfolding inactivity of its opening hours with anything more than similar moderation doomed it to a failure which had more far-ranging implications. During 7 August Hamilton had an uneasy suspicion that time was being wasted, 'but if the mildness of his first application of the spur can be taken as a measure of his uneasiness, it would seem that the Commander in Chief was still convinced that there was no real cause for anxiety'.[78] Even Dawnay, Aspinall's friend and colleague during these difficult days, objected to Aspinall's assertion, which nevertheless remained unaltered, that had Hamilton gone ashore on 7 August and insisted to Stopford on an immediate advance he might have ended the war by two years. Instead he sent Aspinall to report back and, in response to his staff officer's dismay at what he found on shore, Hamilton despatched a telegram to Stopford:

> I am in complete sympathy with you in the matter of all your men and officers being new to this style of warfare, and without any leaven of experienced troops on which to form themselves. Still I should be wrong if I did not express my concern at the want of energy and push displayed by the 11th Division.[79]

Stopford, however, remained reluctant to countenance any advance without more water and ammunition and when piecemeal attempts were made on the following day in the face of far greater Turkish opposition, they were unsuccessful. Still Hamilton refused to accept or admit that he was beaten and when, three days later, the whole edifice of his plan lay in ruins and in the midst of a 'miasma of defeat' that was now infecting all ranks of the corps, he recorded: 'The Turks . . . knew they were done unless they could quickly knock us off our Chunuk Bair. So they have done it. Never mind: never say die.'[80]

Hamilton's stoic reticence in the face of adversity was also to colour his subsequent approach to his treatment by Aspinall in the Official History. Despite this damning portrait painted by Aspinall, Hamilton refused to criticise the work and indeed publicly supported it. He described Aspinall's work to a lecture audience in 1932 as 'being something entirely out of the line of official histories and having by some miracle escaped from the official mill still trailing a few wisps of battle smoke and glory after it'.[81] Part of this response can be explained in the fact that, whilst the work was critical of Hamilton in specific respects, by far the greatest thrust of its attack was aimed at the government. Whilst Hamilton failed operationally, the vacillation of the government in committing the necessary resources to Gallipoli fatally tied his hands and made his objectives considerably more difficult to accomplish. Indeed notwithstanding Aspinall's criticisms of Hamilton's leadership and strategic competence, Aspinall recognised the scale of the problem he faced. He concluded his volumes with the assertion that 'no British General [had] ever been given a more difficult task than that which confronted Sir Ian Hamilton from the outset of operations'.[82] However, this might mitigate but it did not disguise the explicit nature of Aspinall's revelations of Hamilton's failings and Hamilton did have quite strong reservations about parts of Aspinall's work. It was a mark of his character that he scarcely offered a complaint. He informed Daniel that if Aspinall's work had been private he would have remained totally silent; it was only because it was written under the aegis of the Historical Section that he felt inclined to pass any comment at all. Indeed on the one occasion when Hamilton did speak up for himself it was in specific response to a request to do so from the Historical Section:

Whenever in his work General Aspinall-Oglander passed judgement upon my character, motives or actions I stood out: you will understand this. Now, however, the Historical Section of the CID asks me a specific question as to the facts I shall have no hesitation in answering quite frankly.[83]

Furthermore, the mildness of his complaint and the breezy humour of his tone was typical of the manner in which Hamilton approached all matters, not least those concerning his public reputation.

Hamilton had two specific objections to comments made in the final volume. The first was on the matter of military principle as to whether, once a battle has begun, a Commander-in-Chief should interfere with his generals' tactical command of operations. Aspinall had suggested in his first volume that Hamilton's failure to interfere in Hunter-Weston's direction of events during the landings at Helles had resulted in the loss of vital opportunities. Similarly, Hamilton's failure to involve himself directly in Stopford's activities at Suvla was said by Aspinall to have cost Britain an early end to the war. However, Hamilton objected only to the suggestion that he should have borne any responsibility for Stopford's misrepresentation of his plan to his divisional command and specifically to the comment that he had 'approved these [divisional] orders before issue and thereby assumed as much responsibility for them as if they had been his own'.[84] Having commanded brigades under Buller, the Duke of

Connaught and White and divisions under Roberts and Kitchener, Hamilton had never known a Commander-in-Chief examine his orders to his troops. He informed Aspinall that:

> We must remember that this history will be critically read in all War Academies in the world and it is quite an unorthodox idea that the C.-in-C. should examine divisional orders. If he does he had better command the divisions.[85]

Hamilton instead offered a number of suggested inclusions which would have justified his failure to intervene. Aspinall accepted the inclusion of one typically Hamiltonesque phrase concerning Stopford's change of emphasis in the plan: 'Here the student may see reflected as in a mirror the breath of uncertainty and indecision beginning to blur the outlines of a scheme.'[86] However, the suggestion that this change of emphasis was Hamilton's ultimate responsibility remained. Aspinall recorded that Hamilton returned the draft copy of Stopford's flawed orders 'without comment on 1st August'.[87]

Hamilton's second concern centred around the oft-cited suggestion that he was too meek in his dealings with Kitchener, particularly with regard to reinforcements, because he remained in awe of his former Commander-in-Chief. In particular, he requested the removal of two paragraphs and a 'quite superfluous and tiresome footnote' which described the timidity with which he approached Kitchener before the Suvla landings in asking for the brigade of Gurkhas. Hamilton wished Aspinall to make clear that the mildness of his requests was founded upon the promises he had made before leaving England not to place difficult demands on Kitchener and upon the sympathy he felt for 'poor K' left 'in London without anyone to help him'.[88] However, Hamilton's defence against this charge was in fact a clear illustration of its substance. He claimed that the source of the myth was the interpretation placed upon his communications by the Dardanelles Commission, which was 'unaccustomed to the deference in which a General cloaks himself when he enters into the presence of a Field Marshal'.[89] Furthermore, if Hamilton did possess a 'full share of the awe due to a national hero occupying the autocratic and altogether outstanding position of Lord K[itchener]', he was nevertheless less timid in approaching him than anyone else then at the War Office. Indeed, in an intriguing insight into the relationship between these two men, Hamilton suggested that his long familiarity had bred 'not contempt but affection mingled with amusement at such threats as that if I did not look to it I should find myself in civilian kit next morning'.[90]

It was as clear then from Hamilton's own words, as it was from the analysis of Aspinall to which he objected, that Hamilton viewed the Secretary of State for War not as a member of the Cabinet but still as his

Commander-in-Chief, to be defended against the demands of alarmist politicians but to be revered for the power of summary dismissal he held over his generals. The Dardanelles Commission highlighted the importance of this relationship in explaining Hamilton's failure to secure the necessary reinforcements and resources to achieve success at Gallipoli. For Aspinall to have ignored it would have been to lessen considerably the value of his conclusions. Thus, whilst Aspinall did incorporate part of Hamilton's suggested inclusion, a part which on its own did little to support Hamilton's defence, his account clearly highlighted the significance of his deferential relationship with Kitchener. Aspinall explained, for example, that having spent the last six months of the South African War living under the same roof as Kitchener, Hamilton was still 'under the domination of that forceful personality'.[91] Lord Kitchener, as a soldier Secretary of State, acted to all intents and purposes as his own Chief of General Staff. All messages from Commanders-in-Chief in the field had to be addressed to him directly. Demands for reinforcements were adjudicated by him alone. 'His position was pre-eminent, his power almost supreme. Sir Ian Hamilton had seen him, in South African days, reply to an officer's appeal for reinforcements by taking half his troops away from him.'[92] Whilst this might be considered as in some way mitigating Hamilton's conduct towards his old chief, the footnote which Hamilton considered made little of his appeal for the Gurkha brigade remained unaltered. In addition, Aspinall revealed that, although Hamilton was anxious for reinforcements, he was equally anxious to avoid the impression that he was actually asking for them. On hearing of the possibility of a further French division, Hamilton informed Kitchener that 'just in case there is truth in the report, you should know that Mudros harbour is as full as it will hold'.[93] What Hamilton suggested was a tiresome irrelevance, Aspinall considered as appropriate to understanding the nature of the relationship, which resulted in a vital deprivation of adequate forces from the peninsula. Notwithstanding then the appeals of his former Commander-in-Chief this important criticism remained.

IV

Thus a comprehensive, frank and truthful account of considerable historical value became part of the series of Official Histories of the Great War. Aspinall's two volumes, published on Anzac Day, 25 April 1929 and 1932, received almost universal public praise from the press and the political and military establishment. The government sold the serial rights of Volume II to the *Daily Telegraph*, which serialised its own edited version of the work in the newspaper. Its reviewer, Capt. B.H. Liddell Hart, was well placed to know the true nature of the process of the compilation of official works.

As a result, his comments were particularly accurate when he wrote that the feeling of depression aroused in the work was

> in itself a tribute to the compiler and his assistants for a history written under official auspices and subject to the sensitive objections of every interested party has to overcome immense obstacles on its way to truth and true criticism.[94]

Indeed, even Aspinall's previous critics recognised in his completed volumes a work of great skill and value. The Historical Section congratulated Aspinall on the 'admirable achievement' of his completed work in 1932 and was 'much gratified to learn how well it has been received by all competent judges'.[95] The second volume sold 1,600 copies in the three weeks following publication and Daniel saw this as testimony to the author and a 'masterly telling of a thrilling story'.[96] Birdwood too congratulated Aspinall on the completion of Volume II and informed him that he liked his writing very much and kept the volume by him as a reminder of those days.[97] Jean Hamilton, the wife of Sir Ian Hamilton, congratulated Aspinall on the way in which he had carried out a difficult task and on his writing which was stated with great clearness and fairness.[98] General Sir Charles Monro, Hamilton's successor at Gallipoli, considered Aspinall's work to be so accurate that he concluded that he must 'have had a devil of a time getting the War Office to let some of [his] story appear'.[99] Furthermore, the Australian official historian, Charles Bean, notable for his own forthright views on the conduct of operations during the Great War and himself knowledgeable of the workings of the government with regard to the publication of official histories, informed Aspinall that the public had accepted his work as the standard authority. He told Aspinall that he felt sure 'that you will never regret having adopted the freedom which you employed in stating your own views'.[100]

7

Military Operations: France and Belgium 1918, Volume I: The German March Offensive

I

After publication of his Somme volume in 1932 Edmonds proceeded to complete his volume on the German offensive of March 1918. It will be remembered that Edmonds, and the War Office, had been anxious to complete this volume out of sequence and ahead of other volumes. A series of problems with previous writers employed for this task had delayed completion considerably beyond the desired timescale. The writing of this volume is of considerable importance to an understanding of the process and historical value of Edmonds' work. As with his Somme volume, the impact of the evidence of hundreds of participants in shaping the content and conclusions of this work will be considered alongside the level of influence exercised by Edmonds' more senior colleagues. Of significance is the degree to which Edmonds exposed failings where they occurred and thereby highlighted the undoubtedly important lessons of this experience for future generations of military students. A number of his critics have suggested that in four major areas Edmonds allowed lessons to be ignored.

II

This particular volume of Official History was one of the most complex to write and its compilation was fraught with difficulty from the outset. Edmonds had first suggested in 1922, to the Subcommittee responsible for the production of Official Histories, that the 1918 volume should be published as soon as possible. At this time the first Western Front volume had just been published and Edmonds envisaged that it would be possible to complete the work on 1918 within two to three years.[1] The decision

6. Edmonds as Deputy Engineer-in-Chief (1915–18), November 1918.

to proceed with these volumes out of sequence was taken seven months later when Col. Daniel reported to the Subcommittee that the War Office was equally anxious to see an early publication.[2] Haig's former Chief of Staff, Lt-Gen. Sir Launcelot Kiggell, was chosen for the task but made such little progress over the next two years that the Subcommittee in 1926, under pressure from the Treasury, determined to replace him. Edmonds too had been concerned about Kiggell's lack of progress but his main objections were based on his work's lack of 'colour and atmosphere'.[3] This is an important observation when it is borne in mind that a number of Edmonds' critics have complained about the lack of value which Edmonds placed on literary style. Edmonds initially intended to use Aspinall to continue Kiggell's work. Edmonds noted that, whilst Haig was 'anxious' that he should write it himself, he preferred, for the sake of continuity, to complete the volumes on 1915 and 1916 on which he was currently working.[4] Work continued during the late 1920s on compiling the 1918 'narrative', which Edmonds was concerned should be circulated to the 'principal actors' before they died. However, Aspinall was not going to be free to write the 'history' before the completion of his second Gallipoli volume, which he anticipated he would finish in 1932. Accordingly in 1930 Edmonds decided to take over the writing of the three 1918 volumes himself, starting with the volume on the March 1918 German offensive.

Given the nature of the battles which took place during the five days following the launch of Operation Michael, the work involved in writing this volume was particularly complex. Not only was the mass of documentation immense but it was also unreliable. As a result of the chaos of these five days, diaries were not written up until weeks later. In the case of one artillery brigade the entries for the seven days from 21 March were covered simply by two words: 'In action'.[5] Eight corps and 40 divisions had been involved in the battles and the confusion, exacerbated by the heavy use of codes in their diaries and despatches, made the task of unravelling the movement of units even more difficult. 'To write about March 1918', wrote Edmonds, 'is like writing about a cathedral from the knowledge of one window only.'[6] This placed a heavier reliance than normal upon the evidence submitted to Edmonds by participants. It also made his normal process of using this information to corroborate what he had learnt from the documentation that much more flimsy. As a result, much of this evidence was incorporated by Edmonds in his text simply on the grounds of its apparent credibility as he was, in most cases, unable to verify it in any other way.

The narrative draft was circulated to 1,500 participants and, from the responses of over half of those who furnished corrections and additions, Edmonds was able to build up an accurate picture. The best test of its accuracy, Edmonds wrote, was 'that nearly all the various fragments of information provided by so many hands fitted into their places to form the picture like the pieces of a jig-saw puzzle'.[7] Indeed it is remarkable, given the nature of the events of these five days, that an account emerged which was almost universally recognised by participants as authoritative and reliable. Lt-Col. Percy Beddington, Gough's Chief of Staff, pronounced Edmonds' draft 'a very true and impartial story' in which he had presented 'the real facts which ought to have been known even though to some people they are somewhat damaging'.[8] Col. Groncard of 16th Division, who witnessed the battle from a very different perspective, admitted to having been 'exceedingly surprised at the comprehensiveness with which the whole subject ha[d] been treated'.[9]

III

The issues surrounding the events of March 1918 and the writing of its Official History are arguably of far wider importance than the one action alone. For three long years the British army had fought a number of large set-piece offensives which had cost the lives of thousands of its best soldiers with little to show on the face of it but the gain of a few hundred yards of ground. On the morning of 21 March 1918 the Germans launched their first great offensive since Verdun: Operation Michael. Employing tactics rarely used by the British (except in isolated engagements) of a short bombardment followed by rapidly moving units of storm troops, they quickly succeeded in breaking through the stalemate of trench warfare. Within five days they had driven over 40 miles behind the allied lines, from where they could have potentially threatened Paris or the Channel ports. They were, of course, more than considerably aided by the heavy fog that covered the area of their attack on the first morning, combined with the redoubt system of defence employed by the British Fifth Army who had recently taken over the line from the French.

A number of questions are thus raised by the events of these five days. How did the German army succeed in breaking through when the British had consistently failed, and were there any tactical lessons to be learnt from their methods? Why did the British army appear to perform so poorly in defence? Was the target and direction of the attack sufficiently appreciated by Haig and GHQ in advance, and, on that basis, was the distribution of the forces at their disposal sound? Finally, to what extent were the actions fought by the British part of an ordered withdrawal or to what extent were they undisciplined and ill-coordinated retreats in which the direction from the higher command had completely broken down? Not unnaturally those critics of Haig's military competence and his strategy have found much in the events of these few days to justify their criticisms. As a result of this offensive the Commander of Fifth

Army, Sir Hubert Gough, was dismissed by the government. Haig might have suffered a similar fate but for the immediate difficulty of finding a suitable replacement at a time of national crisis.[10]

The degree to which Edmonds' Official History dealt with these issues has been the basis on which a number of critics have judged his work to be lacking. Liddell Hart believed Edmonds had ignored the most vital lessons of the campaign and in so doing did little service to the army's ability to learn from these events. Britain's part in the battle was essentially a military failure in which Haig's distribution of his forces, his failure to recognise the direction of the attack and the subsequent breakdown of communication played a far greater role than external factors such as the British government or their French allies.[11] Travers has criticised Edmonds for playing down the chaos of the army in retreat. Like Liddell Hart he has accused Edmonds of overlooking Haig's sanguine attitude before the offensive and of ignoring the breakdown in the command structure once it began.[12] On a more general point, G.C. Wynne, one of Edmonds' own official historians, believed that Edmonds had failed to distinguish German tactics from British and thereby hidden the superior German tactical doctrine from the next generation of military leaders.[13] It is therefore particularly instructive in an assessment of Edmonds' impartiality and motivation to consider how far he used his writing of this action to defend the senior commanders involved.

Let us then consider how Edmonds formed and amended his narrative and opinions from the mass of this evidence submitted to him by his correspondents. The scale of this correspondence was unprecedented and considerably in excess of that relating to any other volume, either previously or subsequently. Because of the confused and disorganised nature of the fighting, much of this correspondence concerned very minor actions, often involving units no larger than companies. It is not practicable to reproduce here the level of detailed information which was made available to Edmonds. What does become apparent in studying this correspondence, however, is that the great weight of evidence from a huge variety of different sources helped to form Edmonds' opinion of a crucial and controversial aspect of the events of March 1918: namely, the degree to which the British army stood and fought in the face of the German whirlwind advance or the degree to which it turned and fled. Other important features of the action also proliferate in these first-hand accounts: the speed and novel tactics of the German attack, the great confusion caused by the breakdown of communication and, notwithstanding this, a strong determination by the British not to give up. All these features became an important part of Edmonds' final work which could not have been determined from a study of the available documentation alone.

Lt-Col. Birch was the commanding officer of the 7th Battalion Kings

Royal Rifle Corps. On 21 March this formed part of the 14th Division operating within III Corps on the far right of Fifth Army. Following an extremely heavy bombardment on the morning of the 21st as much as three-quarters of his battalion was wiped out. Almost before they were aware that a general advance had begun Birch's battalion witnessed German troops already heading north away from them towards Essigny le Grand. According to Birch:

> the German advance was carried out in accordance with the best principles laid down for divisions in attack. Small parties snaked forward mostly with machine guns, they immediately opened fire on halting and covered the forward rushes of other groups. Field artillery was also close up with the leading waves and appeared to open fire at once on any suitable target. I was informed later by a German Staff Officer that two divisions attacked on a 3000 yard front and the attacking divisions were four deep, a leading division when exhausted being leapfrogged by a fresh one in the rear. It was obvious that points of resistance like ours were ignored by the first attacking waves who pushed through rapidly and left subsequent troops to mop up.

Having seen their position overrun by the enemy, and having completely lost touch with units on their flanks, Birch's men were given the less than comforting news from Brigade HQ that there was nothing behind them, so they had to hold on to the end. In the event, they managed to withdraw by degrees with grenades and rifle fire to the village of Jussy where, that night, the battalion's adjutant, Capt. Maurice St Aubin, led a party of cooks and clerks on a bombing raid to dislodge some German infantry which had gained a foothold on one of the bridges. The mixture of various units that passed back through the Jussy–Cugny road the following day was described by Birch as 'panic-stricken' and could not be persuaded to stand fast on his line of defence.[14]

This view was corroborated by R.M. Burke, who suggested that the whole draft of the events of the first three days of the offensive would give the misleading impression to readers of the future that the battle was a comparatively well-ordered affair. He criticised the narrative for implying that

> timely orders were issued for the movement of units and formations and that these were generally complied with except for a gradual retirement westwards under overwhelming enemy pressure. In reality, as most of us who took part in the battle are aware, at times the chaos was indescribable and the sudden change from trench warfare to the quickly moving events of open warfare con-

ditions proved to some extent beyond the capacity of the existing organisations.[15]

Col. R. Sandilands, Commander of 104th Brigade in 35th Division, noted a similar chaos but revealed that it had spread to the highest formations. Returning to France from leave on 25 March, Sandilands found it impossible not only to locate his brigade but to be given reliable information as to the current location of the front line. At Amiens, a 'place full of the wildest rumours', he managed to locate General Gough's HQ on the morning of the 26th. Gough's HQ was 'in a state of great confusion' and no one had any clear knowledge not only of the whereabouts of 35th Division but in which corps it was currently![16]

Yet despite this chaos a corresponding picture emerged of the courage and determination of the troops, who were prepared to fight to the last. A company commander, William Golden, was in a position west of Gricourt on the morning of the 21st. His trench was heavily shelled and at 8.30 a.m., with visibility down to five yards, the enemy appeared practically in Golden's trench. His unit beat them off with fire. They were then attacked on both flanks by bombing parties, which they were again successful in repelling. Golden continued:

> No sooner had they withdrawn than a heavy attack was delivered from our rear and almost at the same time a party attacked on the front and our right flank. We lost a big number in this fight but in the end the enemy again withdrew and left about 20 men in a fit condition.

German troops continued to advance behind Golden's lines and at 2 p.m. they returned and attacked Golden's men from three sides. 'Our ammunition gave out', he wrote, 'and we finished our stand with our hand grenades.' Having inflicted this much damage on the advancing Germans there is little doubt that these men knew they were fighting to the death. They were ultimately saved by a German officer who entered their trench and prevented his troops from killing them. Golden and his 20 men had held out for six hours. On his march back through German lines, for mile after mile Golden passed every vehicle that he had ever seen, army wagons, farm carts and even small traps drawn by dogs but he saw not a single fighting battalion. According to Golden, there were no troops left in the old German front lines.[17]

One final account deserves mention which not only revealed the fluidity and confusion of the events of those days but also established the pluckiness which characterised the British spirit in adversity. On the night of 22 March the bridge at Ham, like that at Jussy, divided the British and German lines. A battalion officer in the 20th Division and his adjutant had lost touch with their unit and attempted to come over the bridge from behind the German lines. They were stopped by a German sentry who claimed to take them prisoner. The British officers said that on the contrary they were taking him prisoner. After some discussion the colonel asked the German what the devil he meant by talking like that to an officer whereupon the sentry allowed them to pass unmolested to the British side.[18]

These letters, and many more like them, provided Edmonds with a unique vantage point of the various actions which took place in the days after 21 March. Official messages, reports and diaries were not, on their own, sufficient to form an accurate picture. As Edmonds told one of his correspondents: 'it is now essential to obtain corrections and additional information from actual participants in the fighting'.[19] This evidence significantly shaped Edmonds' conclusions on the issue of the confusion and communication breakdown which afflicted the forces of Third and Fifth Army. Travers has claimed that:

> understandably the Official History made little mention of surrenders or command breakdowns and instead concentrated on an exceedingly complicated narrative of interlocking units and their stands and retreats. The result was a text which was dense and impenetrable which thus concealed the actual breakdown of the command structure.[20]

Liddell Hart also believed Edmonds had concealed this feature of the action.[21] Yet this cannot be reconciled with either the majority of the narrative or indeed with Edmonds' conclusions, as this brief consideration will reveal.

Concerning the first day of the offensive Edmonds wrote:

> In the fog and in the confusion which followed, owing to the breakdown of communications, each party fought as best it could, and the battle was mainly carried on by battalions and small bodies, assisted by the divisional batteries.[22]

With regard to the breakdown of command at a higher level Edmonds wrote of the same morning:

> No general situation report was sent from the Fifth Army to GHQ until 11 a.m. Being naturally several hours behind events, these were by no means clear, tinged with optimism, giving little more than the names of places held or lost with little indication of what was taking place. It was, and is, quite impossible to deduce the real situation from them.[23]

Where units had been forced to give themselves up, Edmonds made this clear.[24] By the night of 23–24 March:

> no words . . . could convey any picture of the confusion . . . troops wandering about to find their brigades and battalions, in an area without landmarks, devastated a year before by the enemy; dumps burning and exploding; gaps in the line; the Germans attacking almost behind the V. Corps front; the atmosphere charged with uncertainty and full of the wildest reports and rumours.

On Fifth Army's front, by the morning of 24 March, divisions were 'now fighting and moving in small bodies, often composed of men of different units, frequently with parties of Germans mixed up with them, so that it was impossible for the corps or divisional staffs to ascertain the position of the front line'. 'Communications grew more and more precarious, and, in the absence of orders, battalions, even brigades, acted as seemed best.' Indeed, so small and intermingled did the fighting units now become that Edmonds proceeded to follow thereafter only a broad outline, presuming to leave 'the confusion which prevailed . . . to the imagination'.[25]

It is difficult to conclude, therefore, that there was any attempt made by Edmonds to disguise either the confusion or the obvious breakdown in command. According to Edmonds, there was confusion, a degree of panic and a number of unwarranted retreats. However, under fire the spirit of the men was rarely broken. It is true that Edmonds did not explicitly refer to the breakdown of command in his conclusions. Continuing to tread that careful path of revealing failings, but discreetly and between the lines, Edmonds reported surrenders and confusion, as clearly demonstrated above, but it was the acts of courage and resistance which attracted the final and stronger comment.[26] The inefficacy of the higher command remained apparent, but probably only to an informed reader who was able to draw his own conclusions from the almost complete absence of any reference to its influence on events. In five days' fighting involving 40 divisions the high command rarely warranted a mention. Instead, as Edmonds pointed out, 'the control of infantry operations . . . lay mainly in the hands of the infantry brigadiers, often in the dark as to the intentions of the higher commands'.[27] In continuing to adhere to the conflicting constraints placed upon him by the various objectives of the Official Histories, Edmonds exhibited a commendable skill.

With regard to the supposedly dense, impenetrable text, it is not practical to expect a staff history of military operations to ignore the many, and piecemeal, actions which were taking place across a 126–mile front. Certainly the ability to present these movements in both a comprehensive and, at the same time, interesting way, was an issue which taxed Edmonds. Whilst Kiggell was writing the volume, Edmonds proposed that he should show the movement of units through sketch maps 'rather than a narrative that is bound to be monotonous'. When Edmonds took over this task himself he came to the conclusion that the events of this offensive were of 'such great interest that it is proposed to cut down the description of operations – which in the first draft are very long – and to describe troop movements each day mainly by maps and sketches'.[28] What emerged in the published work was a narrative which was in no manner impenetrable but was, instead, a fascinating and comprehensive patchwork of the hundreds of individual actions which took place during those first five days.

IV

Let us now consider the influence of information and objections submitted to Edmonds from some of his more senior military colleagues. This will establish the degree to which Edmonds was subjected, and responded, to pressure from high-ranking participants to soften the tone of any criticism in his account. General the Honourable Sir Julian Byng was the Third Army commander at the time of the German offensive. Whilst Fifth Army bore the brunt of the attack, it was the split which opened up between the two armies as a result of their failure to keep in touch with each other which allowed the German army to progress so rapidly through the British lines. Byng was particularly sensitive about the accusation in Edmonds' draft that it was Third Army which bore the prime responsibility for this split. He wrote in 1934 that:

> the wording . . . is, in our opinion hypercritical and the point of responsibility for keeping in touch is unduly laboured. For touch to be maintained there must be a partnership. The left of the Fifth Army had disappeared.[29]

However, Edmonds' justification for thus apportioning the blame was his belief that the difficulties directly flowed from Byng's reluctance to abandon the Flesquieres Salient, held at the start of the battle by V Corps. The Flesquieres Salient was a large bulge in the front line which had been created during the Cambrai tank offensive of 1917 and was vulnerable to being pinched out by German forces attacking from the flanks. It was for this reason that Douglas Haig, after visiting the area on 10 March, issued instructions to the effect that the salient was to be held *only* as a false front, in sufficient strength to check raids. If seriously attacked, the occupying troops were to fall back immediately to the rear to avoid being trapped and in order to retain contact with the two neighbouring corps, one of which was Fifth Army's VII Corps. Edmonds clearly emphasised these instructions in his official volume.[30] Byng argued in his defence that Edmonds should judge the situation from the facts as they were known at the time. He admitted that with hindsight it would have been strategically better to have fallen back on the green line (the rear zone) on the night of 21 March but asked, 'What would have been the effect on the troops of what would have seemed to them an unnecessary retirement?' He cited Edmonds' own words, taken from later in his work and offered in a different context, regarding the distaste felt by troops in evacuating ground without being driven out of it. He claimed too that orders from GHQ were quite definite as to the holding of the salient for reasons of observation, the cover provided by the old Hindenburg line and the denial to the enemy of a strong jumping-off place.[31]

Edmonds was unmoved and failed to amend his account or even to add a kind word in mitigation. It remained graphically and unsparingly critical of Byng in this respect. First Edmonds related the German plan of attack, which made clear that one of its primary intentions in the first wave was to pinch out the Flesquieres Salient. Indeed, as he had in his Somme volume, Edmonds was quite prepared to disregard the advice he had given his own writers, in order to strengthen the force of his argument. Ignoring his own view that subsequent knowledge of enemy activities or intentions was unfair to the British commander, who did not have this knowledge at the time, Edmonds cited von Hindenburg's orders of 10 March, which began: 'the first great tactical object of Crown Prince Rupprecht's Group of Armies will be to cut off the British in the Cambrai Salient'.[32] When Edmonds subsequently turned to that theatre in his narrative of the fighting he reminded his readers once more that the enemy had had no intention of assaulting the salient but had always intended to 'pinch it out'.[33] More damningly, if one accepts that Byng could not have known this in advance, Edmonds stated that at the outset of the bombardment mustard gas was used against the salient. 'A sure sign', he argued, 'as the Director of Gas Services pointed out, that no attack was intended against it.'[34] As the German advance began it soon became evident that the troops retaining this salient were extremely vulnerable, and the enemy's progress on its flanks constituted, in Edmonds' words, a 'serious threat'.[35] Constant shelling by mustard gas made its retention very costly and the longer troops remained the harder would be any chance of later withdrawal. However reluctant the commanders of Third Army and V Corps were to abandon strong positions won only four months before, by the evening of 21 March the enemy's plan to pinch out the salient was obvious and at the very least the apex must be abandoned. Edmonds wrote:

Many officers now hold the view that it would have been wise, and in any case would have saved many gas casualties, if a retirement from the Salient had been ordered directly the signs of the German offensive became unmistakable. Its retention, acquiesced in by GHQ as a false front, proved a source of weakness; the delay in ordering evacuation when the Fifth Army was forced back left the V Corps lagging behind the general line for several days, a result which added to the difficulties of keeping touch and gave the Germans the opportunity to drive the Corps north-westwards, thus contributing to enlarge the break which arose between the Fifth and Third Armies.[36]

In response to correspondence from participants (and appearing in a footnote, as was typical of amendments made after the first drafts) Edmonds had added:

Regimental officers at the time protested against being left in a salient deluged with gas shells and from the front line of which the field of fire was indifferent; whereas by withdrawal the enemy would be forced to advance over ground where he could be dealt with far more easily.[37]

Instead, Edmonds wrote, 'Byng gave ground grudgingly'[38] and for that 'optimistic retention' the British army was made to pay 'in more ways than one'.[39] It is not difficult to see why Byng should have wished to register his concern at such direct criticism. However, he was forced to accept, after Edmonds justified his treatment of this episode to him, that no useful purpose would be served in continuing the argument.[40]

Travers has highlighted this episode as indicative of Edmonds' bias, which sought to discredit Byng in order to favour Gough. He has written that:

It can be argued that Edmonds was critical of Byng partly in order to defend Gough; partly because Byng was a cavalry man against whom Edmonds had an established bias; and partly because Edmonds had a poor opinion of Byng following his conduct of the later stage of the Cambrai tank battle.[41]

Certainly, Edmonds' opinion of Byng, as expressed to Liddell Hart, was that he was the 'most incompetent of all the Commanders'.[42] This does not necessarily suggest bias. It is far more plausible that once again Edmonds had come to this opinion from his own research, and his footnoted comments concerning the views of many regimental officers acknowledged this. Indeed, initially, Edmonds' original draft of the narrative had suggested that it was Gough's Fifth Army which was responsible for the split. As Lt-Gen. Sir W.N. Congreve, Commander of VII

Corps, who later served under Byng in Third Army, informed Edmonds in 1927:

> I feel sure that anyone rising from perusal of your account of the battle of the Third Army would say Mr Lloyd George was justified in his first announcement of the battle i.e. that Third Army had had to retire because Fifth Army ran away . . . But I thought that idea had long since been abandoned. In my opinion the real cause of constant gaps between V. and VII. Corps was due in the first instance to the retention of the Cambrai salient from which the V. Corps never recovered.[43]

At the time, Edmonds did little to satisfy Congreve that he would amend his account, for Congreve answered Edmonds' response by noting that it did not 'at all remove from [his] mind this anxiety [he felt] lest the Lloyd George myth be perpetuated and confirmed by the Official History'.[44] However, following correspondence from numerous more junior officers which corroborated this view, Edmonds began to alter his opinion of these events. As he told Gough in 1932:

> I have been in communication with dozens of your divisional and regimental officers and the story of the fighting as it works out is, I think, more than gallant . . . The base of the trouble seems to me to be that GHQ or Third Army hung on too long to the Flesquieres Salient. So that when the garrison did at last clear out it was forced North away from the Fifth Army and a gap between the armies was created.[45]

In fact, notwithstanding his accusations of bias Travers agrees with this. He wrote that although one can feel sympathy for Byng, 'it *does appear that Edmonds was correct* – Byng *was* too slow in evacuating the salient'.[46] So by Travers' reckoning Edmonds came upon the correct analysis of the situation purely by the accident of his own bias. Travers might then find it difficult, using the argument of bias, to reconcile Edmonds' predisposition to defend Gough in this volume with what he considers his more critical treatment of the same officer in his Passchendaele volume. He overcomes this by suggesting that in criticising Byng in his March 1918 volume Edmonds was showing the early signs of a growing penchant for fixing on certain commanders to blame which later came to focus on Gough. In fact, it will be seen that Edmonds exhibited no more predisposition for blaming Byng in this volume than he did for blaming Gough in his Passchendaele volume. A far more plausible explanation is that Edmonds thought highly of Gough's conduct in the March action but less so of his conduct in 1917.

Gough's own Chief of Staff, Lt-Col. Percy Beddington, had come to the same conclusion. After receiving Edmonds' completed draft in 1934 he congratulated him on a very 'true and impartial story'. Gough had not been free from blame over Passchendaele, Beddington admitted, and had attacked with insufficient strength against the advice of his staff. On 21 March 1918, however, his conduct had been 'all that could be desired'.[47] Even Travers admits that with only limited GHQ support and reserves Gough 'fought the battle in retreat as well as could be done'.[48] So why, then, should we question the bases for Edmonds' conclusions and speculate that they were influenced by personal preferences rather than historical judgement?

If personal bias were indeed Edmonds' greatest influence, then he would have ensured the views of his supposed 'favourites' were consistently expressed in his published work. Yet in one important instance Edmonds ignored the testimony of Gough in favour of that of Haig's DMO, Sir John Davidson. Gough himself had complained to Edmonds that many of the difficulties facing Fifth Army stemmed from the fact that neither Haig nor anyone else at GHQ had taken the trouble to visit him during the opening stages of the offensive:

> Why GHQ entirely neglected the Fifth Army even in the very early stages . . . why they never took any steps to get in touch with us by coming to see me personally and thus understand the desperate nature of the problem and the task they had set Fifth Army – why they did or did not do these things beats me – I consider it was because neither Lawrence nor any of his underlings had the faintest conception of how to command in battle . . . If I in the midst of this terrific storm could have gone round my four corps commanders and covered 60 miles, surely to heaven Lawrence or his deputy, or even Haig should have come to me, even if it had been in the middle of the night.[49]

However, Davidson advised Edmonds in a subsequent meeting and letter that Lawrence had, in fact, visited Fifth Army HQ on the afternoon of 24 March. He wrote:

> I would like to emphasise again the desirability, even necessity, for referring to General Lawrence's visit to the Fifth Army HQ on Sunday afternoon, 24th March. It is important as Lawrence proceeded direct from there at Haig's request to meet him (Haig) at Byng's HQ at 8 p.m. the same evening. There is no doubt that Lawrence and Haig were that evening when they met at Byng's HQ at 8 p.m. as fully acquainted as they could be with the position on the Third and Fifth Army fronts at the time.[50]

It was this view, and not Gough's, which Edmonds incorporated into his account as follows:

> Lt-General Sir H. Lawrence, the C.G.S., visited Fifth Army head-quarters during the afternoon . . . On leaving General Gough, after making himself thoroughly acquainted with the local situation, he proceeded to Third Army headquarters where he was to meet the Commander-in-Chief at 8 p.m.[51]

In assessing whether Edmonds' work was either balanced or biased, it is important to recognise that his criticisms were not limited to Byng alone, or indeed to Third Army. Other senior officers were clearly criticised, two of whom, Maxse and Congreve, were corps commanders. Both were censured for allowing, or in the case of the latter for ordering, their corps to retreat when retreat was unnecessary and potentially disastrous. The case of Congreve is of particular interest, specifically because the evidence which revealed his failure, and indeed his attempts to cover it up, came to Edmonds' attention from a more junior participant, Brig.-Gen. R. Sandilands. (Some of his evidence has already been cited previously in connection with the confusion at Army HQ.) Sandilands' letter to Edmonds was one of many similar unsolicited representations made by a number of officers to the Historical Section in the hope that a forth-coming Official History might endorse their side of a dispute. In Sandilands' case he was attempting to overturn the accusations made against his divisional commander, General Franks, that he had abandoned the strong Bray position on 26 March on his own initiative. The corps commander, Congreve, had claimed that when he discovered this, he telephoned Franks on the afternoon of 26 March and instructed him to return. When Franks refused he was dismissed from his command. Sandilands' evidence, however, showed that the reverse had been the case.

On returning to France from leave, Sandilands eventually discovered that his division, the 35th, now formed part of General Congreve's VII Corps at Vadencourt. He arrived at Corps HQ in the afternoon of 26 March. He informed Edmonds that:

> I had never seen General Congreve before and was quite shocked by his appearance. He struck me as absolutely down and out and incapable of any clear thinking. He was evidently suffering from want of sleep and both mental and physical fatigue.[52]

Congreve told Sandilands to report to General Franks at Divisional HQ with instructions that the 35th Division was to withdraw as soon as possible to the line of the Ancre and on no account to risk being implicated in a battle with the enemy. In fact Franks had already informed Corps HQ earlier that morning that his men were quite capable of remaining at the Bray position throughout the day; they were 'full of fight and not in the least bit rattled . . . and very confident of being able to repel any attack'. Nonetheless, he had been specifically instructed by Corps HQ to withdraw. However, by the time Sandilands arrived with his message from Congreve, Franks had just received a contrary instruction ordering him instead to return to his original position. The 35th Division had been fighting a rearguard action all day before the corps suddenly changed their orders and told Franks to reoccupy the position, eight miles in front, which he had abandoned that morning. Sandilands was incensed that the corps later claimed that it was Franks who had taken the decision to withdraw from Bray on his own initiative and requested that Edmonds set the record straight in his Official History.[53]

Had Edmonds wished to protect the reputations and sensibilities of his more senior military colleagues it would have been easy to have ignored this request. Had he possessed scant regard for historical accuracy, little, bar the personal injustice to Franks, would have induced Edmonds to alter the already 'official' version of events. Instead Edmonds' account made clear the true facts about the withdrawal, correctly apportioned blame and highlighted the disastrous consequences that ensued. He wrote: 'In the Third Army the operations of the 26th were marked by an *unnecessary* wheel back of the bulk of the VII Corps . . . from the line Bray–Albert to behind the Ancre.'[54] Edmonds noted the GHQ warning on the night of 25 March which stated that every effort must be made to check the enemy's advance by disputing ground. Furthermore it was to be distinctly understood that no retirement was to take place unless the tactical situation imperatively demanded it. Edmonds explained that no corps commander issued any orders on receipt of this warning except Lt-Gen. Congreve whose instructions incorporated a vital change of emphasis as follows:

> The VII Corps will fight today on the line Bray–Albert in order to delay the enemy as long as possible without being so involved as to make retirement impossible. Retirement when made will be to the North of the Ancre.[55]

Congreve then spoke personally by telephone, at length, to General Franks and 'gave him to understand that the retirement to the west bank of the Ancre would definitely take place during the afternoon of the 26th'.[56] Franks assured his corps commander that he could hold on much longer than that but Congreve told him on no account to risk infantry or guns. Furthermore, the corps had already made arrangements to move their HQ to a position beyond the Ancre and no provisions were made for refilling supplies or ammunition on the Bray–Albert line. This left Franks in no doubt as to what was required of him or indeed with little alternative.[57]

Until 1 p.m. on the 26th, 35th Division had remained untroubled on the Bray–Albert line. At 1.20 they began to face growing pressure from German patrols along the entire front line but the liaison between infantry and artillery was excellent and their combined fire brought the enemy to a standstill. Franks then issued the order for retirement to begin at 3 p.m. if no new attack developed. Almost simultaneously with news of this retirement reaching VII Corps HQ, a message was also received there from Third Army which, Edmonds made clear, in support of Sandilands' assumption, was one of the first consequences of the Doullens conference. It informed Congreve that 'there must be no withdrawal . . . The position at Bray is to be maintained with the utmost determination.' Congreve then telephoned this instruction to Franks but, at this point, it was too late to call back any of the division but the last 500 men of 106th Brigade. Such action, however, was now futile.[58]

> Bodies of German troops could now be seen across the valley north of the Bois des Tailles, offering magnificent targets; but as the entire artillery with the exception of two batteries had gone back, it was impossible to take full advantage of such opportunities.[59]

Edmonds concluded:

> Had it not been for the unnecessary swing back of the VII Corps from Bray . . . which left a long transverse gap along the Somme, between its right and the left of the XIX Corps the British line would have been continuous.[60]

Apparent in these amendments, as with his volume on the Somme, is Edmonds' self-proclaimed preference for the credibility of the accounts of junior officers over their more senior colleagues.

V

Having considered how Edmonds built up his narrative and conclusions from the evidence of participants, and how he failed to be swayed by pressure from his more senior colleagues to tone down criticism, it remains to consider the issue of academic value. Liddell Hart, as has been shown, accused Edmonds of having ignored some vital lessons of the campaign concerning Haig's poor distribution of forces and defensive doctrine, inadequate training given to troops in retreat, and GHQ and

Haig's misjudgements concerning the thrust and direction of attack.[61] Wynne has suggested that Edmonds has denied the opportunity of future generations to study the superior German tactical doctrine. French, too, whilst not considering Edmonds' history on this campaign, has laid the principal blame for Britain's performance in March 1918 on GHQ's failure to recognise the new German tactics witnessed at Cambrai the previous December, on a faulty defensive doctrine and on Haig's over-optimism and misjudgements surrounding the location, speed and scale of threat posed by the attack.[62] To what extent did Edmonds either high-light these failings or ignore these lessons, and to what extent did he lay the responsibility for the failure to hold the German offensive on exter-nal factors?

With regard to Britain's defensive doctrine, Edmonds acknowledged that this was faulty. 'It must be freely admitted', he wrote, 'that the British Armies of 1918 . . . were not well trained to stand on the defensive and deal with an attack by infiltration.' More importantly, '[t]raining in the conduct of retreat, and of a retreat extending over many days, never entered anyone's mind'.[63] Edmonds noted that there were excellent reasons for adopting the principles of defence in depth laid down by the German General Staff after three years' experience of defence on the Western Front. However, the British forces were unable to observe the first principles that the forward zone was only to be a means of delaying the enemy whilst the battle and rear zones were to be an elaborate laby-rinth of trenches, wire, 'pillboxes', machine-gun nests and deep dug-outs. Actually the British forward zone was 'stronger in every way than the zones in the rear of it'. Time and labour had been lacking, in the six weeks since the British had taken over 40 miles of front from the French, to reproduce what the Germans had taken years to build. Whilst Haig's dis-tribution of forces was sound from the perspective of the different stra-tegic importance of the various sectors, 'it hardly took into account the relative strength of [these] defences'. Whilst the troops 'fought magnifi-cently' and defended their 'isolated posts to the death', there were too many 'inexperienced young officers and too many untrained young sol-diers'. Their instinct was to 'fight it out' where they stood with no thought of 'elastic yielding' and no knowledge that the 'men on the spot' could use their own discretion in extreme circumstances. Whilst not explicitly stated, GHQ must bear responsibility for this, for '[n]o warning seems to have been given to any brigade or battalion commanders, and therefore none to the lower ranks, that in certain circumstances there might be an ordered retreat'. During the retreats, although again it is not explicitly stated, there was little direction from the higher command:

The general policy should have been to hold on during daylight and slip away a couple of miles or so to a new position during the night . . . It was simply courting disaster to hold on and be found at daybreak in the position occupied the night before, already registered by the enemy's artillery.

'There was, in fact, little co-ordination of the retreat.' Even the most vital of GHQ's responsibilities was neglected, and, as Edmonds noted with masterly understatement: 'The junctions of Armies often require the attention of the high command.'[64]

What of the novel German tactics in attack which have purportedly been ignored? It was normally true that enemy movements and objectives rarely formed part of the main body of text; they usually appeared as footnotes or appendices to chapters. However, in this volume Edmonds devoted an entire chapter to the German plans and preparations. He not only dealt with the objectives of their plan, to split the junction between the French and British armies, but clearly revealed the essential features of their novel tactics. Divisional generals and staff, as well as the troops, were given special courses in training based upon a flood of official German literature on offensive warfare. This emphasised the great lengths required to maintain the element of surprise and stressed the demand for mobility. The success of a breakthrough was not only a question of tactics and strategy but essentially one of reinforcements and supply. The tactical breakthrough was not, indeed, an object in itself, but a means only to apply the strongest form of attack, envelopment. The object of the first day must at least be the enemy's artillery but, beyond that, objectives would depend upon the first day's success for there 'must be no rigid adherence to plans made beforehand'. The advance had to be fluid with units pressing on regardless of whether touch was maintained with their flanks; touch with the enemy was 'the desideratum'. In a further important point, the advance of the infantry must be organised 'in most complete combination with that of the artillery'. The bombardment was to be short, to ensure surprise, but 'unprecedented' in its force and concentration. The infantry were warned that the bombardment would ensure that the enemy took cover but it would not annihilate him. It was therefore important to advance rapidly behind the 'creeping barrage' before the enemy had a chance to man his guns. The storm troops, who led the first to advance, were sometimes small units armed with light machine-guns, trench mortars and flame projectors, sometimes whole special battalions. They were to be constantly maintained at full strength, to push on past and through weakly held trenches, leaving centres of resistance and machine-gun nests to the infantry waves following behind them.[65] As Prior and Wilson have demonstrated, and indeed as Edmonds noted in his volume on Third Ypres published 13 years later, the British army was to employ similar techniques to good effect some months later.[66]

Finally, what of the issue of Haig's overconfidence and misjudgement with regard to the timing, location and strength of the forthcoming attack? It has already been seen that Edmonds was critical, although very much in a passing reference, to Haig's distribution of his forces and the lack of any intervention by the high command when the junction between Fifth and Third Army was threatened. Concerning the timing and location of the offensive, Liddell Hart accused Edmonds of ignoring the GHQ summary of 10 March in which it was stated that no serious attack was 'to be expected south of the Bapaume–Cambrai road'.[67] However, Edmonds described the army commanders' conference of 16 February at which Brig.-Gen. Cox, head of the Intelligence Section of the General Staff, had reported that the Germans were about to launch a major attack against the British on a 32-mile front. Haig summed up that meeting by informing his commanders to expect an attack on a potentially wider front from Lens to the Oise. As Edmonds explained in a footnote, the eventual attack was from Croiselles, 16 miles south of Lens, to the Oise.[68] Edmonds, in fact, did record the full intelligence summary of 10 March, which Liddell Hart had claimed he had ignored. He did so, though, as part of a deliberate method of relating the process by which various pieces of information, from enemy activity to the accounts of captured prisoners, allowed the British high command to build up a picture of where the attack would take place. In this instance, Edmonds' practice of revealing only by stages what was known to the high command at the time has a dramatic impact on the reader's sense of the impending onslaught. By 19 March:

> the last pieces of evidence regarding the approaching storm were gathered on the Fifth Army front. A captured German artillery N.C.O., a group of infantry prisoners, and Alsatian deserters from a trench mortar battery, all told the same story, each in his own way, and in some cases unwillingly . . . They had been warned that an offensive was imminent: there was a state of nervous tension: the men were being worked very hard and urged to greater exertions in carrying up the ammunition: the back areas were full of troops: there were no tanks about but a new pattern gas mask had been issued: and operations were expected to begin on the 20th or 21st.

As a result, the intelligence officers of Third and Fifth Army were able to agree that the attack would come against Fifth and Third Armies within the next two days and that only minor operations could be expected further north.[69]

Once the battle had begun, Edmonds chose barely to mention Haig. Whilst this undoubtedly contributes to the reader's sense of any lack of involvement or coordination by the high command in the turbulent events, it could be argued that Edmonds avoided an opportunity to pass comment on the accusation that Haig deliberately abandoned Fifth Army to protect the Channel ports. Gough made this point to Edmonds, after this volume had been published. He believed, with Liddell Hart, that Haig had misjudged the direction of Ludendorff's offensive and had 'piled all his reserves behind or within reach of the Third Army', despite Fifth Army information revealing that the attack would come south of the Bapaume–Cambrai road, not north of it. Once the offensive had begun Haig, according to Gough, had been 'in such a temper by being forced by Lloyd George to extend his front southwards that he abandoned the Fifth Army in order to let the consequences fall on Lloyd George and the French'.[70] Edmonds himself had informed Liddell Hart during the preparation of this volume that 'the deeper he went into the history of the war, the less opinion could he keep of Haig'.[71] Yet in an otherwise complete account, Edmonds found no place to assess the role of the Commander-in-Chief in the tactical outcome of the events of 21 to 26 March. (Edmonds did deal with Haig's part in the creation of a supreme command under a *Generalissimo* in order to sacrifice Britain's specific strategic objectives of protection of the Channel ports to the wider good of safeguarding the alliance with France.[72])

VI

Ultimately, Edmonds concluded, it was external factors which were primarily responsible for the great dangers facing the British army in these turbulent five days of fighting: the British government consenting to an extension of the front without an appropriate level of reinforcement and the French contemplating a separation of the Allied armies. Whilst directing the reader to this conclusion it cannot be disputed that Edmonds' own narrative repeatedly revealed avoidable failings on the part of the British higher command. He demonstrated the lack of training of the troops either in defensive doctrine or in fighting a retreat. He highlighted, too, that instead of a coordinated rearguard action, the events of 21 to 26 March were 'just a series of retirements' and 'unnecessary retreats'.[73] Some of the senior army and corps commanders, specifically Byng, Congreve and Maxse, had been sufficiently negligent in their command as to avoid disaster only narrowly. By contrast, the superiority of the German tactics in the offensive was clearly evident and was assessed. So, whilst it might be argued that some of the points which Edmonds made could have been more forcefully put, the work is, nevertheless, a frank and comprehensive exposition of success and failure. This, no doubt, is what Liddell Hart meant when he said that 'the facts necessary for judgement are given, with few exceptions, but . . . a subtle twist is given to them so that the reader is likely to miss the natural conclusions and jump to a judgement which is contrary to the facts'.[74] This is perhaps a somewhat unjust appraisal but it nevertheless reflected the careful literary path which Edmonds trod and his commitment to provide the true lessons to those who could read between the lines. The extent to which Edmonds approached his final work, on Third Ypres, in the same way, has been the subject of considerable further controversy.

8

Military Operations: France and Belgium 1917, Volume II: *Messines and Third Ypres (Passchendaele)*

I

As with *March 1918*, this volume of the Official History series covered one of the more contentious of the Great War's battles. In order to provide a comprehensive and historically legitimate account this work would have to deal with major and controversial issues surrounding Haig's strategic vision and tactical responsibility. Strategically, what was Haig's motivation for fighting this offensive and for continuing to fight it once the appalling weather conditions had all but precluded any chance of success? Haig subsequently claimed that he was driven on by his own private knowledge of the mutinous state of the French army and by the appeals of Pétain. Furthermore, did Haig intend the action as a decisive breakthrough or, as he subsequently contended, as a step-by-step advance as part of a steady process of wearing down the German army? Did the tactical preparations for the advance support this strategy and, importantly, to what extent did they draw on lessons of previous tactical success? The work would have to consider how successfully Haig was able to communicate both his strategic intentions and his tactical direction to his army commanders, and, indeed, the degree to which Haig himself, as opposed to these commanders, assumed tactical responsibility. The extent to which Edmonds was able to raise and answer these questions, and the degree to which these conclusions stand up to the scrutiny of current research, will be considered in due course.

This volume is also important in assessing the historical validity of Edmonds' work by virtue of the manner in which its writing progressed. Edmonds' treatment of its original historian, Capt. G.C. Wynne, has been cited as evidence of his increasing authoritarianism in the direction of the Historical Section and of his growing determination, as time progressed, to defend and protect the reputation of Sir Douglas Haig in his official work.[1] This view of bias is not challenged by the fact that, in contrast to Edmonds' previous volumes, a single and high-ranking participant, Hubert Gough, was allowed to play a more significant role than any individual hitherto in shaping the eventual tone and conclusions of the work. In particular, Edmonds' dissatisfaction with Wynne's draft ultimately resulted in him taking it over himself and rewriting large tracts.

II

Work began on the Flanders offensives of late 1917 during September 1939, immediately after completion of the first 1917 volume. But for the fact that Edmonds eventually took over its completion himself, it would have been published after this and prior to the remaining two volumes on 1918. The original compiler, Captain Cyril Falls, left within a month of beginning work to join the staff of *The Times*. Captain Wynne took over and continued to write drafts until April 1943 when he was assigned to serve in North Africa. It would seem that in his absence Edmonds undertook to follow his usual practice of circulating the drafts for comments to senior participants in the battle, for on Wynne's return in early 1944 Edmonds wrote:

> I am sorry I cannot send you the top copy of chapters VI, VII and VIII but I decided that the last of these chapters should be sent to the more important people on the staffs of Fifth Army and its Corps. You shall have them back as soon as the extra six copies have been run off.[2]

One such recipient was General Sir Hubert Gough, Commander of Fifth Army, who, as Edmonds had anticipated, did not 'altogether agree with [Wynne's] conclusions', although he had no quarrel with the facts.[3] In a long letter with extensive marginal notes to the draft text Gough highlighted the issues which were to continue to prove contentious throughout numerous subsequent exchanges until the final rewriting and publication of the work was completed. Principally, these were: whether Haig intended the action to be a breakthrough; whether he communicated his intentions correctly to Gough; and whether it was his responsibility to interfere in Gough's plan and tactics if he was dissatisfied. With regard to the scope of the attack Wynne's original draft had clearly suggested that it was Gough who was overly ambitious and that it was Haig who had had to restrain him. Wynne had written:

In the marginal note of the GHQ copy of [the Fifth Army plan] Sir Douglas Haig remonstrated that the task he had set 5th Army was not of such far-reaching magnitude. He referred General Gough to the decision made at the conference at Doullens on 7th May that the objective of the 5th Army offensive was to 'wear down the enemy but at the same time to have an objective. I have given two, the Passchendaele–Staden ridge and the coast'. This reminder did not suffice to restrain General Gough who throughout the preparatory stages and <u>later</u> had the single idea of breaking through the German defences on a wide front and the <u>early</u> employment of the cavalry beyond.[4]

Gough took exception to what he termed this 'very exaggerated assertion', which implied that he, single-handedly, planned to defeat the German army and march on Berlin. Gough, according to his own account, had been clearly led to believe in a meeting on 28 June that Haig intended the action as an attempt to break through the German lines. In fact, Gough had confided in Robertson when he visited Gough's HQ with George V on 3 July that 'he was not under the illusion that seemed to be in Sir Douglas Haig's mind that our advance would be rapid. [He] told him that "we shall be lucky if we take Roulers in 2 months".' Gough also argued that the proposal to use the cavalry to exploit a success was not his but that of GHQ. This was proven by the fact that long before he was appointed to lead the attack a sleeper roadway had been specially prepared and kept constantly clear in order to allow the cavalry to burst through the infantry's lines.[5] It was true that Gough had a reputation as a 'thruster' but this, as Gough later pointed out with much justification, merely strengthened the view that Haig, in appointing him, intended the action as a breakthrough.

It was certainly the case that Haig had initially asked Plumer and Rawlinson to propose a plan for his Flanders offensive but had turned to Gough when dissatisfied with their limited and cautious proposals.[6] What Gough had argued for was that the attack should not be *limited* by specific objectives. He told Edmonds that he had had in mind the many operations which had achieved much less than they should have done as a result of excessive caution, such as Loos, Gallipoli or the Somme. Gough wrote:

In all these operations victorious troops were halted on a prearranged line at the moment where the enemy was completely disorganised and was given time to bring up fresh troops with the result that ground which lay completely open to us and could have been seized without almost any opposition was occupied by the enemy and subsequently cost us very many valuable lives before it was captured. This was the argument which I used with complete justification with Douglas Haig.[7]

Wynne's draft had also cited Davidson's memorandum of 26 June which had criticised the unlimited objectives of Gough's plan and expressed concern at the 'ragged' line which might result. Gough wrote that such arguments were 'born of minds that were mediocre, pedantic and who accepted no risks and lacked enterprise'. He argued that the lessons of previous missed opportunities such as Loos were 'not that the advancing troops should go on and seize unoccupied ground but that the reserves must be pushed closer up behind the assaulting troops and be on the spot to take advantage of any gifts of fortune which she may hand on'.[8] Gough had argued almost precisely these points in his reply to Davidson's memo at the time in June 1917, a full copy of which was eventually reproduced as an appendix to the Official History.

Edmonds passed these comments on to Wynne with the instruction that he thought Gough's 'point of view should be fully represented'.[9] Wynne responded, almost by return, that he did not agree. His view was that Gough had misinterpreted Haig's intention at the time and continued to misinterpret, therefore, the whole point of the story. His view was that:

Haig told [Gough] that he was to 'wear out the enemy but have an objective'. To wear out the enemy means to destroy his divisions by degrees and to do that . . . a strictly limited objective was essential. General Davidson's memorandum could not be bettered on the subject and was not in the least 'pedantic' or 'over-cautious', it was plain common sense. Gough put the objective first – as he says again in his comments he wanted to push on as far as he could with the attack and tried to impress his Corps and Divisional Commanders with 'this spirit' which he knew 'most of them possessed'. But it was not that kind of spirit which the campaign of Haig's instruction asked for.[10]

Wynne admitted that Haig had originally intended the attack as a breakthrough but Wynne had gathered from General Davidson that Haig's outlook had been changed by his meetings with the War Cabinet on 25 June.[11] His modified instructions to Gough to 'wear the enemy down but have an objective' were written a few days later on 30 June.

Having originally instructed Wynne fully to represent Gough's view, Edmonds now appeared to accept Wynne's opinion that Gough was neither suitable nor inclined to conduct the particular offensive that Haig had required. He instructed Wynne to

[l]et Gough have his say but you have the last word and I am certain you have got to the bottom of the affair . . . Gough was out to fight and get forward. He had no idea how to conduct the action Haig

required and would not take advice. I heard him complain that the troops had no 'blood lust', the officers no 'spirit of the offensive'.[12]

In order to emphasise his point, and perhaps reflecting his own personal lack of sympathy for Gough, Edmonds related how he had been having tea in the mess at Gough's HQ when Gough had come in and said, 'I want to shoot two officers':

> There was an astonished pause and the APM said 'Beg your pardon Sir there are no officers under sentence'. Gough looked at him as if to say 'you fool' and explained 'Yes I know that but I want to shoot two officers as an example to the others'. And he got them.[13]

A month later, Gough wrote again to Edmonds, insisting that it was Haig who had originated the strategy of a breakthrough and not him. He wrote:

> [Haig] quite clearly told me that the plan was to capture the Passchendaele ridge and to advance as rapidly as possible on Roulers. How many miles does Roulers lie behind the German lines? 40 miles. I was then to advance on Ostend. By the time I had reached and taken Roulers Haig considered that the 4th Army on the coast would have advanced sufficiently to cover my left and combine with me in clearing the coast. This was very definitely viewing the battle as an attempt to breakthrough and moreover Haig never altered this opinion till the attack was launched as far as I know. He confirmed this general idea on several occasions.[14]

In response, and in striking contrast to his letter to Wynne a month before, Edmonds now wrote to Gough:

> I thoroughly agree with you about the carping criticism in Wynne's narrative. I have already told him that a narrative of events is required, not criticism. He will have to re-write the greater part of the story. Part of the explanation is that Wynne fell into the hands of Tavish Davidson.[15]

He added: 'Later on I shall trouble you with an improved version. With very many thanks for the trouble you have so kindly taken.'[16]

This inconsistency partly reflected a particular weakness of Edmonds' which goes some way to explaining why his motivations and dealings with his colleagues have been generally misunderstood. Rather than suggesting an autocratic approach to his writers, it suggested a lack of courage in his convictions and a desire to appear accommodating. Terraine has summed this up most succinctly with his suggestion that Edmonds wished to be 'all things to all men'.[17] Notwithstanding that, it is more than likely that, convinced by Gough's letter of 18 March, Edmonds had returned to his original view and this was ultimately the view which he expressed in the Official History.

The question of whether the objective of the 1917 offensive was to be a decisive breakthrough or a limited advance aimed at wearing down the enemy is important for a number of reasons, not merely in measuring its success. On a strategic level it must be remembered that the government, whilst desiring a morale-boosting success, had only sanctioned the offensive on the basis that it was to be a series of step-by-step advances with strictly limited objectives which were capable of being called off if they looked like degenerating into another attritional struggle. Tactically, the eventual plan for 31 July, if intended as a breakthrough, was fatally flawed because it failed to mass sufficient men or artillery for the purpose.[18] Whether, therefore, it was Haig or Gough who had envisaged such a breakthrough is a matter of considerable relevance to assigning responsibility for the ultimate failure. There was plenty of evidence, in addition to Gough's own protestations, to suggest that Haig himself had intended the Flanders offensive as a decisive breakthrough. In contrast to Wynne's original draft, which had placed the reponsibility for this exclusively on General Gough, this evidence was eventually incorporated by Edmonds into the published account.

This account first described how the 1917 Flanders offensive had originated as part of a combined attack with the French in a plan devised by General Nivelle. Haig had asked Plumer in January 1917 to prepare a plan whose 'whole essence . . . is to attack with rapidity and push right through quickly'.[19] Despite Haig's demand for a breakthrough Plumer proposed a cautious advance, insisting on two features whose neglect was ultimately to bedevil the operation which took place seven months later. Plumer argued that the first day's objective should be limited to the German second line on the reverse slope of Pilckem Ridge so that a subsequent advance might have adequate and observed artillery cover. In addition, a gap of 2,000 yards existed at the point of the Ypres Salient between the northern and southern thrusts of the attack. Plumer argued that it was vital that this gap should be closed in order to gain a foothold on the Gheluvelt plateau, which was essential to protect the right flank of the northern attack. General Rawlinson, asked to comment on Plumer's scheme, emphasised yet more strongly that the attack should not progress until the high ground of the Gheluvelt plateau in the centre was in British hands. Rawlinson agreed with Plumer that insufficient space existed to assemble the necessary volume of artillery to mount three attacks simultaneously, and so he proposed a southern attack, followed 48 to 72 hours later by an attack against the centre and the north. Haig, wrote Edmonds, believed both schemes to be too cautious and wrote in the margin of Rawlinson's proposals: 'Our objective is to break through rapidly.' By April, Haig had suggested that the objective of the third day could be achieved on the first. As Edmonds noted dryly: 'The task of capturing the Ridge was accordingly telescoped into one day, or rather into five morning hours; and in the afternoon the advance was to be continued down the eastern slope to the Oosttaverne Line.' Still not satisfied, though, with the spirit in which his army commanders proposed to carry out this plan, Haig sought, in General Gough, a commander who 'would be more sympathetic to his own changed outlook'.[20]

After the failure of the Nivelle offensive in April it became clear that the French were not going to be able to support the British in their offensive. Despite the fact that the War Cabinet, on 16 May, made French support a condition of any British attack and '[d]espite the lamentable state of the French Army having completely altered the situation', Haig determined to press ahead with his plans. 'On his own responsibility, without further reference to the War Cabinet', Haig proceeded with his first stage of the attack against the southern flank at Messines. At the end of June, Haig outlined the second stage of his Flanders offensive to the War Cabinet. Having been advised by General Robertson not to argue that he could finish the war in 1917, Haig nevertheless detailed how he planned to clear the Channel coast of German submarine bases in an advance of 25 miles. Once his forces had advanced 40 miles the French would be asked to advance towards Metz–Valenciennes, and once they had reached 60 miles the Germans would be falling back across the entire front. Edmonds noted that 'to some readers the outline of the campaign may seem super-optimistic and too far-reaching, even fantastic', although a Commander-in-Chief usually held quite distant objectives in mind.[21] Nevertheless, Edmonds had made it quite clear that Haig specifically intended the campaign to break through the German front.

In Edmonds' subsequent amendments to Wynne's chapter dealing with the Fifth Army plan, he demonstrated how Haig's strategic objectives directly influenced Gough's tactical preparations. The chapter began with the assertion that Sir Douglas Haig:

> did not contemplate a prolonged campaign in the Ypres district and hoped that the Fifth Army would be approaching the Roulers–Thorout railway fifteen miles from the start in time for the coastal operations by the 4th Army to catch the high tides on the 7th and 8th August.[22]

On 14 May General Gough was handed the 'Northern Operations' file which contained the GHQ 1917 plan. In this the first day's objective was limited to the capture of the German second line, an advance of about a mile. This was to be followed by a two-day pause to allow the capture and consolidation of the Gheluvelt plateau. Edmonds wrote: 'This plan did not appear to provide for the speedy progress which General Gough had understood was required according to the verbal instructions he had received from Sir Douglas Haig.'[23] Edmonds then took the somewhat unusual step of citing in a footnote Gough's letter of 18 March 1944, in which he referred to Haig 'definitely viewing the battle as an attempt to breakthrough'.[24] As a result of this view Gough modified this scheme to aim for further objectives, involving an advance of 4,000–5,000 yards on the first day with only limited pauses at each stage to consolidate. Despite Davidson's memorandum of 26 June urging a succession of deliberate attacks with objectives limited to about a mile within the range of artillery support, Haig allowed the plan to stand: 'it seemed, perhaps, worth trying an all-out attack on the first day'.[25] Haig did, however, stress the vital importance of securing the Gheluvelt plateau before advancing further north. The Official History pointed out that the Fifth Army scheme, in spreading the front and reserve divisions of the four attacking corps equally across the front, did not provide for this consolidation of the plateau. Nor was any alteration made and 'Sir Douglas Haig did not press the points he had made'.[26] Indeed, Edmonds emphasised that Haig still clung to the hope that a strong blow in Flanders might break the German resistance and he wished to be ready to exploit to the full such an opportunity. At a conference on 5 July he 'used the words: "in the operations subsequent to the capture of the Passchendaele–Staden Ridge, opportunities for the employment of cavalry in masses are likely to offer"'.[27]

Edmonds' clear interpretation, then, was that Haig had intended to break through and had encouraged the army commander whom he specifically selected for this task to plan for such a strategy. The flaw in this approach was that, whilst Haig recognised the necessity of concentrating his resources to secure the Gheluvelt plateau and thereby protect the northern advance, Gough was driven to spread his forces uniformly across the entire front to pursue Haig's desired breakthough. Indeed, Haig had refused to permit the originally proposed step-by-step advance which would have secured this plateau (and which was later to succeed in September) and insisted instead on a rapid advance without pause beyond, crucially, the range of artillery support. As Prior and Wilson have pointed out 'the gap between the high command's aspirations and power to accomplish them could not have been clearer'.[28]

Furthermore, Edmonds consistently reinforced the view that Haig continued to cling unrealistically to an anticipated breakthrough as his narrative progressed from planning to the different stages of the battle. On 4 August Haig informed the War Cabinet that the action of 31 July (despite having failed to secure the vital Gheluvelt plateau) had been 'highly satisfactory and the losses slight for so great a battle'.[29] Edmonds commented that whilst the losses of 31,850 for the four days to 3 August were 'moderate' when compared with the opening day of the Somme, they were 'in themselves severe'.[30] He added that '[t]he situation was, however, only relatively satisfactory'.[31] The nine leading divisions of the four corps of the Fifth Army had been intended to reach their third and fourth objectives on the first day and then to advance on the Passchendaele–Staden ridge before relief. In fact as Edmonds highlighted after four days they were less than half way to the first day's objectives and had already lost 30 to 60 per cent of their fighting strength. By 29 August, following the persistently unsuccessful attempts to secure the Gheluvelt plateau and the radical revision of *Haig's*[32] tactical scheme placing leadership of the offensive with Plumer and Second Army (envisaging a succession of steps with strictly limited objectives), Edmonds wrote:

> Although the objectives with which the campaign had started were still far distant, Sir Douglas Haig hoped that any one of the heavy blows he proposed to deliver might yet demoralise and crack the German defence, with far-reaching consequences.[33]

On 21 September, following the successful attack against this plateau, Edmonds wrote:

> Sir Douglas Haig still hoped that any one of the blows he intended to deliver might cause the disintegration of the German opposition, and all available British strength in France, including the five cavalry divisions, was to be assembled ready to exploit any opportunity thus created by pushing through the new Fifth Army front north-eastwards towards Roulers and Staden.[34]

Haig, Edmonds wrote, now made 'special preparations for the long-awaited opportunity of a breakthrough'.[35] By this point, however, both Gough and Plumer wrote independently to Haig to the effect that they believed 'any idea of extensive exploitation to be premature'.[36] By early October, having been informed by both army commanders that they would 'welcome a closing down of the campaign', and with the weather turning the battle area into a 'porridge of mud' and a 'vast wilderness of slime', Haig nevertheless begged the Cabinet to have 'firm faith in the possibility of final success'.[37] Edmonds' work therefore could scarcely be clearer on this issue; the 'breakthrough' was Haig's plan and one which he continued to anticipate against the views of his senior colleagues and government long after the realistic prospects of its success had evaporated.

Edmonds also altered Wynne's draft over another issue with which Gough had expressed concern. With regard to the malign influence of poor weather during the August fighting, Wynne's original draft had suggested that Haig allowed Gough to proceed against his own better judgement that conditions made progress impossible. This issue convinced Gough that Wynne was a biased observer, intent on discrediting him. Gough objected to Wynne's assertion that he ought to have postponed the attacks in August because the likelihood of poor conditions was predictable, since the 'weather broke early in August with the familiarity of an Indian monsoon'.[38] He wrote:

> It certainly did not in 1914–1915 . . . I was as closely in touch with Meteor as [I was] with GHQ. It was laid down that November was the wettest month of the year. NO ONE expected August to be a wet month.[39]

Again in May 1944 Gough restated his objections to this comment:

> As an instance of the absurd lengths to which the author will go to find something with which to throw discredit on me and on the 5th Army I would mention his remarks in one of the earlier chapters about it being well known that August was one of the wettest months of the year and that rains broke with the regularity of a monsoon. Out of the four years of the war August was a fine dry month in three of them. Even in the four years of this war has August been anything but a fine month or has the rain broken in Flanders with the regularity of a monsoon?[40]

Gough, in fact, claimed that on 16 August he had told Haig that 'owing to rain and mud the whole operation should be abandoned'.[41]

Edmonds passed this on to Wynne who responded that the statement about the monsoon had been taken from Charteris's book and he had accepted as written that the intelligence section had 'most carefully prepared statistics of previous years'. Wynne complained that Gough had taken this quotation from Charteris as an indication of his 'jaundiced mentality and [showed] the absurd lengths etc'.[42] Nevertheless, in this matter as with others, Edmonds again supported the view of Gough. When he came to rewrite Wynne's narrative he not only expunged this reference but actually countered it. As he wrote in his preface: 'It is simply not true that, as asserted, "Flanders was the wettest area on the front" and that "in Flanders the weather broke early each August with the regularity of an Indian monsoon".'[43] If this were not sufficient Edmonds repeated this identical assertion at the end of his chapter on the August actions in a note which devoted two pages to meteorological statistics and Bigourdan's *Le Climat de la France* giving average annual rainfall for four frontier *départements* over 50 years.

Was this view simply indicative of the fact that Edmonds tamely accepted Gough's persistent objections? If it was, one might have expected Edmonds to bend to all Gough's complaints. However, on a number of issues Edmonds allowed Wynne's narrative to stand in spite of strenuous efforts on the part of Gough to have it amended. One such issue raised by the Official History's treatment of the planning of the Flanders offensive was the degree to which the Commander-in-Chief devolved tactical responsibility for the battles to his army commanders. The Official History implicitly suggested, by describing his active involvement in framing the plan and vacillating between potential commanders, that Haig exercised considerable tactical influence. However, Wynne's original draft explicitly adhered to the view that Haig defined strategy and did not interfere in the tactical preparations made by his commanders to carry that out. Gough had again complained to Edmonds that Wynne's draft chapters

> set forth almost as a principle the abrogation of authority and responsibility of commanders to command by the frequent references that are made to Haig disapproving of my plans and yet not interfering to alter them. This is quite a new light on Haig's character and one which I fail to recognise. I doubt whether he would be very pleased! I doubt the wisdom of emphasising this point although it may shift responsibility from Haig's shoulders – for I take it that the function of an Official History is not only to tell the true story but also to point out the true lessons and surely this is not a lesson to be inculcated.[44]

He called Wynne's work a 'vicious distortion of the facts . . . deliberately written with the object of absolving Haig and almost more so GHQ from all responsibility by placing every possible reason for failure on my shoulders'.[45] Maj.-Gen. Neil Malcolm, Gough's Chief of Staff, came to a similar conclusion. He informed Gough that he simply could not understand how anyone could allow himself to produce such a 'farrago of malicious nonsense':

> The picture [Wynne] draws of Haig as a commander is very far from the truth, allowing himself to be flouted by you, an army commander, while at the same time you were stamping on your corps commanders, with his full knowledge.[46]

Whilst all references to Gough 'stamping' on the views of his corps commanders were dropped in the published version, Wynne's original comments concerning Haig's abrogation of tactical responsibility remained.

The published volume retained Wynne's conclusion, to which Gough had strenuously objected:

> Having settled on the general plan at conferences, Sir Douglas Haig did not interfere with his army commanders as regards details of execution, indeed he often gave way to them and their wishes in spite of his better judgement. Notably, he yielded to General Gough as regards distant objectives and the neglect of the Gheluvelt plateau.[47]

This impression remained in brief glimpses elsewhere in the volume, such as in the suggestion that Haig officially approved Gough's plan 'yet had some doubts as to the distant objectives given for the first day'.[48]

III

The question of the weather remained a controversial issue with which the Official History of the Third Ypres campaign would have to deal. Edmonds acknowledged in his preface that '[m]uch has been said – without exaggeration as regards the last four weeks – of the dreadful conditions under which the British and Dominion troops fought'. The name 'Passchendaele' had come to connote a long and persistent struggle in mud and rain. However, Edmonds' narrative did little to redress the misconception which he had identified in his preface that these conditions applied only to the last four weeks from 12 October to 10 November. On 31 July rain set in and continued for 'three days and nights almost without cessation'. Edmonds wrote:

> For the time being it converted the shelled areas near the front into a barrier of swamp, four thousand yards wide and this had to be crossed in order to reach the new front line. The margins of the overflowing streams were transformed into long stretches of bog, passable only by a few well-defined tracks which became targets to the enemy's artillery; and to leave the tracks was to risk death by drowning.[49]

Reviewing the August battles, Edmonds wrote:

> The memory of this August fighting, with its heavy showers, rain-filled craters and slippery mud, was so deeply impressed on combatants, who could not be told the reasons for the Commander-in-Chief's persistency, and such stories were spread at home by the wounded, that it has remained the image and symbol of the whole battle.[50]

This question of the reason for Haig's persistence in the face of such adversity is an important one. The War Cabinet had sanctioned the Flanders offensive on the condition that it was a series of step-by-step advances, limited to the range of artillery support, which could be terminated if casualties were disproportionate to the results achieved. On 18 July 1917 Sir William Robertson had assured the Cabinet that this was precisely the kind of operation which Haig had been planning. On 21 July the Cabinet asked to be informed of the first objectives so that they might judge whether the operation had been successful. As the Official History pointed out:

> Sir Douglas Haig's reply is important. He wrote that 'even if my attacks do not gain ground, as I hope and expect, we ought still to persevere in attacking Germans in France. Only by this means can we win: and we must encourage the French to continue fighting'. That principle was to guide his decisions throughout the Flanders campaign.[51]

After the war, Haig claimed that he had agreed to attack in Flanders because the French had begged him to do so in order to prevent the Germans from exploiting disorders in their own army.[52] David French has shown that not only is there no contemporary evidence for this, but that senior French commanders had in fact deprecated the notion of an attack in Flanders. Whilst it is recognised that there were mutinies in the French army in 1917, recent studies have suggested that morale was not so low as to threaten a collapse if the French army had been attacked.[53] It is therefore interesting to consider the degree to which the Official History supported Haig's justification.

It has been suggested that Edmonds took over the writing of this volume from Wynne and rewrote much of his narrative in order to make it more defensive of Haig.[54] In fact, Wynne's original conclusion, which was ultimately altered by Edmonds, contained a lengthy justification of Haig's action in this campaign. This rested heavily upon the mitigation which Haig had subsequently used in his own defence: that during 1917 the Commander-in-Chief feared the imminent collapse of the French army and maintained an offensive attitude during that year in order to divert the enemy's attention and resources from the French front. Moreover the danger of a French collapse was, according both to Haig in his diaries and to Wynne, known on the British side to Haig alone. The British Cabinet, ignorant of this danger, opposed any further offensives by the British army until the following year. However, despite clear instructions from the government to avoid further action, Haig, according to Wynne, fought the Messines battle on his own initiative 'and thenceforward continued to carry the responsibility for the campaign largely upon his own shoulders'. Gough had noted in the margin against this view:

> This may be in many respects greatly to the credit of D.H. but it must be conceded that such a lack of confidence between a Chief and his government is most regrettable and I do not think D.H.'s example should be encouraged. It is one thing to act on one's own initiative without waiting for orders in emergencies – it is quite another to act completely contrary to orders and to conceal facts from the Government, however bad the Government may be.[55]

Thus, Wynne argued, despite Lloyd George's reluctance to fight a campaign in Flanders, it was Haig who continued to push for every available man to be sent. He alone had been confided in by Pétain 'in the strictest confidence' that the French army could not stand up to a new German offensive and was on the point of breaking. Wynne cited Haig's own words to Davidson of March 1927 on the subject of criticism in the press:

> The mere suggestion of a pause in our attacks in the north at once brought Petain in his train to see me and to beg me to put in another effort against Passchendaele without delay. Knowing as I did the rotten state of the French army in 1917 (for Petain told me more than once about his awful anxieties) I felt thankful when the winter came and the French army was still in the field. For this the price paid was not excessive.

Wynne added in support of this contention the view of the German official historian that the requirement to meet the British offensives of 1917 with all available reserves, guns and ammunition resulted in the failure of the high command to exploit the Nivelle disaster and 'settle finally with the French Army'. Furthermore, by early June mutinies had broken out in 48 divisions of the French army and wholesale absence without leave and refusal to obey orders were widespread. Even the construction of the Maginot line after the war was taken by Wynne as 'additional proof of the "rotten" state to which the French Army had sunk . . . it was the outward visible sign of an army and a nation which had lost hope in a free destiny.'

To these points Gough asked two important questions. Firstly: 'Was Haig justified in placing such confidence in Petain's judgement? Petain was a well-known pessimist. In addition he hated the English and never hesitated to sacrifice them for the French however petty the reason.'[56] Secondly, if Haig's great concerns about the state of the French army were the driving force behind his efforts first to gain approval for a campaign in Flanders and then doggedly to persist in the fight, why did he not share these concerns with the government? In justification Wynne had stated that Lloyd George had himself admitted that ministers could not keep information to themselves. Furthermore, Wynne also pointed out that Ludendorff had stated in his *Memoirs* that the German high command were completely unaware at the time of the scale of French mutinies and poor morale. However, as Gough had noted: 'The information need not have been given to Ministers, nor on paper – but it should have been given verbally to the PM and to the CIGS at home.'[57] Wynne concluded however:

> Sir Douglas Haig has been accused of exaggerating the weak state of the French army as an excuse for the continuation of the Flanders campaign until the breakthrough which he expected occurred. The facts do not support this contention. Throughout those critical months his constant instructions to the army commanders were to 'wear down the enemy but at the same time have an objective'. The objective was not gained but the enemy's divisions were worn down so effectively that the great crisis of 1917 was surmounted.[58]

As a result of this strategic success the Passchendaele campaign could be regarded among the elect few:

> which have shaped decisively the fate of Europe and the history of the British Commonwealth . . . [B]y the dogged tenacity and steadfast faith of . . . Sir Douglas Haig, the mighty task was accomplished. The most dangerous crisis of the War was surmounted, and during the process 87 German divisions were so hammered and reduced in efficiency that the foundation was laid for victory in 1918. The British people, who accepted the red poppy of Flanders as symbol of the great sacrifice made in the War, will give the Flanders battles of 1917 their rightful place in its memory.[59]

Given that Edmonds has been accused of exhibiting a growing bias in defence of Haig, it is interesting to note that Wynne's conclusions were almost completely altered in Edmonds' version and the lengthy explanation of Haig's self-justification greatly reduced and toned down.[60] Dealing briefly with the French mutinies, Edmonds wrote that General Debeney had informed Haig, 'behind closed doors and without witnesses, as a military secret, of the deplorable state of the French Armies'. He concluded that to 'secure that the enemy should not exploit this temporarily enfeebled condition of the French became the first and immediate purpose of the British Commander-in-Chief, and continued to be so until the end of the year'.[61]

IV

By this point in the compilation process it was clear that Edmonds had firmly sided with Gough against the view of his official historian. Furthermore the supposed evidence of bias which Gough monthly brought to Edmonds' attention had coloured Edmonds' attitude to Wynne irreparably. In May 1945 Wynne was instructed to meet with Gough to settle the remaining issues of contention. Wynne did so and found Gough 'agreeable throughout the interview and most willing to help'.[62] In this interview Gough reiterated his view that Haig's verbal instructions to capture the Passchendaele ridge and then to advance as rapidly as possible on Roulers was definitely an 'attempt to break out on a wide front'.[63] He framed his plans accordingly spreading his divisions out equally in the orthodox manner. With hindsight Gough accepted that he should have massed his reserves behind the most important tactical objective, i.e. the Gheluvelt plateau. However, he was clear that Haig neither criticised nor even commented on his plan.[64] During his interview Gough had

> stressed most emphatically that he had acted throughout on Haig's instructions and that Haig had made no comment or disapproval of his action either before or after the campaign. It was for this reason that he had so strongly objected to the inference in the first draft that he was acting as a freelance contrary to Haig's wishes. His position throughout had been as an Army commander acting on the orders of Douglas Haig.[65]

Following this interview, Wynne did, in fact, alter his own view and amended his text in a number of instances. He removed a reference made to a conference held by Haig to consider Davidson's memo of 25 June at which Haig was swayed to accept the Fifth Army scheme by Plumer's recommendation to 'go right through the ridge on the first day'. Gough had told Wynne that although Plumer was a wily old fox and would quite likely have urged such a course, knowing he would be in no way responsible for the job, he had no personal recollection and did not believe it.[66] Although this would have supported Gough's defence, Wynne agreed to omit it as based solely on Davidson's memory. In addition Wynne deleted his reference to Lt-Gen. Cavan's alleged offer of infantry and artillery support to allow Gough to concentrate maximum resources against the Gheluvelt plateau. Gough had told him this was 'pure invention'.[67]

Finally Wynne accepted Gough's arguments concerning Haig's responsibility for approving his plan. Wynne informed Gough that this point of view was in fact to be adopted in the final draft and that when he read it he would not find much fault with it.

In June 1945 Wynne submitted this draft to Edmonds. Edmonds, however, was not satisfied and wrote that 'careful editing of the volume is required . . . I have drafted a preface and am putting together the final reflections, those drafted by Wynne being quite unsuitable'.[68] From this point the relationship between Director and official historian deteriorated dramatically and echoes of Edmonds' treatment of a previous historian, Aspinall, became apparent in his widely offered and rather acrimonious criticism. He wrote to the Joint Secretary of the Official History Committee that 'Captain Wynne is lacking in military judgement and is indolent and careless. I have no further use for him.'[69] To another official historian, A.M.R. Topham, Edmonds accused Wynne of falsifying documents and of bias. He wrote:

> Wynne's behaviour has been strange for some time (he was 4 years a prisoner of war in 1914–18) and got a shock when he went to North Africa in April 1943 . . . I will tell you more and give you specimens of the dear lunatic's stuff when we next meet.[70]

It was, therefore, Edmonds' version that went to press and Wynne requested that his name be deleted from the list of authors. Edmonds explained in his preface that owing to the war one after another of the authors involved in the compilation of this volume were transferred to employment on more important work. He stated that it had therefore been left to him to collate and edit their unfinished drafts and to complete the book. He admitted that 'for any comments and any opinions expressed in it I am solely responsible'.[71]

We have already seen how these comments and opinions were influenced by Edmonds' correspondence with Gough. However, it is equally the case that Wynne substantially modified his view following his own meeting with Gough and one must accept that Gough's evidence was credible. (It was undoubtedly strengthened by the fact that he was one of a very small handful of senior participants still alive in 1945 to provide any first-hand evidence whatsoever.) Whilst the level of Gough's influence is therefore clear, it is difficult to argue that the incorporation of his evidence in the account necessarily damaged the historical validity of the work. If anything one might consider that it made the work *more* accurate. In particular, if we compare the respective concluding chapters of Wynne and Edmonds it will be seen that the conclusion that was finally published was more balanced and considerably less defensive of Haig and GHQ.

Wynne's concluding chapter attempted to consider whether the 'unparalleled exertions' and 'untold sufferings' of the Flanders battles of 1917 were justified.[72] (To this Gough had added the comment: 'Is the use of the adjective "unparalleled" and "untold" a correct impression to leave on the reader when other battles are considered; where the exertions and the sufferings were quite as great?'[73]) Wynne argued that there were two purposes to the campaign which had to be considered separately: a strategic one to prevent a German offensive against a demoralised French army and a tactical one to clear the German submarine bases along the Belgian coast. Whilst the strategic purpose 'succeeded admirably', the 'tactical failure was complete'. 'No previous campaign undertaken by Sir Douglas Haig had terminated so unsatisfactorily.' Wynne believed that the sorry outcome to a campaign which had started with such great expectations was due mainly to an underrating of the opposition and the attempt to break out on a wide front. The responsibility for this attempt he lay squarely at the door of Gough and Fifth Army. He emphasised the fact that several GHQ plans for a Flanders offensive had *all* stressed the need for limiting the first day's objectives to about a mile in order to obtain observed artillery support for the subsequent infantry advance. They had all advised, too, that the high ground of the Gheluvelt plateau must be occupied before pressing further north. Wynne wrote that, '[d]espite . . . the great strength of the German position, the Fifth Army scheme rejected the safeguards'. Whilst Sir Douglas Haig approved this scheme 'at a special conference on the subject at the end of June':

> his later instruction on 6th July to General Gough ... . did in fact contradict it. Doubly underlined in blue pencil was the instruction 'to wear the enemy down but at the same time to have an objective; I have given two, the Passchendaele–Staden ridge and the coast'.

This passage was subsequently scored out by Wynne and replaced by the contention that 'evidence show[ed] that [Haig] had his doubts about [the Fifth Army scheme] but did not press them'. Despite this amendment Wynne nevertheless argued that, had Fifth Army followed the original GHQ plan of February 1917 for a series of limited 'wearing-down' battles, 31 July might have 'gone with the same victorious swing' as had the battle on Messines Ridge on 7 June. 'Instead, the attempt at a deep penetration on a wide front, without adequate close support by artillery and tanks, played into the enemy's hands.' Long spells of heavy rain turned the shell-torn waterlogged battlefield into a clayey mud and subsequent operations were further hampered by the 'continued failure to appreciate the strength of the German defence'. By contrast, when by late

September Haig regrouped his order of battle and adopted the original GHQ plan under Plumer, in 'three brilliantly executed steps' across the Gheluvelt plateau 'full account was taken of the German defence and it was outwitted and outfought'.[74]

Thus Wynne's conclusion placed his thesis firmly in the Haig camp. On a strategic level it justified the continued struggle and sacrifice in the light of the subsequent failure of the German offensive in 1918. It also emphasised, as has been shown, the supposedly imminent collapse of the French army, of which contemporary knowledge was available to Haig alone at the time. On a tactical level it sought to underpin this strategic vision by emphasising Haig's supposedly persistent instructions to his army commanders to 'wear down' the enemy. For evidence to support these conclusions, Wynne had drawn heavily on Haig's own diary and information supplied by Davidson. Had this been the work that was finally published then it might have justified the criticism of those who have suggested that the Official Histories were overly defensive of Haig. However, Edmonds considerably altered the narrative in the light of Gough's concerns so that it became far more critical of the Commander-in-Chief. His conclusions now contained a much-toned-down version of Wynne's overt support for Haig; there was no reference to Haig's instructions to Gough to 'wear down the enemy'; and there was no more than a passing reference to Haig's fears about the imminent collapse of the French army. The outcome was a far more balanced and far less justificatory assessment.

Edmonds' conclusion was defensive of Haig on a strategic level but was certainly less triumphalistic than Wynne's. Edmonds, too, cited the German view that but for the exhaustion of their best divisions in Flanders in 1917, complete success would have been theirs in March 1918. In contrast to Wynne, he argued that even the British Prime Minister was 'foremost in demanding that "the enemy must not be left in peace for one moment"' and in recognising that a purely defensive attitude during 1917 'would be the gravest imprudence'.[75] Furthermore he defended Flanders (against Gough's opinion) as strategically the best place for the Allies to attack. Even given the poor conditions of the terrain after the rains began, Edmonds cited examples of campaigns under Malborough and Wellington which had triumphed in the face of similar adversity. Haig, he wrote, 'possessed exceptional persistence and tenacity; it had been dinned into him at Staff College that "the man who gives the last kick wins . . .".[76]

In dealing with the tactical preparations for the battle Edmonds did direct some criticism towards Gough. He remarked that the outstanding value of the Gheluvelt plateau was frequently mentioned at conferences before the battle but was not made the foremost objective by Fifth Army in the opening phase. However, Edmonds reiterated that:

it must be held, in any case, that it was an error of judgement on the part of the Commander-in-Chief in the first instance to super-sede General Plumer and his staff who knew the ground – 'every puddle', in the Ypres Salient, it was popularly said – by a general and staff unacquainted with it. This change over was also the cause of the loss of precious time.[77]

Gough had all the qualities which might be expected to ensure he seized an opportunity and Haig did not want a repetition of the loss of such opportunities at Messines. He was a cavalryman with drive and quickness of judgement – 'qualities which made the late General George Patton . . . remarkable in 1944–1945' – and not at all suited to siege operations in the field.[78] Again, whilst not specifically stated in his conclusion, the implication here echoes Edmonds' previous remarks that if Haig had genuinely sought a step-by-step 'wearing-down' advance, then his selection of Gough to play the principal role was a strange decision.

The clear view that therefore emerged from Edmonds' work was that Haig, whilst limited by constraints beyond his control, was to a great degree the author of his own destiny. Haig desired a famous break-through, selected a thrusting general to undertake it and encouraged him in the firm belief that this was the strategic goal. The concerns of the Cabinet and his own GHQ tempered his faith in this eventuality and led Haig to develop misgivings which he was woefully inadequate at commu-nicating, particularly in respect of securing the Gheluvelt plateau. Finally when it became clear that the series of battles was destined to failure and his own army commanders urged restraint, Haig continued to argue that the enemy was on the point of collapse and that one more push would achieve the intended breakthrough. These views and conclusions con-trasted significantly with those expressed by Wynne.

V

As with Edmonds' volume on March 1918, the Passchendaele volume and the process by which it was written has been dealt with by Travers in a chapter of *The Killing Ground*. In this Travers has argued that the Passchendaele volume swung through four remarkable 'if not scandalous' changes in viewpoint from anti-Haig to anti-Gough to 'anti-Haig but still partly anti-Gough' (Wynne's final draft) to finish as pro-Haig and anti-Gough (Edmonds' final version).[79] Travers seems to have based his con-clusion that Edmonds' final version was pro-Haig simply on the single assertion in his last chapter that Haig gave way to Gough 'as regards distant objectives and the neglect of the Gheluvelt plateau'. In fact, this had been Wynne's opinion which Edmonds had left unaltered in the final version.[80] 'In other words', wrote Travers:

> the *Official History* is once more strongly pro-Haig, for Edmonds argues that the fatal plan for 31 July 1917 was really Gough's and not Haig's; that Gough attempted a breakthrough against Haig's advice; and that he neglected the Gheluvelt plateau against Haig's advice.[81]

However, this argument can be challenged on a number of counts. First, on the point of neglect of the plateau Travers agrees with Edmonds in any case and states that there is 'considerable justification for this particular criticism'.[82] This might explain why Edmonds chose to leave it in the account, in spite of Gough's objection to it! Secondly, with regard to the breakthrough, the weight of Edmonds' argument both in his conclusion and earlier in the work is, in fact, firmly behind Haig as the author of the ambitious plan, as has been shown. Finally, Edmonds' suggestion that Haig gave way to Gough over these issues in spite of his better judgement does not specifically suggest that Gough was necessarily aware of these concerns and therefore acting against Haig's *advice*. There is a crucial difference in interpretation between demonstrating that Gough had acted against Haig's advice and demonstrating, as Edmonds had in fact done, that Gough acted according to what Haig, who harboured his own private doubts, had led him to believe. As Gough pointed out on a number of occasions to Edmonds, if he had been aware of these concerns he most certainly would have acted upon them. Edmonds' comments dealing with the selection of General Gough had shown that Haig clearly wanted a 'decisive defeat' and distant objectives, even if he later came to have concerns about Gough's specific objectives for the first day.

Thus, Travers concludes that Edmonds' Official History version was 'plainly wrong':

> Broadly speaking, Gough should be absolved for attempting a breakthrough – he was led by Haig to emphasise this and was even specifically told on 28 June 1917 to try for a breakthrough. Subsequently it was not made abundantly clear to Gough that a step-by-step advance was required and not a breakthrough.[83]

Yet a reading of Edmonds' work leads one to precisely the same conclusion. Travers then states that 'Gough remains at fault in not immediately recognising the critical importance of the Gheluvelt plateau . . . and for not accepting Haig's clear instructions regarding the necessity of capturing the whole Gheluvelt plateau'.[84] Notwithstanding the issue of the clarity of Haig's instructions, on this point Travers has already stated that

Edmonds' conclusion was justified. Finally Travers contends that Haig was at fault for not thrashing out properly the differences and problems inherent in the campaign, particularly when many of these problems stemmed from his own very poor choice of Passchendaele as the front to launch this offensive. However, Edmonds' work clearly highlighted the confusion caused by Haig's inability to communicate the same message consistently to all his commanders.

To attempt to support a theory of bias by viewing Edmonds' work as merely pro-Haig or anti-Gough is an oversimplification which leads one to conclusions which are difficult to reconcile. Thus Travers asserts that Edmonds' Passchendaele volume was anti-Gough yet he recognises that Gough was broadly satisfied with its final version. He explains this by suggesting that Gough had been 'finally worn down by the long drawn-out arguments over the various drafts and viewpoints'.[85] This was certainly not the case as Gough maintained his defence of his long-standing position even after he had read the final draft. He told Edmonds that '[a]s regards the analysis of myself as a commander, I do not think the facts justify everything you say'.[86] He was no doubt referring in particular to the inclusion in Edmonds' conclusion of the view that Haig yielded to Gough in respect of the neglect of the Gheluvelt plateau against his better judgement. Gough had earlier informed Edmonds with regard to this specific passage:

> I do not think this is at all correct. DH never made any objection to the choice of objective – he made no protest or argument. If he had I would have naturally been impressed and in all probability he would have carried the day.[87]

On the other hand, because there remained a number of conclusions like this with which Gough was not entirely satisfied, it would be equally wrong to claim this work was simply a defence of Gough. It is quite clear that, notwithstanding Gough's many interventions, Edmonds did not simply defer to Gough's sensitivities. Nevertheless Gough believed the final work was 'an immense improvement on Wynne's'. The concluding chapters were 'most readable and very instructive for the student and the historian'. He thanked Edmonds for having written them in such 'a fair and friendly spirit'.[88]

VI

Let us finally consider how Edmonds' last work, published in 1948, compares with current studies of this offensive. We have already seen how Edmonds specifically avoided the opportunity overtly to justify Haig's persistence by reference to his subsequent claims about the parlous state of the French army. Interestingly, the claim made by Haig, that the disastrous seven-week delay between the two phases of the campaign (Messines and Pilckem Ridge) was caused by the pressing need to take some immediate pressure off the French, is not supported by the Official History. Haig in fact proposed the two distinct phases of the attack at his army commanders conference at Doullens on 7 May. He was not informed of the problems within the French army until 2 June by which time the Messines attack was only five days away.[89] The Official History in fact stated that the Messines attack was to be delivered early to overcome the problems, highlighted by Plumer and Rawlinson, of delivering three attacks simultaneously. The subsequent delay of seven weeks, whilst not explicitly stated, was due to Haig having decided to transfer the campaign to General Gough. Whilst not explicitly associating the dangers inherent in giving the enemy a seven-week warning with the subsequent failure of the attack against Pilckem Ridge, Edmonds nevertheless described in detail the loss of opportunity which followed the inability to exploit the Messines victory.

Wynne had made the point, considered earlier, that Edmonds had failed to reveal to future generations the superior offensive tactics of the German army. Prior and Wilson have shown that British tactics on the Western Front had been evolving successfully during 1917 but that their lessons were not always so successfully applied. The battles of Third Ypres provided a good example. To what extent did Edmonds' volume highlight these lessons?

In considering, first, the battle of Messines, Edmonds in fact emphasised that the final objective had been strictly and deliberately limited to an advance of one to two miles. Pamphlets had been issued summarising the lessons learnt at the Somme dealing with artillery, the infantry advance and forward communication. The plan also incorporated several progressive features which had been first introduced at Arras on 9 April: greater attention was paid to counter-battery work and the timetable of the barrage throughout the operation. Aside from the explosion of mines directly under the German front lines immediately before the assault, the plan was unique in the level of artillery preparations. A total of 2,266 guns and howitzers were assembled for the operation along with 144,000 tons of ammunition. At zero hour each 18-pounder gun had an average of 1,000 rounds. As Edmonds revealed, though only in figures in a footnote, this represented a concentration of artillery and shells two and a half times greater than was available for the battle of the Somme.[90]

To discharge this unprecented concentration of firepower the artillery plans also revealed the British high command to be learning from previous experiences. The artillery plan was designed to counter the German system of deep defences based on immediate counter-attack. Strongpoints and machine-gun nests were to be battered and destroyed by the preliminary bombardment and the front divisions were to be harassed and exhausted by artillery and machine-gun fire by day and night. Field artillery was to concentrate on wire entanglements in the forward zone and strong counter-battery fire was to continue against the enemy artillery. During the advance the barrage was to become a protective screen creeping 150–300 yards ahead of the infantry, sweeping and searching the area to check any local counter-attacks. Two further belts of fire would provide the infantry with a dense protective screen 700 yards in depth. The infantry were trained in the method of pillbox fighting which had been so successful against the deep dug-outs at Vimy, and careful instruction was given to the mopping-up parties who followed quickly in the rear to take the outflanked or surrounded enemy positions. These tactics resembled the system of infiltration recommended by a French infantry officer, Capt. Laffargue, in May 1916. According to Edmonds, a copy of these instructions was soon after found by the Germans, who issued it for tactical training at the new storm-troops schools.[91] As a result of the employment of these new techniques a 'great victory' was won at Messines with a 'swift completeness beyond that of any previous major operation of the British Armies in France and Flanders'.[92]

Of course, as Prior and Wilson point out, these lessons were largely dispensed with seven weeks later at Pilckem Ridge as Haig overruled Plumer's, Rawlinson's and Davidson's attempts to repeat them. The value of these new techniques, made possible by significant improvements in both the accuracy and, crucially, availability of artillery ammunition, lay in their ability to suppress the enemy whilst the infantry advanced. They were of little value if the objectives lay, as they did on 31 July, beyond the range of the guns. Edmonds, too, acknowledged that the experiments of strictly limited offensives at Vimy Ridge and Messines had proved the 'most perfect examples' of the efficient use of artillery. He wrote:

Often the method had been stretched beyond its proper limitations. In the opening offensives at Loos, on the Somme and at Arras the British artillery had been asked to neutralize the defence on a wider front and to a greater depth than was reasonably practicable with the available resources. Heavy casualties to the assaulting infantry, which the method had been designed expressly to prevent, had been the consequence. Once again, in the battle about to begin, the limitations of bombardment had been left out of account; particularly as the German defence now relied chiefly on immediate counter-attacks by divisions which were held back beyond artillery range. The destruction of the German strongpoints was not practicable and, as the later battles of the campaign

190

were to show, a short concentrated bombardment by heavy and medium artillery, sufficient to stun the garrisons of the strong-points at the moment of assault, would have been equally effective at a fraction of the cost.[93]

Instead, as Edmonds concluded, the efforts of the artillery arm were 'handicapped by the excessive demand' placed upon its limited resources and the need to spread its fire over the entire German position.[94]

By the end of August, after successive failures to secure the Gheluvelt plateau, Haig recognised that it was necessary to alter his tactics to the step-by-step advance originally proposed by General Plumer. Edmonds noted that the tactical scheme to secure the plateau was 'radically revised'. The fullest possible weight was to be massed against the plateau, the occupation of which was to be carried out by a succession of assaults with strictly limited objectives. Plumer intended to advance in four separate steps with an interval of six days between each to allow time to bring forward artillery and supplies; the distance between each step, governed by the need to meet German counter-attacks with fresh infantry supported by an effective artillery barrage, was to be limited to about 1,500 yards. Special emphasis was placed on the need for heavy and medium artillery both to smash the concrete shelters and machine-gun nests and to engage in effective counter-battery work before the assault. Plumer asked for twice the amount of guns allotted to the same frontage as 31 July but, given that he had halved the depth of the attack, this represented a density of bombardment four times as great as 31 July.[95]

Commenting on these preparations, and highlighting how lessons were now being learnt, Edmonds wrote:

> The gathering artillery potential had been shown in the battles for the Vimy and Messines ridges, where the frontage and depth of the area attacked had been within the power of the artillery to over-whelm with shell . . . The keynote of the Second Army plan was the systematic concentration of fire on definite targets such as strongpoints, battery positions and counter-attack formations, both before and during the assault . . . In addition, a barrage of artillery and machine gun fire a thousand yards deep was to move ahead of the infantry, in order to keep down any enemy troops lying in shell holes in the open.[96]

The infantry tactics had also been developed from previous experience. The infantry would still be required to fight skilfully across shell-cratered ground but fresh troops would be at hand to consolidate any objective and to hold it against immediate counter-attack:

From the lessons learnt in the Messines battle, General Plumer had worked out a more flexible attack organisation for the infantry to deal with the new German method of defence . . . Radical changes were made in the scheme of attack. The assault was led by one or two lines of skirmishers, at five paces' interval, to act as an advanced guard in order to afford freedom of manoeuvre to groups in the rear. The loose distribution of the infantry in groups for the purpose of outflanking enemy strongpoints and fortified shell holes became a recognised battle drill.[97]

Edmonds then described how, at the start of the assault, the artillery barrage was beyond precedent. 'Massively supported in this manner, it [was] no wonder that the four assaulting divisions advanced with the utmost resolution.' The barrage was magnificent in accuracy and volume and moved forward in lifts of 50 yards every two minutes. The German outposts and counter-attack groups were overrun before they could emerge from their shelters. The barrage then slowed to lifts of 100 yards every six minutes. 'The Western half of the plateau was soon covered with small assault groups worming their way in single file between the shell craters deep into the German defence system.' Unnerved and stunned by the concentrated blast of heavy high-explosive shell, the Germans were completely demoralised and had 'but one idea, to surrender as soon as possible'. After five days' fighting, and despite numerous and determined counter-attacks by the enemy, Plumer had succeeded in gaining all his objectives and had driven the Germans from the major part of their key positions on Gheluvelt plateau:

> Thus ended, with complete success . . . the first step in Sir Douglas Haig's first trial of step-by-step advance: the much vaunted new German defence tactics had failed to stop the new method. The change was not appreciated in England or in France, and the success was underrated by the public, but not by the troops themselves, or by their adversaries.[98]

Edmonds cited Ludendorff's concerns, in confirmation of this, that 'the enemy managed to adapt himself to our method of employing counter-attack divisions'.[99] As Prior and Wilson have noted, though, it was a measure of the diminishing expectations which now accompanied this campaign that Plumer's success should have been greeted so triumphantly by the British high command. The Belgian coast remained, but for three and a half miles of gain, as far away as it had on 31 July. The high ground of the Passchendaele ridge was still 4,500 yards distant.[100]

Haig, as Edmonds made clear, had not learnt the lessons of this operation. As Edmonds dryly noted, the success of the first two steps against the Gheluvelt plateau led him 'to make special preparations for the long awaited opportunity of a breakthrough'. The next steps could be 'less strictly limited' as Haig believed the Germans to now be on the point of collapse.[101] The attacks at Broodseinde, Poelcappelle and Passchendaele through October and early November were inadequately prepared for, insufficiently supported by artillery and made by exhausted troops in atrocious conditions. The three chapters of Edmonds' Official History covering these battles make grim reading. At Poelcappelle on 9 October, the 'porridge of mud' made accurate artillery fire impossible and many guns were unable even to participate. Regardless of this scant artillery protection, battalion commanders, spreading out their companies to cover the wide gaps in the line, ordered their men to advance into a 'morass' 30 to 50 yards wide and, in places, waist deep. As Edmonds remarked, that 'the attacks ordered were so gallantly made in such conditions stands to the immortal credit of the battalions concerned'.[102] By 12 October:

> [t]he sodden battlefield was littered with wounded who had lain out in the mud among the dead for two days and nights; and the pillbox shelters were overflowing with unattended wounded, whilst the dead lay piled outside. The survivors, in a state of utter exhaustion, with neither food nor ammunition, had been sniped at by Germans on the higher ground throughout the 10th, with increasing casualties.

Yet despite these atrocious conditions, Sir Douglas Haig remained typically sanguine. He told a meeting of war correspondents on the 11th that mud alone had caused the failure on the 9th, remarking that 'we are practically through the enemy's defences'. He added 'the enemy has only flesh and blood against us, not blockhouses; they take a month to make'.[103] In the battle for Passchendaele on the following day, 13,000 'gallant men' were lost and virtually no ground gained.[104]

VII

Edmonds' final volume of Official History was published at the end of 1948. The *TLS*, reviewing it in February 1949, remarked that had it appeared 'twenty years ago . . . it would have aroused the widest interest and might have created what is called a "sensation"'.[105] Passchendaele had become a word which embodied all criticism against Haig, and imputations levelled at the high command had taken the form of attacks on personal integrity and honesty. In 1948, however, a great war had come and gone and once fierce and angry controversies had now subsided.

Nevertheless it has been seen that there was much within Edmonds' work to reawaken these controversies, particularly surrounding the issues of strategy and the weather. Tactical failings were also revealed and set in contrast to the evolving techniques which were known at the time to have advanced the art of the offensive on the Western Front. There is little within this volume that does not accord with recent studies of this period of battles and there is barely a flicker of the widespread bias of which Edmonds is often accused. At the time the *TLS* reviewer acknowledged that, whilst Brig.-Gen. Edmonds often appeared as Haig's defender, he did not, himself, refrain from criticism. Certainly, as with previous volumes, Edmonds' conclusions directed readers to consider the external factors of want of manpower and the demands of the French as responsible for failure.[106] Within the narrative, however, the military failures were clearly apparent. Edmonds demonstrated the optimistic attempts of Haig to break through the German lines and his failure to temper these strategic desires to the reality of his tactical situation. He revealed Haig's failure effectively to communicate his intentions and his concerns to his army commanders. Finally, Edmonds highlighted Haig's dogged persistence in the face of atrocious conditions, in spite of the reluctance of his senior commanders and in ignorance of the tactical lessons of previous success. In contrast to the more triumphalistic and defensive account of his colleague, Wynne, Edmonds produced a work of lasting authority and value.

9

Conclusion

I

With the publication of Edmonds' final volume on Third Ypres in 1948 the 33-year long process of compiling the Official Military Histories of the Great War came to an end. Founded on the objective of the government to 'place before the public an absolutely reliable and impartial account' of that conflict, the Historical Section and its authors encountered many obstacles on the path to completing their task.[1] Their work remained constantly at the mercy of the Treasury and prey to financial considerations which hampered progress and, on occasions, threatened to destroy the project altogether. Their volumes of Official History, as Hankey had correctly predicted, had regularly to 'run the gauntlet of departmental criticism' on their way to publication.[2] However, Hankey was wrong on a number of counts. Far from emasculating them and depriving them of half their interest, two works were notably able to resist pressure from both the War Office and Foreign Office for major revision. Aspinall's Gallipoli volume and Edmonds' Somme volume emerged unchanged from persistent governmental attempts to protect the reputations of Haig and Hamilton by softening the tone of their criticisms. In so doing, these volumes not only testified to the literary independence of their authors but revealed that the ultimate authority for the content of these official works rested not with any political or service faction but with the Cabinet itself. As Aspinall pointed out, the Official Histories were not General Staff publications.

Hankey was also wrong in his concern that the Official Histories would always be the subject of public criticism. Certainly, the 'official' label has attracted considerably more critical scrutiny to these works than might be expected of 'unofficial' history. Not only have recent commentators looked for higher levels of academic insight and integrity than they might from other works, but the 'official' title appears to justify suspicions of partisan bias and governmental influence. It has also tempted the uninitiated to assume that the works lacked colour and style. These views are all challenged by a thorough understanding of the volumes and their

195

process of compilation. Nor do these recent views reflect the way in which the press or public perceived the Official Histories at the time of publication, although there remained some reviewers, notably Liddell Hart and Sir William Robertson, who inevitably suspected some 'official' malpractice.

Edmonds' first volume was published in November 1922 and was received with universal acclaim in the press. The *TLS* reported that:

> Though so complete the picture is never overloaded with detail; the compiler's sense of proportion has served him well and is one of the most admirable features of a work which, let it be said at once, is excellently done. The first official history is an absolutely true and accurate account of events without partiality, favour or affection . . . [E]vents have been related frankly and honestly in accordance with the facts, supported by the official documents where relevant.
>
> All these qualities – accuracy, impartiality, lucidity – are those expected of an official historian. But it is the easy style, the touches of colour and a sense of the epic quality that give special dimensions to the book.[3]

In 1925, when Edmonds' second volume was published, *The Times* reported that it 'surpassed the very high level of the first volume'.[4] The potentially more controversial volumes received equal praise.

Aspinall's first Gallipoli volume was published in April 1929. *The Times* acknowledged that great failures in war often held greater attractions for the military reader than the campaigns which ended in victory. Of all the theatres of the Great War, Gallipoli held the most interest for the general public, who would readily welcome this work. Interestingly, its reviewer reserved some criticism for the fact that, whilst the plan of the campaign had been criticised by Aspinall in the light of later knowledge, the difficulties and 'fog of the time' should be borne in mind.[5] The *Greenock Telegraph* may not have been an illustrious journal but it described Aspinall's work as having 'lifted the veil on many things hitherto only partially understood'.[6] *Reynolds Illustrated News* referred to the war's most monstrous muddle and the truth about Gallipoli having been revealed at last. The Official History was, according to their reviewer E.C. Buley, 'literally a shocking book', revealing, in what was already the parlance of the time, one more story of lions led by asses.[7]

By contrast, Sir William Robertson, reviewing the first Gallipoli volume in the *Sunday Times*, said that the history did not actually go far enough in revealing ministerial responsibility and claimed that ministers had forbidden publication. A number of other reviewers, including Liddell Hart, suggested that the War Office and Admiralty sought to prevent publication of Volume II. Liddell Hart referred to a 'hitch at Whitehall' which was common knowledge in military circles concerning a difference of opinion arising over the final pages and which threatened publication.[8] The *Sunday Express* claimed that the War Office and Admiralty sought to replace Aspinall with another writer, and *Reynolds Illustrated News* speculated that the delays between publication of Volumes I and II were evidence of this attempted replacement. This speculation, however, was misplaced. The dates at which Aspinall circulated his draft chapters provided clear evidence as to the timing of his work and he did not begin researching the events from June 1915 to the Suvla landings until after publication of Volume I in 1929. He was still in correspondence with participants concerning the Suvla operations in 1931 and 1932. However, the presence of such speculation, and indeed the eager reception of a work which appeared to have broken new ground, revealed both the public interest in and concerns over the Official Histories. The inherent suspicion of contemporary critics was that these works were unlikely to be truthful and of historical value and the allaying of these fears by Aspinall's volumes was in itself evidence of his accomplishment.

Similarly, Edmonds' volume on the Somme, published in January 1932, was recognised at the time as having exposed the great failings of the British army's tactical doctrine. *The Times*' reviewer highlighted the lessons of Edmonds' work in which 'the flower of British manhood . . . lacking in skill and experience assaulted the German army at the zenith of its confidence in a position they had fortified for nearly two years'. It was, he remarked, 'a tragic day for British arms . . . there fell the best and bravest of the nation'. Drawing on Edmonds' account, he wrote that the real causes of Britain's failure

lay in our insufficient training and unsuitable formations and tactical methods. An infantryman carrying 66 lbs was incapable of rapid movement but the artillery had not grasped the necessity to protect these clumsy, slow moving waves by an equally slow moving barrage; we had not sufficiently good or experienced commanders. In a word, we attacked as amateurs and were repulsed by professionals.[9]

The *Manchester Guardian*, whilst repeating these points, chose to emphasise the skill of Edmonds as an historian. Its reviewer wrote that:

[t]he merits of General Edmonds as a military historian need no fresh advertisement. This latest volume confirms one in the opinion that for knowledge, judgement and clarity he has no really formidable competitor in this country and stands very high

amongst the greatest in the subject . . . [His narrative] is lucid, sober
and as inornate as a fixed bayonet, only now and again, when that
which might have been is hinted at, betraying the emotion that
even the trained historian cannot but feel; an emotion that reaches
the reader even through these unemotional pages.[10]

Edmonds' volume on March 1918 was published in January 1935 and
was received with similarly complimentary reviews. The *TLS* proclaimed
it a 'most interesting volume, compiled with the same care and impartiality, written in the same clear style and seasoned with the shrewd comment
as previous volumes of the Official History have been'. Despite the mea-
greness of official records 'a clear and connected account of the confused
fighting that followed the German breakthrough has been pieced
together'.[11] *The Times*, perhaps providing a valuable insight into the way
in which the entire series of Official History was regarded at the time,
reported that:

[t]he account of this most dangerous period of the war is of absorb-
ing interest. The volume is in every way fully up to the high level
of its predecessors which have already set a standard in style, in
interest and in frank accuracy never before reached by the official
histories.[12]

Certainly, then, the contemporary press had no doubts that the
Official Histories satisfied one of the major objectives of their creators,
which was to provide an interesting and readable account to the general
public. It is evidence, too, from a study of these works that their language
and style is far from bland and impenetrable. In each of the volumes
which have been considered a glimpse of emotion, to use the words of
the *Manchester Guardian*, whether glory or sorrow, reaches the reader
through otherwise unemotional pages. In the capture of Messines Ridge,
Edmonds described how:

in that rosy dawn a host of British and Dominion troops were
surging forward behind the cloud of smoke and dust of the deep
barrage up the great breast of the Messines–Wytschaete Ridge; over
a hundred battalions . . . were moving up the slope, and every man
among them had a pre-arranged and carefully rehearsed task.[13]

At the Somme at 7.30 a.m., Edmonds wrote:

the crisis came. Under a cloudless blue sky which gave full promise
of the hot mid-summer day which was ahead, wave after wave of
British infantry rose and, with bayonets glistening, moved forward

into a blanket of smoke and mist as the barrage lifted from the enemy's front trench . . . No braver or more determined men ever faced an enemy than those sons of the British Empire who went 'over the top' on the 1st July 1916.[14]

Finally, in one of the most poignant passages of an Official History, Aspinall related the final moments before the Second Battle of Krithia:

As far as the eye can reach there is no sign of movement; the world seems bathed in sleep. Only high on the shoulder of Achi Baba – the goal of the British troops – a field of scarlet poppies intrudes a restless note. Yet in half an hour that peaceful landscape will again be overrun by waves of flashing bayonets; and these are the last moments of hundreds of precious lives.[15]

II

The issue of language and style in the Official Histories has a significance beyond the mere attraction of the prose. It was certainly the case that Edmonds placed considerable importance on a fluent literary style. His concerns over Kiggell's lack of 'colour and atmosphere' and Fortescue's squandered opportunity to 'write a thrilling story' have already been noted.[16] In his record of the experience gained in compiling the Official Histories, Edmonds acknowledged that a historian must have literary talents and should ask a civilian friend to read his draft to ensure that it was intelligible to the layman.[17] However, the specific use of language and imagery within Official History is also of importance in the context of the work's place within the historiography of the First World War. The official volumes, published between 1922 and 1948, had to compete for the public's attention with a variety of diverse publications. Against the background of nationalistic and triumphalist works of Buchan and Conan Doyle, Edmonds became convinced by his publishers that his original concept of Official History, which followed the line adopted in despatches, would not have a large number of readers amongst the general public. Nor was the public thirst for such works lost on the Treasury, which remained constantly concerned about the financial burden of producing an Official History series. Notwithstanding the objective of the Historical Section to produce official works precisely in order to counterbalance the host of 'popular' writings, the Treasury proposed to the Chairman of the Subcommittee for Control of Official Histories that:

[as] no really substantial economies can be affected . . . it is for your consideration whether . . . it would not be advantageous, particularly

from the standpoint of increased sales, to associate with the present staff employed on the military . . . histories men of outstanding literary reputation e.g. Mr G.M. Trevelyan, Mr Rudyard Kipling or Sir A. Quiller Couch.[18]

The Official Histories did not, in fact, bear any similarities with the works of these popular authors. Quite how far removed they were from this style of writing can be seen from the fact that Conan Doyle complained to Edmonds that his reference to the panic of some British units at Loos was too vivid and 'could be softened'.[19] Nor did they belong to what the *Daily Telegraph* reviewer of Liddell Hart's *The Real War* termed as the literature of 'distress and disillusionment', which stripped the war of its noble purpose and established the foundations on which the cultural legacy of the Great War was to be built.[20] However, the Official Histories did occasionally become accomplices in building upon the mythology of the war. The enduring themes of a lost generation, the destruction of the flower of British manhood and the daring stoicism in the face of adversity are all present in the words of Edmonds and Aspinall. They were not the first to employ these images but they deliberately used them to good effect to strengthen the impact of their argument. Given the sensitivity of the War Office to the 'picturesque phrases' of Churchill and the view of 'unofficial writers' that the flower of the British New Army was 'wasted through the stupidity of our High Command', the use of such imagery in the official works is significant.

III

If the Official Histories satisfied one of the two principal objectives of their creators, to provide a readable account to the general public, how successful were they in fulfilling their other central aim which was to provide an instructive account for the professional officer? Hankey was quite clear that it was primarily 'by the standard of their value for professional educational purposes that the official histories must be judged'.[21] When Daniel submitted a report on sales to the Subcommittee for Control in 1933 which was 'almost apologetic' in its tone, Hankey objected that 'the histories need[ed] no defence. They were essentially educational.'[22] By 1933 the official works were regularly being set in army promotion examinations.

An illustration of the instructive value of the Official Histories was the fact that even some of Edmonds' critics have had to recognise how future generations of military strategists were considerably assisted by the lessons presented in the official works. Edmonds' Somme volume has been credited by David French with having so shocked Lord Milne, the CIGS at the time of publication, that he established a committee under Lt-Gen. Sir Walter Kirke to discover what lessons might be learnt from the war.[23] Liddell Hart, too, recorded a conversation with Edmonds in 1930 when he had reminded Edmonds of his strong criticism of Liddell Hart's 'Real War on account of the Somme chapter'. Liddell Hart told Edmonds that he was owed an apology because 'if [he] had read [Edmonds'] Somme draft before writing [his] chapter [his] criticism would not merely have been unaltered but stronger still'.[24] Those who have criticised Edmonds for his lack of historical integrity and deliberate attempts to ignore the lessons of the war might note Edmonds' reply: 'I did not know then what I know now. I had not gone so fully through the records.'[25]

For his ability to satisfy the two conflicting demands made upon him of providing both a readable account for the public which did not explicitly reveal fault and an instructive academic work from which professional soldiers might learn lessons, Edmonds deserves considerable credit. This conflict explains his very particular style, which attempted to allow the 'young officers of the Army' to see the mistakes of their predecessors, 'yet without telling the public too much'.[26] To achieve this Edmonds used an array of literary tools. The most obvious was the relegation to footnotes or appendices of any information gained 'after the event', such as enemy intentions or knowledge of subsequent failure. This method followed the Clausewitzean guidelines of critical analysis, which allowed a reader to judge a commander's actions and decisions only in the context of what was known to him at the time. However, it has been seen that on a considerable number of occasions, Edmonds ignored this self-imposed convention in order specifically to strengthen his criticism. Haig, Rawlinson, Byng and Gough, GHQ and the staffs of Third, Fourth and Fifth Armies all fell prey to Edmonds' deliberate flouting of his own guidelines.

Another method by which only an informed reader might be able to detect the real lessons hidden between the lines was Edmonds' practice of employing implicit rather than explicit criticism. This is, no doubt, what he meant when he informed Aspinall that, whilst there were lessons to be learnt from Gallipoli, it was not necessary to 'rub them in'. It is reflected also in Edmonds' instructions to his official historians to 'avoid all but implied criticism'.[27] Edmonds achieved this in practice by stating the facts without drawing undue attention to the real import of what they in fact revealed. In his volume on March 1918, for example, Edmonds reported the surrenders and confusion without specifically calling attention to the breakdown of the command structure. The evidence for this breakdown is readily visible but only to a reader who is knowledgeable enough to question what direction might normally be expected from GHQ during this type of action. The complete lack of coordination of the retreat by the high command is apparent, but predominantly as a result of its absence from the narrative.

This feature is also evident in the apparent discrepancies between the analyses in Edmonds' prefaces and conclusions and the criticism highlighted in the body of the text. It is particularly the case in Edmonds' volumes on March 1918 and Third Ypres that, whilst the text is directly critical of Haig and the higher command in numerous places, the tone of the preface and conclusion is somewhat more defensive. Thus whilst the text of the March 1918 volume does reveal the chaos and unnecessary retreats, the weakness of the British defensive doctrine, the superior German tactics in attack and the failings of senior corps commanders, the work concludes that it was external factors which were primarily responsible for the difficulties and setbacks of the near-disastrous final days of March 1918. The British government had consented to an extension of the front without providing the appropriate level of reinforcements and the French had contemplated separation of the Allied armies in order to fall back to protect Paris. Edmonds concluded that: 'As so often in its history the British Army has been called upon to undertake a task beyond the power of its numbers.'[28]

Similarly with his Third Ypres volume, Edmonds was critical of Haig's over-optimism, his failure to apply the lessons of successful tactical evolution and his dogged and costly persistence in the face of atrocious conditions. Yet Edmonds' preface read like the counsel for the defence in which aspersions 'on the military character of Field Marshal Earl Haig' needed to be corrected. Having highlighted the lost opportunities by failure to exploit the victory after Messines, and having revealed the tactical victory that might have been within Haig's grasp had he not ignored the advice of his army commanders and head of Operations Branch at GHQ, Edmonds' work concluded, in contrast, with the statement that '[a] nation cannot expect great and immediate victories unless it supplies the means, the men and the material'.[29] In much the same way as Edmonds no doubt considered footnotes and appendices as unlikely territory for the lay reader, he perhaps considered that the public would tend to read his prefaces and conclusions and not necessarily the complete text. This was certainly the advice offered by the aforementioned head of Operations Branch, John Davidson, who wrote to *The Times* shortly after the publication of the Third Ypres volume:

As few people are willing to wade through an official history I would recommend that, if interested in Passchendaele, they read 18 pages of the Preface and the 21 pages of the Retrospect to enable them to get a fair and reasonable appreciation of the facts which have been hitherto distorted and misrepresented and to place Lord Haig's responsibilities and decisions in a proper perspective.[30]

This ability of Edmonds to soften the direct nature of his criticism was no doubt what Sir William Robertson was referring to when he likened Edmonds' style to the unsatisfying taste of skimmed milk.[31] However, notwithstanding this careful path along which Edmonds was required to thread his way, it has been shown that the great majority of Edmonds' work was both explicit in its criticism and comprehensive in its efforts to reveal the lessons of avoidable failure. Of course, external factors had an influence on events and there are few impartial historians who would not consider that the vacillation of the government, the demands of the alliance with the French and the lack of manpower and resources had considerable bearing on the outcome of the great offensives in 1916 and 1917. As such it is unreasonable to expect Edmonds not to cite these. Where Edmonds' critics are wrong is in suggesting that he allowed blame to fall on these factors alone.

Of the Somme offensive it has been shown that Edmonds was unstinting in his efforts to reveal failings at all levels of the higher command. Despite Rawlinson's intention for a battle with strictly limited objectives, and despite the warnings of his artillery adviser at GHQ that this would be stretching the artillery and men too far, Haig 'more optimistically contemplated a breakthrough'. Crucially, this significantly weakened the concentration of the artillery bombardment by expending on the German 'second position ammunition badly wanted to demolish the first'. Haig's original condition that the infantry were not to advance until the corps commanders were satisfied that the enemy's defences had been sufficiently destroyed 'seems to have been dropped as time passed'. Rawlinson's rigid tactical plan then ensured that densely packed waves of infantry, weighed down by 66 lb of kit, attempted to cross a no man's land, in places 4,000 yards wide, in the face of an unsuppressed German defence. They did not even have the protection afforded by surprise because insufficient attention had been paid to maintaining it in the days prior to the assault. Across almost the entire 20-mile front the waves of infantry were 'swept down dead and wounded' by 'murderous machine gun fire'. By 6 p.m., in the bloodiest day in British military history, Fourth Army had suffered 57,470 casualties and, as Edmonds concluded, for 'this disastrous loss of the finest manhood of the United Kingdom and Ireland there was only a small gain of ground to show'.[32]

In March 1918 Edmonds revealed similar failings at senior command level. Haig's distribution of forces in anticipation of the forthcoming attack may have been strategically sound but 'it hardly took into account the relative strength of [his] defences'. No warning was given by GHQ to brigade or battalion commanders that when the assault began there might, in certain circumstances, need to be an ordered retreat. Nor had the necessity of training or preparing the men for fighting a rearguard action 'entered anyone's mind'. 'In the fog and in the confusion' of the first five days of the assault, the structure of command completely broke down. Divisions fought and moved in 'small bodies, often composed of men of different units'. In the absence of orders the control of infantry operations 'lay mainly in the hands of the infantry brigadiers, often in the dark as to the intentions of the higher commands'. In these circumstances battalions, and 'even brigades, acted as seemed best'. A critical junction was allowed to open up between Fifth and Third Armies because of the reluctance of Third Army commander, Byng, to evacuate his salient despite clear evidence available at the time that the enemy intended to 'pinch it out'. The retention of the Cambrai Salient 'acquiesced in by GHQ as a false front, proved a source of weakness' for which the British army was 'made to pay in more ways than one'. Corps commanders Maxse and Congreve conducted unauthorised and unnecessary withdrawals which nearly proved disastrous and prompted Edmonds' remark that 'the junctions of Armies often require the attention of the high command'. Finally, the weakness of the British defensive doctrine was contrasted with a detailed consideration of the highly successful tactics of the enemy in attack.

Edmonds' volume on the Flanders battles of 1917 is also a remarkable work. Ostensibly a defence against the manpower restrictions forced upon the British army by Lloyd George, and viewed by critics as a partial account in which Edmonds exhibited his growing bias in favour of Haig, the Official History nevertheless revealed some vital military lessons. A recent work has shown that the elements of limited tactical success on the Western Front were becoming increasingly acknowledged by army commanders by 1917. Well-trained and well-equipped forces with the support of massed artillery could achieve striking success if their advances were limited to short steps within the range of their guns. Furthermore advances in the accuracy of shells and of artillery techniques, combined with a far more plentiful supply of ammunition, allowed the commanders in 1917 considerably better opportunities for success than existed in 1916.[33] Edmonds' own work clearly described the evolution of these elements of artillery and tactical success and graphically revealed the contrasting results when these lessons were ignored. Edmonds showed how Haig's ambitions for a decisive and final victory resulted in the appointment of the 'thruster', Gough, to command his Flanders offensive. They led, too, to the fatal change of planning which more than doubled the depth of the advance and thereby crucially halved the concentration of the initial bombardment. The lessons learnt by Haig's more experienced army commanders, Plumer and Rawlinson, during 1916 and early 1917, were discarded as too cautious. In Haig's quest for a rapid breakthrough, their recommendations for periods of consolidation to bring artillery forward for each subsequent advance were ignored. Haig heeded only their warnings to capture the high ground in the centre of the assault before pushing north, but he failed woefully to communicate this to Gough. The value of Plumer's methods became apparent when he successfully conducted the attack against the Gheluvelt plateau in September. These would not, however, produce the decisive and far-reaching results which Haig consistently believed were within his grasp. Once more ignoring the lessons of this tactical progression, Haig believed subsequent steps could now be 'less strictly limited' in order to secure the 'long-awaited opportunity of a breakthrough'. Despite the atrocious conditions in which these subsequent, ill-prepared and ill-supported attacks were made, Haig remained optimistic of this breakthrough to the end.[34]

In contrast, then, to the views of his critics, Edmonds did not excuse Britain's military performance by reference to external factors alone but did reveal considerable evidence of military failure. As a result, his volumes have left a detailed record of tactical lessons, much of which is in accordance with current academic thought. It should also be noted that the basis for these revelations was the thousands of first-hand accounts submitted to Edmonds by a variety of participants who experienced military action at all command levels. As a body of academic work, the Official History must be unique in the unprecedented access which its authors enjoyed to such a wealth of first-hand evidence. Edmonds approached the weighing of this evidence with diligent care. In the majority of cases he went to extreme lengths to corroborate the information he received and, when satisfied of its reliability, amended his account. Often the evidence of quite junior participants was given greater credence by Edmonds than a contrasting view of a more senior colleague. Indeed it was extremely rare for the more personal pleas of high-ranking officers to present their own particular view in the official works to have any influence on Edmonds whatsoever. Despite the constraints of loyalty to colleagues and his service which acted upon Edmonds, he was clearly determined to retain his literary and academic integrity.

IV

Aspinall's Official History has similarly left an enduring mark on almost all subsequent works of the campaign which have rested heavily upon its evidence and cited extensively from its conclusions.[35] Few, if indeed any, of these have seriously questioned its historical validity. The authority of Aspinall's work has survived intact the academic scrutiny of the documents and information to which its author alone had access at the time it was written. This on its own is not surprising for the author approached his task with diligence and energy, researched his material exhaustively, and questioned participants and witnesses extensively in order to establish the truth. In addition, he himself participated at an important level in the events of which he wrote and was thus able to write with veracity and compassion of their effects upon the men who shaped them, as well as being able to see their significance in the wider context.

Even acknowledging the value of Edmonds' official work, Aspinall's Gallipoli volumes are indeed remarkable for their depth, their clarity of vision and their integrity of expression. It was a mark of the strength of Aspinall's convictions that he refused steadfastly to bend to the numerous and concerted attempts by government departments to amend his work and to sacrifice what he saw as its central lessons. Whilst Edmonds expressed grave reservations that the Gallipoli volumes would tarnish the whole body of official work, in fact the value of the entire series could be said to have been enhanced as a result.

It was, however, above all else the explicit manner in which criticisms were revealed in the Gallipoli volumes which was exceptional. In the expression of these, Aspinall was motivated by his own determination to produce a work of real and lasting value and was aided crucially by the support of Winston Churchill. Moreover, the campaign of which he wrote provided in many ways the ideal opportunity in which to express these views. Not only were its lessons starkly clear and its opportunities tantalisingly fleeting but it played out in microcosm the tactical issues of the war as a whole. The classical nature and beauty of its setting allowed the employment of a language and a colour to the work which enhanced its literary value beyond anything applicable to accounts of the Western Front. As Aspinall himself concluded:

> The drama of the Dardanelles campaign, by reason of the beauty of its setting, the grandeur of its theme and the unhappiness of its ending, will always rank amongst the world's classic tragedies. The story is a record of lost opportunities and eventual failure; yet it is a story which men of British race may ponder if not without pain yet certainly not without pride; for amidst circumstances of unsurpassed difficulty and strain, the bravery, fortitude and stoical endurance of the invading troops upheld most worthily the high traditions of the fighting services of the Crown.
>
> To the student of military history the campaign offers the unusual advantage that, though it formed only a relatively small episode in the World War, its varied incidents stand out as a dramatic whole, with a beginning, a middle and an end; they facilitate

to a remarkable degree the study of cause and effect and point with unerring finger to the retribution which almost inevitably follows the neglect of age-old principles.[36]

Therein were encapsulated the dual roles that the creators of the Official Histories envisioned for their works: a valuable discourse for the military student and an uplifting story for 'men of British race'. The difficulty which most of their authors, including Edmonds, found in walking this path resulted from the additional constraints placed upon them by the particular requirements of the interested parties allowed an involvement in the process. In his determination and his ability to ignore these influences Aspinall succeeded in producing a work of great character and great value which has stood the test of time and of academic scrutiny.

V

By almost every standard by which the Official Military Histories of the Great War might be judged, one must conclude that the works were of substantial historical, military and literary value. Not only did they admirably conform to the objectives of their original creators but they must be recognised as full and accurate accounts of sound academic integrity whose conclusions remain valid over 50 years later. Even those who have accused Edmonds of bias have had to acknowledge that his assessments and conclusions are correct. They are therefore left with trying to bring into question Edmonds' motivations for arriving at such conclusions. In this area there is little evidence that Edmonds was interested in publishing anything other than a truthful account. His method of data collection and analysis was painstaking; the influence of thousands of first-hand observations and criticisms was balanced and judicious. Attempts by senior colleagues or government departments to alter the content or tone of his work were predominantly ignored. In scrutinising the documentary evidence on which Edmonds based his work and the records of his activities from 1919 until 1949 there is very little to support the claims of his critics. Indeed, it is inconceivable that a man who had devoted the greater part of his working life to this enormous undertaking, and who approached this task with such dedication and scrupulous care, should wish its future legitimacy to rest on suspect foundations. As Edmonds remarked to Swinton in 1950:

It seems to me that providence brought me [into the world] to write the history of World War I. Looking back all my career seems to have been a preparation for that one thing.[37]

In the end, the official works can be judged for themselves. The 14 volumes on the Western Front and 15 volumes of subsidiary actions stand as a comprehensive and unique insight into the military operations of the Great War. They must therefore stand too as a testament to the tenacity, academic integrity and intellectual prowess of their authors and of their editor, James Edmonds.

Notes

Introduction

1. For the historiography of the Great War, see Brian Bond (ed.), *The First World War and British Military History* (Oxford: Clarendon Press, 1991).
2. See Hankey memorandum, Oct. 1919, PRO, Cab 103/82 and Cab 103/83; also Liddell Hart to Edmonds, 13 Nov. 1934, KCL, Liddell Hart Papers, 1/259/95.
3. Liddell Hart to Edmonds, 6 Nov. 1934, KCL, Liddell Hart Papers, 1/259/93; Liddell Hart to Edmonds, 25 June 1934, 1/259/84.
4. David Lloyd George, *War Memoirs*, Vol. II (London: Odhams Press, 1936), p. 1755.
5. David French, 'Sir James Edmonds', in Bond (ed.), *First World War and British Military History*, Tim Travers, *The Killing Ground: The British Army, the Western Front and the Emergence of Modern Warfare 1900–1918* (London: Allen & Unwin, 1982).
6. Denis Winter, *Haig's Command: A Reassessment* (London: Viking, 1991).
7. John Keegan, *The Face of Battle* (London: Pimlico, 1976), p. 31; Travers, *Killing Ground*, p. 239.
8. Cecil Aspinall married Florence Joan Oglander on 25 May 1927, and on 1 July 1927 changed his name to Cecil Aspinall-Oglander. As the text relates to periods of his life both before and after his change of name he will be referred to as Aspinall so as to avoid confusion. His book is published under his name of Aspinall-Oglander and he is therefore referred to as such in the notes and bibliography.

1: The Origins, Purpose and the Workings of the Historical Section

1. Esher memorandum, 6 Sept. 1906, PRO, Cab 103/102.
2. Hankey memorandum, 26 Aug. 1919, PRO, Cab 103/82.
3. Maj.-Gen. Sir Frederick Maurice and M.H. Grant, *Official History of the War in South Africa, 1899–1902*, 4 vols (London: Hurst & Blackett, 1906–10).
4. Hankey memorandum, 26 Aug. 1919, PRO, Cab 103/82.
5. First Report on work of Historical Section 12 May 1915 to 22 Dec. 1919, PRO, Cab 103/1.
6. Hankey memorandum on formation of Historical Section, 14 July 1922, PRO, Cab 27/212 and Daniel memorandum, 12 July 1922, PRO, Cab 103/82.
7. Hankey memorandum, 26 Aug. 1919, PRO, Cab 103/82.
8. Daniel memorandum, 12 July 1922, PRO, Cab 103/82 and Cab 27/212.
9. Ibid.
10. Progress Report, 9 July 1917, PRO, Cab 103/1.
11. Hankey memorandum, 26 Aug. 1919, PRO, Cab 103/82.
12. Ibid., Hankey to Daniel.
13. Hankey memorandum, Oct. 1919, PRO, Cab 103/82 and Cab 103/83.
14. Daniel to Raleigh, undated but late 1919, PRO, Cab 103/83.
15. Progress Report, 30 June 1919, PRO, Cab 103/1.
16. Edmonds to Daniel, 16 Feb. 1919, PRO, Cab 103/97.
17. Ibid.
18. Edmonds to Daniel, 1 Dec. 1919, PRO, Cab 103/1.
19. Ibid.

20. Progress Report, 30 June 1919, PRO, Cab 103/1.
21. Ibid.
22. Board of Education to Daniel, 28 July 1922, PRO, Cab 103/73.
23. Codling to Daniel, 17 June 1922, PRO, Cab 103/73.
24. Daniel memorandum, 12 July 1922, PRO, Cab 27/212.
25. For minutes of the seven meetings between 27 July 1922 and 28 Dec. 1923, see PRO, Cab 27/212, and for minutes of the 16 meetings between 9 Jan. 1924 and 11 July 1939, see PRO, Cab 16/53.
26. Meeting of Committee for Control of Official Histories, 19 Jan. 1926, PRO, Cab 16/53.
27. J. Edmonds, 'Experience Gained in Compiling Official Military Histories of 1914–1918', KCL, Edmonds Papers, VIII/11.
28. Meeting of Committee for Control, 9 Jan. 1924, PRO, Cab 16/53.
29. Meeting of Committee for Control, 23 Mar. 1933, PRO, Cab 16/53.
30. Meeting of Committee for Control, 13 Mar. 1930, PRO, Cab 16/53.
31. Meeting of Committee for Control, 12 Mar. 1931, PRO, Cab 16/53.
32. Meeting of Committee for Control, 11 Feb. 1927, PRO, Cab 16/53.
33. Romer to Edmonds, 27 Nov. 1922, KCL, Edmonds Papers, II/1.
34. Progress Report, Oct. 1924, PRO, Cab 103/2.
35. Meeting of Committee for Control, 9 Jan. 1924, PRO, Cab 16/53, and Meeting of Subcommittee of CID, 1 Feb. 1923, PRO, Cab 27/212.
36. Edmonds, 'Experience Gained in Compiling Official Military Histories'.
37. Ibid.
38. Progress Report, Oct. 1924, PRO, Cab 103/2.
39. J. Edmonds, 'Memoirs', KCL, Edmonds Papers, III/16.
40. Ibid.
41. Progress Report, Nov. 1929, PRO, Cab 103/7.
42. Ibid.
43. Ibid.
44. Meeting of Subcommittee of CID, 31 July 1922, PRO, Cab 27/212.
45. War Office to Edmonds, 24 Aug. 1927, PRO, Cab 103/77.
46. Edmonds to Daniel, 27 Aug. 1927, PRO, Cab 103/77.
47. Progress Report, Nov. 1927, PRO, Cab 103/5.
48. See Chapter 6.
49. E.E. Bridges to Gen. Ismay, 23 Jan. 1939, PRO, Cab 103/102.
50. R. Howarth to Edmonds, 6 Feb. 1939, PRO, Cab 103/102.
51. Daniel to Treasury, 'Appreciation on Official Histories', Jan. 1939, PRO, Cab 103/102.

2: Sir James Edmonds

1. Edmonds, 'Memoirs', KCL, Edmonds Papers, III/1.
2. Ibid.
3. Edmonds, 'Memoirs', I/1.
4. Edmonds, 'Memoirs', III/1.
5. Gerard J. DeGroot, 'Ambition, Duty and Doctrine: Douglas Haig's Rise to High Command', in B. Bond and N. Cave (eds), *Haig: A Reappraisal 70 Years On* (Barnsley: Leo Cooper, 1999), p. 39.
6. Ibid.
7. H.J. Creedy to Duff Cooper, 21 May 1935, KCL, Edmonds Papers, I/1/18b.
8. Edmonds, 'Memoirs', III/1.
9. See Chapter 3.
10. Edmonds, 'Memoirs', III/1.
11. Ibid.
12. John Terraine, *Sir Douglas Haig: The Educated Soldier* (London: Leo Cooper, 1963), p. 5.
13. Edmonds, 'Memoirs', III/1.
14. Ibid.
15. Report on Army Manoeuvres 1912, WO 279/47, PRO. I am grateful to Andrew Whitmarsh for providing details of this reference.
16. Ibid.
17. Ibid., III/11.
18. Ibid., III/1.

19. Ibid., III/10.
20. Ibid.
21. Ibid., III/11.
22. *Times Literary Supplement*, 29 Sept. 1905, 11 Oct. 1934 and 15 Jan. 1938.
23. Ibid.
24. David French, 'Sir James Edmonds', in Bond (ed.), *First World War and British Military History*, p. 70.
25. David French, 'Spy Fever in Britain 1900–1915', *Historical Journal*, 21, 2 (1978), p. 357.
26. See French, 'Spy Fever in Britain', and Christopher Andrew, *Secret Service: The Making of the British Intelligence Community* (London: Sceptre, 1985).
27. Thomas Fergusson, *British Military Intelligence 1870–1914: The Development of a Modern Intelligence Organisation* (New York: University Publications of America, 1984), p. 203, and Andrew, *Secret Service*, pp. 30–1.
28. Edmonds, 'Memoirs', III/4.
29. Andrew, *Secret Service*, p. 31.
30. Working with Kitchener, Edmonds found him to be not at all the dour, silent worker and misogynist of legend. He enjoyed good stories, good living and practical jokes. Edmonds also witnessed first-hand the poor relationship between Kitchener and French. Kitchener's attempts to ginger French up would be met with what they called at the time 'French's soothing syrup'. According to Edmonds, Kitchener would gladly have sent French home to England but did not feel strong enough with the British public, who had made a hero of French after his ride to Kimberley. The meeting of the two men in September 1914 when French, just before the Battle of the Marne, wanted to re-embark the BEF and Kitchener crossed the Channel to stop him, held a special significance for Edmonds, who knew of the earlier relations of the two men. Edmonds, 'Memoirs', III/4.
31. Fergusson, *British Military Intelligence 1870–1914*, p. 220.
32. In Edmonds 'Memoirs', III/4, he relates how at a cipher class for junior officers held in Liverpool the German consul was discovered in the audience.
33. KU 3/1, PRO contains a memorandum from Colonel F.J. Trench, Military Attaché in Berlin, 'Measures Protecting Military Information', dated 24 June 1909, concerning German intelligence and counter-intelligence activities and legal jurisdiction. Also a translation of an article by A. Rezanov from *Voenni Sbornik* printed in Oct. 1911 details French and German espionage from 1870. Various foreign newspaper cuttings in the same file detail German balloon flights over Verdun in 1908 and Belgian fortifications in 1909 and the theft of a new French machine-gun in 1909.
34. Fergusson, *British Military Intelligence 1870–1914*, pp. 183–4.
35. 'Organisation of Secret Service', Note prepared for DMO on 4 Oct. 1908, WO 106/6292, PRO.
36. Andrew, *Secret Service*, p. 50.
37. Ibid., p. 54.
38. French, 'Spy Fever in Britain', p. 356.
39. 'Organisation of Secret Service'.
40. Edmonds, 'Memoirs', III/4.
41. Edmonds memo, 9 Feb. 1909, Kell MSS, IWM, cited in Andrew, *Secret Service*, p. 54.
42. Andrew, *Secret Service*, pp. 53–8.
43. Conclusions of the subcommittee requested to consider how a secret service bureau could be established in Great Britain, 28 Apr. 1909, WO 106/6292, PRO.
44. Ibid.
45. See KU 3/1, PRO on laws relating to espionage in Germany, Holland, Denmark, Sweden and Switzerland, 1 Feb. 1905, Police regulations re: espionage in Austria, 16 Aug. 1908, Laws and regulations protecting military information, 15 Dec. 1909, Penal Code in Austria and Germany for passing under an assumed name and being in disguise, Aug. 1911.
46. Edmonds, 'Memoirs', III/4.
47. Maj.-Gen. Sir Edward Spears, Liaison Officer with the French high command, related how during the retreat in August 1914 Wilson had been the only officer who could translate so that Lanrezac and Joffre could communicate with Sir John French. Maj.-Gen. Sir Edward Spears, *Liaison 1914* (London: Cassell, 1930), p. 229.
48. Ibid.

49. Hew Strachan, '"The Real War": Liddell Hart, Crutwell and Falls', in Bond (ed.), *First World War and British Military History*, p. 49.
50. Ibid., p. 50.
51. B. Liddell Hart, 'Impressions of the Great British Offensive on the Somme by a Company Commander who saw 3½ weeks of it', 18 Sept. 1916, PRO, Cab 45/135. Author's italics.
52. Ibid.
53. Ibid., III/8.
54. George Cassar, *The Tragedy of Sir John French* (London: Associated University Presses, 1985), p. 117, and Richard Holmes, *Riding the Retreat: Mons to the Marne 1914 Revisited* (London: Jonathan Cape, 1995), pp. 169–70.
55. Cassar, *Tragedy of Sir John French*, pp. 117–20. See also A.J. Smithers, *The Man Who Disobeyed: Sir Horace Smith-Dorrien and his Enemies* (London: Leo Cooper, 1970).
56. Ibid.
57. Edmonds, 'Memoirs', III/9.
58. Ibid., III/9.
59. Ibid.
60. Cassar, *Tragedy of Sir John French*, p. 123.
61. Wilson diary, 29 Aug. 1914, Henry Wilson Papers, cited in Cassar, *Tragedy of Sir John French*, p. 128.
62. Edmonds, 'Memoirs', III/9.
63. Ibid.
64. Edmonds to anon., 7 Apr. 1950, Edmonds Papers, I/2B/5A.
65. Edmonds to Swinton, 1934, Edmonds Papers, III/1.
66. Edmonds, 'Memoirs', III/1.
67. E.C. Bentley in *Daily Telegraph*, Liddell Hart Papers, 11/1930/23, cited in Hew Strachan, '"The Real War": Liddell Hart, Crutwell and Falls', in Bond (ed.), *First World War and British Military History*, p. 49.
68. At a dinner in 1889 at which Gladstone was present, Edmonds contradicted the former Prime Minister, whom he felt was talking a 'volume of tosh' concerning drug abuse in Hong Kong jails. He was later passed a note from Catherine Gladstone saying 'Please do not contradict the Prime Minister' ('*sic*' added Edmonds, as Gladstone had been out of office since 1886). Ibid., III/2.

3: Edmonds' Method and Writing

1. Brig.-Gen. Sir James Edmonds, *Official History of the Great War: Military Operations: France and Belgium 1914* (London: Macmillan, 1922), p. vii.
2. Keegan, *Face of Battle*, p. 31.
3. Liddell Hart to Edmonds, 6 Nov. 1934, KCL, Liddell Hart Papers, 1/259/93.
4. Brook memorandum, 17 Apr. 1945, PRO, Cab 103/112 (author's italics).
5. French, 'Sir James Edmonds', in Bond (ed.), *First World War and British Military History*, p. 73.
6. Liddell Hart, 'Talks with Edmonds', 27 Oct. 1933, KCL, Liddell Hart Papers, 11/1933/26.
7. Edmonds to Daniel, 27 Feb. 1922, PRO, Cab 103/73.
8. Edmonds to Daniel, 1 Dec. 1919, PRO, Cab 103/1.
9. B. Bond, *British Military Policy between the Two World Wars* (Oxford: Oxford University Press, 1980).
10. Cited in D. French, 'Sir Douglas Haig's Reputation 1918–1928: A Note', *Historical Journal*, 28, 4 (1985), pp. 935–60.
11. Haig to Edmonds, 21 Apr. 1927, KCL, Edmonds Papers, II/4.
12. Haig to Edmonds, 26 Mar. 1924, PRO, Cab 45/183.
13. Haig to Edmonds, 18 July 1927, PRO, Cab 44/20.
14. Haig to Edmonds, 20 Feb. 1927, PRO, Cab 44/20.
15. Haig to Edmonds, 6 Aug. 1925, KCL, Edmonds Papers, II/4.
16. Progress Report, Nov. 1928, PRO, Cab 103/6.
17. Liddell Hart, 'Talks with Edmonds', 27 Oct. 1933 and 28 Dec. 1933, KCL, Liddell Hart Papers, 11/1933/24 and 31.
18. Liddell Hart, 'Talks with Edmonds', 10 Jan. 1935, 11/1935/58.
19. Liddell Hart, 'Talks with Edmonds', 8 Dec. 1930, 11/1930/15.
20. Liddell Hart, 'Talks with Edmonds', 7 Dec. 1933, 11/1933/26.

21. Brig.-Gen. Sir James Edmonds, *Official History: France and Belgium 1914* (rev. edn 1933), p. vii, cited in French, 'Sir James Edmonds', in Bond (ed.), *First World War and British Military History*, p. 73.
22. Solly Flood to Edmonds, 28 Oct. 1927, KCL, Edmonds Papers, II/1/125A.
23. Lloyd George, *War* 'Memoirs', Vol. II, pp. 2014, 2018, 1311.
24. Ibid., p. 1755.
25. N. Birch to Edmonds, 29 June 1938, PRO, Cab 45/132.
26. Edmonds to Liddell Hart, 4 Feb. 1935, KCL, Liddell Hart Papers, 1/259/109, cited in French, 'Sir James Edmonds', in Bond (ed.), *First World War and British Military History*, p. 77.
27. Draft letter to *The Times*, 20 Jan. 1939, KCL, Edmonds Papers, VII/8.
28. Note by Frederick Palmer, KCL, Edmonds Papers, VII/8.
29. J.E. Edmonds, 'Mr Lloyd George and the Shell Shortage in 1914–1915', *Army, Navy and Air Force Gazette*, 8 June 1933, KCL, Edmonds Papers, V/4/1/14.
30. Ibid.
31. Edmonds, 'Memoirs', III/16.
32. Brig.-Gen. Sir James Edmonds, *Military Operations: France and Belgium 1916*, Vol. I (London: Macmillan, 1932), p. 124.
33. Ibid.
34. Liddell Hart to Edmonds, 25 June 1934, KCL, Liddell Hart Papers, 1/259/84.
35. Liddell Hart to Edmonds, 13 Nov. 1934, KCL, Liddell Hart Papers, 1/259/95.
36. Meeting of Committee for Control of Official Histories, 19 Mar. 1928, PRO, Cab 45/241.
37. Edmonds to Historical Section, undated but 1919, PRO, Cab 103/1.
38. Cited in Brian Bond, *Liddell Hart: A study of his Military Thought* (London: Cassell, 1977), p. 82 (author's italics).
39. Edmonds to Liddell Hart, 8 Mar. 1932, KCL, Liddell Hart Papers, 1/259/46.
40. J.E. Edmonds, 'The Necessity of Collecting and Recording War Experiences', undated but early 1900s, KCL, Edmonds Papers, VIII/11.
41. Edmonds to Liddell Hart, 15 July 1928, KCL, Liddell Hart Papers, 1/259/16.
42. Edmonds to Liddell Hart, 5 Jan. 1935 (letter states 1934 but it was in response to Liddell Hart's of 4 Dec. 1934), KCL, Liddell Hart Papers, 1/259/64.
43. J.E. Edmonds, 'Old Men at Suvla', *The Army and Navy Gazette*, 8 Nov. 1930, KCL, Edmonds Papers, V/4/1.
44. Edmonds, 'Experience Gained in Compiling Official Military Histories', VIII/11.
45. Ibid.
46. C. Horden to Daniel, 19 Aug. 1938, PRO, Cab 103/88.
47. C. von Clausewitz, *On War*, ed. and trans. M. Howard and P. Paret (Princeton, NJ: Princeton University Press, 1976), p. 164.
48. Ibid., p. 165.
49. Edmonds to Daniel, 13 July 1922, PRO, Cab 103/74.
50. Edmonds to Aspinall, undated but 1928, Newport RO, Aspinall Papers, 112.
51. Edmonds draft notes to Historical Section, Newport RO, Aspinall Papers, 112.
52. French, 'Sir James Edmonds', in Bond (ed.), *First World War and British Military History*, p. 70. See Liddell Hart to Edmonds, 13 Nov. 1934, KCL, Liddell Hart Papers, 1/259/95.
53. Liddell Hart to Edmonds, 6 Nov. 1934, KCL, Liddell Hart Papers, 1/259/93.
54. Ibid.
55. Edmonds to Liddell Hart, 9 Nov. 1934, KCL, Liddell Hart Papers, 1/259/94.
56. Ibid.
57. Edmonds, 'Memoirs', III/16.
58. Edmonds, Progress Report 1924, PRO, Cab 103/2.
59. Edmonds, 'Experience Gained in Compiling Official Military Histories', VIII/11.
60. Ibid.
61. Edmonds, Progress Report 1932, PRO, Cab 103/10.
62. Edmonds, Progress Report 1929, PRO, Cab 103/7.
63. Winter, *Haig's Command*, p. 247.
64. Edmonds to Newbolt, Feb. 1931, KCL, Edmonds Papers, VII/11.
65. Winter, *Haig's Command*, p. 247.
66. Ibid.
67. Edmonds, 'Experience Gained in Compiling Official Military Histories', VIII/11.
68. Winter, *Haig's Command*, p. 247.

69. Edmonds, 'Experience Gained in Compiling Official Military Histories', VIII/11.
70. Edmonds, 'Memoirs', III/16.
71. Ibid.
72. Edmonds, Progress Report 1929, PRO, Cab 103/7.
73. French, 'Sir James Edmonds', in Bond (ed.), *First World War and British Military History*, p. 85.

4: Military Operations: France and Belgium 1916, Vol. I: The Somme

1. Kiggell to Edmonds, 4 June 1938, PRO, Cab 45/135.
2. Kiggell to Edmonds, 11 June 1938, PRO, Cab 45/135.
3. Kiggell to Edmonds, 16 June 1938, PRO, Cab 45/135.
4. Travers, *Killing Ground*, pp. 204–5.
5. A. Montgomery to Edmonds, 9 Aug. 1930, PRO, Cab 45/136.
6. R. Luckock to Edmonds, 8 Aug. 1930, PRO, Cab 45/135.
7. Ibid.
8. Montgomery to Edmonds, 5 Nov. 1930, PRO, Cab 45/132.
9. R. Prior and T. Wilson, *Command on the Western Front: The Military Career of Sir Henry Rawlinson 1914–1918* (Oxford: Blackwell, 1992), p. 88.
10. Ibid., p. 106.
11. Edmonds, *Military Operations: France and Belgium 1916*, Vol. I, pp. 251, 252, 254, 255.
12. Ibid., p. 288.
13. Ibid., p. 289.
14. Ibid., p. 313.
15. Ibid., p. 290.
16. Ibid., p. 292.
17. Ibid., p. 292.
18. Ibid., p. 293.
19. Ibid., p. 298.
20. Ibid., p. 480.
21. Edmonds, *Military Operations: France and Belgium 1916*, Vol. I, p. xii.
22. Ibid., p. xiii.
23. Dobbin to Edmonds, 21 Mar. 1931, PRO, Cab 45/133.
24. D.C. Rees to Edmonds, 14 Nov. 1929, PRO, Cab 45/137.
25. Edmonds, *Military Operations: France and Belgium 1916*, Vol. I, p. 294.
26. G. Moberly to Edmonds, 9 Dec. 1929, PRO, Cab 45/136.
27. D.C. Rees to Edmonds, 14 Nov. 1929, PRO, Cab 45/137.
28. Edmonds, *Military Operations: France and Belgium 1916*, Vol. I, p. 305.
29. S. Gillon to Edmonds, PRO, Cab 45/134.
30. A.C. Sparks to Edmonds, 3 July 1929, PRO, Cab 45/137 (recorded by Edmonds on p. 455).
31. Edmonds, *Military Operations: France and Belgium 1916*, Vol. I, p. 429.
32. A. Hunter-Weston to Edmonds, 12 July 1929, PRO, Cab 45/138.
33. Ibid.
34. A. Whitlock to Edmonds, 21 Jan. 1930, PRO, Cab 45/138.
35. F. Pursly to Edmonds, 22 Mar. 1930, PRO, Cab 45/136.
36. Ibid.
37. Edmonds, *Military Operations: France and Belgium 1916*, Vol. I, p. 430.
38. Ibid.
39. Ibid., p. 431.
40. Ibid., p. 432.
41. Ibid., p. 433.
42. V.A.C. Yate to Edmonds, 18 Oct. 1935, PRO, Cab 45/138.
43. I. Sandell to Edmonds, 1 Nov. 1929, PRO, Cab 45/138.
44. J.C. Mostyn to Edmonds, 15 Mar.?, PRO, Cab 45/136.
45. Edmonds, *Military Operations: France and Belgium 1916*, Vol. I, p. 123.
46. N. Birch to Edmonds, 8 July 1930, PRO, Cab 45/132.
47. Ibid.
48. Edmonds, *Military Operations: France and Belgium 1916*, Vol. I, p. 260.
49. Travers, *Killing Ground*, p. 205.

50. Ibid., p. 218.
51. Ibid.
52. Edmonds, *Military Operations: France and Belgium 1916*, Vol. I, p. ix.
53. Ibid.
54. Ibid.
55. Ibid., p. x.
56. Terraine, *Douglas Haig*, pp. 235, 236.
57. Kiggell to Edmonds, 25 Jan. 1938, PRO, Cab 45/135.
58. Kiggell to Edmonds, 2 Mar. 1935, PRO, Cab 45/135.
59. Kiggell to Edmonds, 25 Mar. 1935, PRO, Cab 45/135.
60. Ibid.
61. Ibid.
62. Edmonds, *Military Operations: France and Belgium 1916*, Vol. I, p. 493.
63. Cited in ibid., p. 495.
64. Ibid., p. 247.
65. Ibid., p. 258.
66. Ibid., p. 260.
67. Ibid., p. 252.
68. Ibid., p. 251.
69. Ibid., p. 254.
70. Ibid., p. 260 fn.
71. Ibid., p. 255.
72. Ibid., p. 258.
73. Ibid.
74. Ibid., p. 251.
75. Ibid., p. 260.
76. Ibid.
77. Ibid., p. 485.
78. Travers, *Killing Ground*, p. 204.
79. War Office to E.Y. Daniel, Historical Section, 12 Nov. 1930, PRO, Cab 103/79.
80. Edmonds, *Military Operations: France and Belgium 1916*, Vol. I, p. 156.
81. Ibid.
82. Ibid., p. 157.
83. War Office to Daniel, 12 Nov. 1930, PRO, Cab 103/79.
84. Ibid.
85. Edmonds to Daniel, 12 Nov. 1930, PRO, Cab 103/79.
86. Edmonds, *Military Operations: France and Belgium 1916*, Vol. I, p. 484.
87. Ibid., p. 260.
88. Ibid., p. 492.
89. Widdows to Daniel, 7 May 1931, PRO, Cab 103/79.
90. Ibid.
91. Edmonds, *Military Operations: France and Belgium 1916*, Vol. I, p. 51.
92. Ibid.
93. Ibid., p. 37.
94. Ibid., p. 315.
95. Ibid., p. 364.
96. Ibid., p. 368.
97. Ibid., p. 377.
98. Ibid., p. 402.
99. Ibid., p. 436.
100. Ibid.
101. Ibid., p. 442.
102. Ibid., p. 454.
103. Ibid.
104. Ibid., p. 483.

5: *Military Operations: Gallipoli*, Part I

1. Brig.-Gen. C.F. Aspinall-Oglander, *Military Operations: Gallipoli*, Vol. I (London: Heinemann, 1929), p. 173.

2. Downing to Atkinson, 26 May 1919, PRO, Cab 45/241.
3. Ibid.
4. Ibid.
5. Ibid.
6. Edmonds, Progress Report 1919, PRO, Cab 103/1.
7. It will be seen in subsequent chapters how Edmonds was quite prepared to ignore his own guidelines in this respect if it suited his purpose to do so.
8. Edmonds, 'Memoirs', III/16.
9. Ibid.
10. See his comment to Daniel that two good soldiers on half or retired pay would cost the section the same as a single civilian at £1,000 a year, PRO, Cab 103/1.
11. Edmonds to Daniel, 1 Dec. 1919, PRO, Cab 103/1.
12. Notes by Ellison on the scope of the Official History of the Gallipoli campaign, 2 Nov. 1923, PRO, Cab 45/242.
13. Ellison to Harington, 3 Mar. 1924, PRO, Cab 45/242.
14. Ibid.
15. Notes by Lt-Gen. Sir Gerald Ellison on the history of the campaign, undated but during 1924, PRO, Cab 45/238.
16. F.R. Maunsell to Ellison, 1 Nov. 1923, PRO, Cab 45/243.
17. Lt-Gen. Sir G. Ellison, *The Perils of Amateur Strategy* (London: Longmans, Green, 1926).
18. Ibid.
19. Ibid.
20. Ibid.
21. Notes by Lt-Gen. G. Ellison on the history of the campaign, undated but 1924, PRO, Cab 45/238.
22. Ibid.
23. Ibid.
24. Edmonds, 'Memoirs', III/16.
25. Aspinall-Oglander, *Military Operations: Gallipoli*, Vol. I, p. 129.
26. Buckley to Aspinall, 22 Dec. 1915, Newport RO, Aspinall Papers, 111.
27. Williams diary, Entry for 2 Sept. 1915, IWM.
28. Ibid.
29. E.Y. Daniel to S. Gaselee at Foreign Office, 3 May 1927, Newport RO, Aspinall Papers, 111.
30. Brig.-Gen. C.F. Aspinall-Oglander, *Military Operations: Gallipoli*, Vol. II (London: Heinemann, 1932), p. 276.
31. Edmonds, 'Experience Gained in Compiling the Official Military Histories 1914–1918', KCL, Edmonds Papers, 5/11.
32. Hamilton to Birdwood, Jan. 1916, Newport RO, Aspinall Papers, 111.
33. Dawnay to Aspinall, 28 Mar. 1916, Newport RO, Aspinall Papers, 111.
34. Mitchell to Aspinall, 27 Feb. 1916, Newport RO, Aspinall Papers, 111.
35. Hankey to Aspinall, 7 Feb. 1916, Newport RO, Aspinall Papers, 111.
36. Aspinall to Hill, 3 Jan. 1993, Newport RO, Aspinall Papers, 111.
37. Aspinall to Downey, 17 Feb. 1931, Newport RO, Aspinall Papers, 111.
38. J.H. Jelson to Aspinall, 13 May 1931, PRO, Cab 45/242.
39. Jourdain to Edmonds, 16 June 1920, PRO, Cab 45/241.
40. Aspinall-Oglander, *Military Operations: Gallipoli*, Vol. II, p. 358.
41. Described by Minchin to Aspinall, 11 July 1929, PRO, Cab 45/243.
42. This has been dealt with in a previous chapter.
43. Leonore Churchill to Aspinall, 1 May 1925, PRO, Cab 45/243.
44. Edmonds to Mrs Churchill, 7 May 1925, PRO, Cab 45/243.
45. Cunliffe Owen to War Office, 27 Sept. 1929, PRO, Cab 45/241.
46. Ibid.
47. Aspinall to MS2R, 6 Oct. 1927, PRO, Cab 45/241.
48. Col. C.M. Wagstaff, General Staff, to MS2R, 30 Sept. 1927, PRO, Cab 45/241.
49. Unaddressed (Dear General) and undated, Newport RO, Aspinall Papers, 112.
50. Hill to Aspinall, 10 Apr. 1930, PRO, Cab 45/242.
51. Hill to Aspinall, 6 Apr. 1933, Newport RO, Aspinall Papers, 111.
52. Downing to Aspinall, 24 Feb. 1931, PRO, Cab 45/241.
53. F. Spring to Aspinall, 26 Jan. 1931, PRO, Cab 45/244.

54. Ibid.
55. Scott to Aspinall, 16 Feb. 1931, PRO, Cab 45/244.
56. Aspinall-Oglander, *Military Operations: Gallipoli*, Vol. II, pp. 258–9.
57. Aspinall to Hill, 31 Mar. 1933, Newport RO, Aspinall Papers, 111.
58. Hill to Aspinall, 6 Apr. 1933, Newport RO, Aspinall Papers, 111.
59. Dixon to Aspinall, 23 Jan. 1929, PRO, Cab 45/241.
60. Aspinall-Oglander, *Military Operations: Gallipoli*, Vol. II, p. 49.
61. Brighton to Aspinall, 19 Dec. 1930, PRO, Cab 45/241.
62. Aspinall-Oglander, *Military Operations: Gallipoli*, Vol. II, p. 323.
63. Haining to Aspinall, 13 Aug. 1931, PRO, Cab 45/242.
64. Aspinall-Oglander, *Military Operations: Gallipoli*, Vol. II, p. 52.
65. J.H. Patterson to Aspinall, 30 Jan. 1931, PRO, Cab 45/244.
66. Aspinall-Oglander, *Military Operations: Gallipoli*, Vol. II, p. 54.
67. Armstrong to Aspinall, 3 Nov. 1929, PRO, Cab 45/241.
68. Aspinall-Oglander, *Military Operations: Gallipoli*, Vol. II, p. 109.
69. Ibid., p. 49.
70. Ibid., p. 139.
71. Ibid., p. 140.
72. Aspinall-Oglander, *Military Operations: Gallipoli*, Vol. I, p. 346.
73. Ibid., p. 343.
74. W. Childs at Foreign Office to Aspinall, 4 Apr. 1927, Newport RO, Aspinall Papers, 111.
75. Braithwaite to Aspinall, 3 Aug. 1927, Newport RO, Aspinall Papers, 112.
76. Aspinall draft letter to CID, undated but late 1928, Newport RO, Aspinall Papers, 112.
77. Ibid.
78. Temperley to Aspinall, 10 Aug. 1926, Newport RO, Aspinall Papers, 112.
79. *The Times*, 7 Oct. 1927.
80. Ibid.
81. Ibid.
82. Edmonds Progress Report, 1927, PRO, Cab 103/5.
83. Bean to *The Times*, 10 Oct. 1927, Newport RO, Copy Aspinall Papers, 114.
84. Note by Aspinall, Newport RO, Aspinall Papers, 114.
85. Aspinall to Historical Section, undated, Newport RO, Aspinall Papers, 114.
86. Marginal note on letter from Edmonds, undated, Newport RO, Aspinall Papers, 112.
87. Aspinall-Oglander, *Military Operations: Gallipoli*, Vol. I, p. 186.
88. Ibid., p. 197.
89. Ibid., p. 268.
90. Ibid., p. 200.
91. Aspinall to Historical Section, undated, Newport RO, Aspinall Papers, 112.
92. Aspinall-Oglander, *Military Operations: Gallipoli*, Vol. I, p. 200.
93. Aspinall to Dawnay, 10 July 1926, IWM, Dawnay Papers, 69/21/3.
94. Dawnay to Aspinall, 7 July 1926, IWM, Dawnay Papers, 69/21/3.
95. Aspinall-Oglander, *Military Operations: Gallipoli*, Vol. I, p. 267.
96. Ibid., p. 268.
97. Ibid., p. 269.
98. Ibid., p. 270.
99. Aspinall to Godley, 11 Mar. 1927, Newport RO, Aspinall Papers, 116.
100. Aspinall to Godley, 3 Mar. 1927, Newport RO, Aspinall Papers, 116.
101. Godley to Aspinall, 8 Mar. and 11 Mar. 1927, Newport RO, Aspinall Papers, 116.
102. Godley to Aspinall, 12 Apr. 1927, Newport RO, Aspinall Papers, 116.
103. Birdwood to Aspinall, 10 Mar. 1927, Newport RO, Aspinall Papers, 116.
104. Godley to Aspinall, 11 Mar. 1927, Newport RO, Aspinall Papers, 116.
105. Aspinall to Birdwood, 7 Apr. 1927, Newport RO, Aspinall Papers, 116.
106. Birdwood to Edmonds, 1 Oct. 1928, KCL, Edmonds Papers, II/1.
107. Birdwood to Aspinall, 4 May 1927, Newport RO, Aspinall Papers, 116.
108. Birdwood to Edmonds, 19 Nov. 1928, KCL, Edmonds Papers, II/1.
109. Birdwood to Edmonds, 7 Apr. 1929, KCL, Edmonds Papers, II/1.
110. Birdwood to Edmonds, 1 Oct. 1928, KCL, Edmonds Papers, II/1.
111. Aspinall to Birdwood, 23 May 1927, Newport RO, Aspinall Papers, 116.
112. Birdwood to Edmonds, 29 Dec. 1928, KCL, Edmonds Papers, II/1.

113. Reported in Birdwood to Edmonds, 7 Apr. 1929, KCL, Edmonds Papers, II/1.
114. Ibid.

6: *Military Operations: Gallipoli,* Part II

1. Aspinall-Oglander, *Military Operations: Gallipoli*, Vol. I, p. 354.
2. Ibid., p. 307.
3. Ibid., p. 303.
4. Ibid., p. 354.
5. Ibid., p. 355.
6. W. Childs to E.Y. Daniel, 26 Apr. 1927, Newport RO, Aspinall Papers, 111.
7. E.Y. Daniel to S. Gaselee at FO, 3 May 1927, Newport RO, Aspinall Papers, 111.
8. Ibid.
9. Ibid.
10. S. Gaselee to Daniel, 28 July 1927, Newport RO, Aspinall Papers, 116.
11. Ibid.
12. Ibid.
13. Gaselee to Aspinall, 2 Aug. 1927, Newport RO, Aspinall Papers, 111.
14. Ibid.
15. Aspinall-Oglander, *Military Operations: Gallipoli*, Vol. I, p. 350.
16. Ibid.
17. Gaselee to Aspinall, 2 Aug. 1927, Newport RO, Aspinall Papers, 111.
18. Ibid.
19. Aspinall to Edmonds, undated but early 1929, Newport RO, Aspinall Papers, 112.
20. Childs to Historical Section, 19 Jan. 1927, Newport RO, Aspinall Papers, 111.
21. Aspinall-Oglander, *Military Operations: Gallipoli*, Vol. I, p. 4.
22. Ibid., p. 7.
23. Ibid.
24. Ibid.
25. Unsigned from Kirkbride to Aspinall, 6 Nov. 19?, Newport RO, Aspinall Papers, 111.
26. Foreign Office to Aspinall, 14 Oct. 1931, Newport RO, Aspinall Papers, 112.
27. Ibid.
28. Ibid.
29. Aspinall-Oglander, *Military Operations: Gallipoli*, Vol. II, p. 485.
30. Ibid.
31. Turkish Foreign Minister to British Ambassador to Turkey, 1 June 1932, *Times*.
32. Rhodri Williams, 'Lord Kitchener and the Battle of Loos: French Politics and British Strategy in the Summer of 1915', in L. Freedman, P. Hayes and R. O'Neill (eds), *War, Strategy and International Politics: Essays in Honour of Sir Michael Howard* (Oxford: Oxford University Press, 1992).
33. Gaselee to Aspinall, 10 Oct. 1931, Newport RO, Aspinall Papers, 111.
34. Ibid.
35. Aspinall-Oglander, *Military Operations: Gallipoli*, Vol. II, p. 398.
36. Comments by General Staff in COH 22, CID Subcommittee for Control of Official Histories, Newport RO, Aspinall Papers, 111.
37. Ibid.
38. Ibid.
39. Ibid.
40. Minutes of meeting of CID Subcommittee for Control of Official Histories, 9 Mar. 1928, PRO, Cab 16/53.
41. Ibid.
42. Ibid.
43. Aspinall-Oglander, *Military Operations: Gallipoli*, Vol. I, p. 69.
44. Minutes of meeting of CID Subcommittee for Control of Official Histories, 9 Mar. 1928, PRO, Cab 16/53.
45. Ibid.
46. Ibid.
47. Ibid.
48. Ibid.
49. Ibid.

50. Draft of Official History, *Military Operations: Gallipoli*, Vol. I, pp. 40–1, Newport RO, Aspinall Papers, 111.
51. Ibid.
52. Edmonds, Progress Report for 1926, 30 Nov. 1926, PRO, Cab 103/4.
53. Minutes of meeting of CID Subcommittee for Control of Official Histories, 9 Mar. 1928, PRO, Cab 16/53.
54. Ibid.
55. Ibid.
56. Edmonds to Aspinall, 2 Apr. 1928, Newport RO, Aspinall Papers, 114.
57. Braithwaite to Aspinall, 20 Apr. 1927, Newport RO, Aspinall Papers, 112.
58. Liddell Hart, 'Talks with Aspinall', 14 Jan. 1930, KCL, Liddell Hart Papers, 11/1930/2.
59. Edmonds to Aspinall, 2 Apr. 1928, Newport RO, Aspinall Papers, 114.
60. Edmonds to Aspinall, 6 Apr. 1928, Newport RO, Aspinall Papers, 112.
61. Newport RO, Aspinall Papers, 114.
62. Edmonds to Historical Section, undated but late 1928, Newport RO, Aspinall Papers, 112.
63. Aspinall to Historical Section, Newport RO, Aspinall Papers, 112.
64. Ibid.
65. Aspinall-Oglander, *Military Operations: Gallipoli*, Vol. II, p. 59.
66. Ibid., p. 65.
67. Ibid., p. 376.
68. Ibid., p. 378.
69. Ibid., p. 379.
70. Ibid., p. 150.
71. Ibid., p. 151.
72. Ibid., p. 232.
73. Ibid., p. 234.
74. Ibid., p. 276.
75. Aspinall-Oglander, *Military Operations: Gallipoli*, Vol. II, p. 145.
76. Ibid.
77. Ibid., p. 136.
78. Ibid., p. 264.
79. Ibid., p. 298.
80. Ibid., p. 312.
81. Hamilton to Aspinall concerning a lecture he had given, 22 Nov. 1932, Newport RO, Aspinall Papers, 111.
82. Aspinall-Oglander, *Military Operations: Gallipoli*, Vol. II, p. 386.
83. Hamilton to Daniel, 19 Jan. 1929, PRO, Cab 45/242.
84. Hamilton to Aspinall, 24 Dec. 1929, PRO, Cab 45/244.
85. Ibid.
86. Ibid. and reproduced in Aspinall-Oglander, *Military Operations: Gallipoli*, Vol. II, p. 151 as 'Here may be seen as in a mirror the breath of indecision beginning to blur the outlines of Sir Ian Hamilton's scheme.'
87. Aspinall-Oglander, *Military Operations: Gallipoli*, Vol. II, p. 153.
88. Aspinall to Daniel, 30 Jan. 1929, PRO, Cab 45/244.
89. Ibid.
90. Ibid.
91. Aspinall-Oglander, *Military Operations: Gallipoli*, Vol. II, p. 122.
92. Ibid.
93. Ibid., p. 124.
94. Copy of review by B. Liddell Hart for *Daily Telegraph*, Newport RO, Aspinall Papers, 114.
95. Historical Section to Aspinall, 6 May 1932, Newport RO, Aspinall Papers, 114.
96. Daniel to Aspinall, 18 May 1932, Newport RO, Aspinall Papers, 114.
97. Birdwood to Aspinall, 13 Apr. 1932, Newport RO, Aspinall Papers, 114.
98. J. Hamilton to Aspinall, 8 Apr. 1932, Newport RO, Aspinall Papers, 114.
99. Monro to Aspinall, 25 Apr. 1932, Newport RO, Aspinall Papers, 112.
100. Bean to Aspinall, 3 Oct. 1932, Newport RO, Aspinall Papers, 112.

7: Military Operations: France and Belgium, Vol. I: The German March Offensive

1. Meeting of Subcommittee of CID, 31 July 1922, PRO, Cab 27/212.
2. Meeting of Subcommittee of CID, 1 Feb. 1923, PRO, Cab 27/212.
3. Meeting of Committee for Control, 19 Jan. 1926, PRO, Cab 16/53.
4. Progress Report, 30 Nov. 1932, PRO, Cab 103/4.
5. Progress Report, Dec. 1932, PRO, Cab 103/10.
6. Brig.-Gen. Sir James Edmonds, *Military Operations: France and Belgium 1918*, Vol. I (London: Macmillan, 1935), p. vi.
7. Ibid.
8. Lt-Col. E.H.L. Beddington to Edmonds, 13 Aug. and 14 Nov. 1932, PRO, Cab 45/192.
9. Col. Groncard to Dixon, 11 May 1928, PRO, Cab 45/192.
10. See David French, *The Strategy of the Lloyd George Coalition 1916–1918* (Oxford: Clarendon Press, 1995), p. 232.
11. Liddell Hart to Edmonds, 6 Nov. 1934, KCL, Liddell Hart Papers, 1/259/93.
12. Travers, *Killing Ground*, pp. 239–43.
13. Cited in French, 'Sir James Edmonds', in Bond (ed.), *First World War and British Military History*, p. 83.
14. Lt-Col. Birch to Lt-Col. A. Bayley, 24 June 1927, PRO, Cab 45/192, and see for its description of these events Edmonds, *Military Operations: France and Belgium 1918*, Vol. I, p. 270.
15. R.M. Burke to Edmonds, 15 May 1927, PRO, Cab 45/192.
16. When Sandilands entered he asked the assembled company, 'What on earth are you all running away for like this?' The remark was received in 'dull silence', whereupon he was shocked to see an officer jump up who had previously been seated having his teeth examined by a doctor. It was Gen. Gough. Col. R. Sandilands to Edmonds, 14 Aug. 1923, PRO, Cab 45/192.
17. W. Golden to Edmonds, 18 Nov. 1927, PRO, Cab 45/192, and see also Edmonds' incorporation of the final detail in Edmonds, *Military Operations: France and Belgium 1918*, Vol. I, p. 263.
18. F. Duncan, Brigadier commanding 60th Brigade, XX Div., to Edmonds, 21 May 1928, PRO, Cab 45/192.
19. Edmonds to Lt-Col. G.S. Knox, 8 Feb. 1928, PRO, Cab 45/193.
20. Travers, *Killing Ground*, p. 239.
21. Liddell Hart to Edmonds, 6 Nov. 1934, KCL, Liddell Hart Papers, 1/259/93.
22. Edmonds, *Military Operations: France and Belgium 1918*, Vol. I, p. 167.
23. Ibid., p. 195.
24. Ibid., p. 177 on surrender of 2/8th Worcestershire and 2/4th Oxfordshire LI, p. 216 on confusion of first day's fighting, p. 221 on troops in forward zone of IV Corps mostly killed, buried or taken prisoner, p. 232 on surrender of 2/6th North Staffordshire, etc.
25. Ibid., pp. 381, 400, 401.
26. Ibid., pp. 199, 206.
27. Ibid., p. 370.
28. Progress Report, 30 Nov. 1926, PRO, Cab 103/4, and Dec. 1931, PRO, Cab 103/9.
29. Byng to Edmonds, 18 Aug. 1934, PRO, Cab 45/192.
30. Edmonds, *Military Operations: France and Belgium 1918*, Vol. I, p. 115.
31. Byng to Edmonds, 18 Aug. 1934, PRO, Cab 45/192.
32. Edmonds, *Military Operations: France and Belgium 1918*, Vol. I, p. 147.
33. Ibid., p. 218.
34. Ibid., p. 162.
35. Ibid., p. 248.
36. Ibid., p. 249.
37. Ibid.
38. Ibid., p. 301.
39. Ibid., p. 377.
40. See Byng to Edmonds, 29 Aug. 1934, PRO, Cab 45/192, in which Byng thanked Edmonds for his letter and acknowledged that, whilst he had every sympathy with Gough, he did not see why criticism should be passed on to other formations which, like him, were doing their best.

41. Travers, *Killing Ground*, p. 236.
42. Liddell Hart, 'Talks with Edmonds', 15 Nov. 1932, KCL, Liddell Hart Papers, 11/1932/44.
43. W.N. Congreve to Edmonds, 6 Jan. 1927, PRO, Cab 45/192.
44. W.N. Congreve to Edmonds, (1)5 Jan. 1927, PRO, Cab 45/192.
45. Edmonds to Gough, 21 Nov. 1932, PRO, Cab 45/192.
46. Travers, *Killing Ground*, p. 237 – author's italics.
47. E.H.L Beddington to Edmonds, 14 Nov. 1932, PRO, Cab 45/192.
48. Travers, *Killing Ground*, p. 241.
49. Gough to Edmonds, 29 July 1934, PRO, Cab 45/192.
50. J.H. Davidson to Edmonds, 7 Sept. 1934, PRO, Cab 45/192.
51. Edmonds, *Military Operations: France and Belgium 1918*, Vol. I, p. 418.
52. Col. R. Sandilands to Edmonds, 14 Aug. 1923, PRO, Cab 45/192.
53. Ibid.
54. Edmonds, *Military Operations: France and Belgium 1918*, Vol. I, p. 508 – author's italics.
55. Ibid.
56. Ibid., p. 509.
57. Ibid., p. 510.
58. Ibid., pp. 511–14.
59. Ibid., p. 515.
60. Ibid., p. 532.
61. Liddell Hart to Edmonds, 6 Nov. 1934, KCL, Liddell Hart Papers, 1/259/93.
62. French, *Strategy of the Lloyd George Coalition*, p. 223.
63. Edmonds, *Military Operations: France and Belgium 1918*, Vol. I, pp. vii, 39.
64. Ibid., pp. 116, 258, 300.
65. Ibid., pp. 156, 157.
66. Prior and Wilson, *Command on the Western Front, passim.*
67. Liddell Hart to Edmonds, 6 Nov. 1934, KCL, Liddell Hart Papers, 1/259/93.
68. Edmonds, *Military Operations: France and Belgium 1918*, Vol. I, p. 104.
69. Ibid., p. 109.
70. Gough to Edmonds, 27 May 1945, PRO, Cab 45/140.
71. Liddell Hart, 'Talks with Edmonds', 15 Nov. 1932, KCL, Liddell Hart Papers, 11/1932/44.
72. See also William Philpott, *Anglo-French Relations and Strategy on the Western Front 1914–1918* (London: Macmillan in association with King's College, 1996), *passim.*
73. Ibid., p. 370.
74. Liddell Hart to Edmonds, 6 Nov. 1934, KCL, Liddell Hart Papers, 1/259/93.

8: *Military Operations: France and Belgium 1917,* Vol. II: *Messines and Third Ypres (Passchendaele)*

1. See Travers, *Killing Ground, passim*, and French, 'Sir James Edmonds', in Bond (ed.), *First World War and British Military History, passim.*
2. Edmonds to Wynne, 12 Feb. 1944, PRO, Cab 45/140.
3. Gough to Edmonds, 2 Feb. 1944, PRO, Cab 45/140.
4. Ibid. (Gough's underlining).
5. Ibid.
6. R. Prior and T. Wilson, *Passchendaele: The Untold Story* (London: Yale University Press, 1996), *passim.*
7. Gough to Edmonds, 2 Feb. 1944, PRO, Cab 45/140.
8. Ibid. (Gough's underlining).
9. Edmonds to Wynne, 12 Feb. 1944, PRO, Cab 45/140.
10. Wynne to Edmonds, 16 Feb. 1944, PRO, Cab 45/140.
11. By June 1917 it had become clear that the French were no longer in a position to assist in a northern offensive. Whilst Haig was prepared to press ahead alone with an ambitious offensive which he hoped would be decisive, Lloyd George at War Cabinet meetings towards the end of June put pressure on Haig to 'wear down the enemy by a punch here and a punch there' with strictly limited objectives.
12. Edmonds to Wynne, 17 Feb. 1944, PRO, Cab 45/140.
13. Ibid.

14. Gough to Edmonds, 18 Mar. 1944, PRO, Cab 45/140.
15. Edmonds to Gough, 24 Mar. 1944, PRO, Cab 45/140. Davidson had opposed Gough's ambitious tactics for the offensive. According to Gough, Davidson had also a personal vendetta against Gough after he had 'deeply offended' Davidson by criticising Haig's disposition of forces before the March 1918 German offensive. See Gough to Edmonds, 27 May 1945, PRO, Cab 45/140.
16. Edmonds to Gough, 24 Mar. 1944, PRO, Cab 45/140.
17. Terraine, *Douglas Haig*, p. 235.
18. French, *Strategy of the Lloyd George Coalition*, and Prior and Wilson, *Passchendaele*, *passim*.
19. Brig.-Gen. Sir James Edmonds, *Military Operations: France and Belgium 1917*, Vol. II (London: HMSO, 1948), p. 14.
20. Ibid., pp. 18, 19.
21. Ibid., pp. 100, 101.
22. Edmonds, *Military Operations: France and Belgium 1917*, Vol. II, p. 124.
23. Ibid., p. 127.
24. Ibid.
25. Ibid., p. 129.
26. Ibid., p. 130.
27. Ibid., p. 131.
28. Prior and Wilson, *Passchendaele*, p. 85.
29. Ibid., p. 177.
30. Ibid., p. 178.
31. Ibid., p. 179.
32. Author's italics – Edmonds commented that Haig transferred the principal role to Plumer and, in changing *his* tactics, now 'agreed that the operation should take the form of a succession of attacks with strictly limited objectives'. Edmonds, *Military Operations: France and Belgium 1917*, Vol. II, p. 206.
33. Ibid., p. 237.
34. Ibid., p. 281.
35. Ibid., p. 296.
36. Ibid., p. 297.
37. Ibid., pp. 325, 327, 329, 330.
38. Gough to Edmonds, 18 Mar. 1944, PRO, Cab 45/140.
39. Ibid.
40. Gough to Edmonds, 3 May 1944, PRO, Cab 45/140.
41. Ibid.
42. Wynne to Edmonds, 9 May 1944, PRO, Cab 45/140.
43. Edmonds, *Military Operations: France and Belgium 1917*, Vol. II, p. vii.
44. Gough to Edmonds, 18 Mar. 1944, PRO, Cab 45/140.
45. Gough to Edmonds, 3 May 1944, PRO, Cab 45/140.
46. Malcolm to Gough, 29 Apr. 1944, PRO, Cab 45/140.
47. Gough to Edmonds, 3 May 1944, PRO, Cab 45/140, and Edmonds, *Military Operations: France and Belgium 1917*, Vol. II, p. 383.
48. Edmonds, *Military Operations: France and Belgium 1917*, Vol. II, p. 128.
49. Ibid., p. 183.
50. Ibid., p. 209.
51. Edmonds, *Military Operations: France and Belgium 1917*, Vol. II, p. 106.
52. French, *Strategy of the Lloyd George Coalition*, p. 110.
53. David French, 'Who Knew What and When?', in L. Freedman, P. Hayes and R. O'Neill (eds), *War, Strategy and International Politics: Essays in Honour of Sir Michael Howard* (Oxford: Oxford University Press, 1992), *passim*.
54. See Travers, *Killing Ground*.
55. Capt. G.C. Wynne, draft of Chapter XVIII, 'Reflections', PRO, Cab 45/140.
56. Ibid.
57. Ibid.
58. Ibid.
59. Ibid.
60. Travers, *Killing Ground*, p. 215.
61. Edmonds, *Military Operations: France and Belgium 1917*, Vol. II, p. 371.

62. Notes on interview between Gough and Wynne, 31 May 1945, PRO, Cab 45/140.
63. Ibid.
64. Ibid.
65. Ibid.
66. Ibid.
67. Ibid.
68. 'The History of Passchendaele', entry for 9 June 1945, PRO, Cab 103/112.
69. Edmonds to Joint Secretary, Official History Committee, 11 Jan. 1946, PRO, Cab 103/112.
70. Edmonds to Topham, 8 Jan. 1946, PRO, Cab 103/112.
71. Edmonds, *Military Operations: France and Belgium 1917*, Vol. II, p. xx.
72. Capt. G.C. Wynne, draft of Chapter XVIII, 'Reflections', PRO, Cab 45/140.
73. Ibid.
74. Ibid.
75. Edmonds, *Military Operations: France and Belgium 1917*, Vol. II, p. 368.
76. Ibid., p. 378.
77. Ibid., p. 385.
78. Ibid., p. 384.
79. Travers, *Killing Ground*, p. 216.
80. See Gough's complaint citing this statement in Wynne's draft of 3 May 1944, PRO, Cab 45/140.
81. Ibid.
82. Ibid.
83. Ibid., p. 216.
84. Ibid.
85. Ibid., p. 215.
86. Gough to Edmonds, 14 Apr. 1946, PRO, Cab 45/140.
87. Gough to Edmonds, 3 May 1944, PRO, Cab 45/140.
88. Gough to Edmonds, 14 Apr. 1946, PRO, Cab 45/140.
89. Prior and Wilson, *Passchendaele*, p. 50.
90. Edmonds, *Military Operations: France and Belgium 1917*, Vol. II, p. 138.
91. Ibid., pp. 32–62.
92. Ibid., p. 87.
93. Ibid., p. 139.
94. Ibid., p. 180.
95. Ibid., pp. 236–9.
96. Ibid., p. 240.
97. Ibid., pp. 241–2.
98. Ibid., p. 278.
99. Ibid., p. 294.
100. Prior and Wilson, *Passchendaele*, p. 131.
101. Edmonds, *Military Operations: France and Belgium 1917*, Vol. II, p. 296.
102. Ibid., pp. 330–1.
103. Ibid., p. 339.
104. Ibid. p. 342.
105. *TLS*, 12 Feb. 1949.
106. Edmonds, *Military Operations: France and Belgium 1917*, Vol. II, p. 387.

9: Conclusion

1. Daniel to Treasury, 'Appreciation on Official Histories', Jan. 1939, PRO, Cab 103/102.
2. Hankey memorandum, Oct. 1919, PRO, Cab 103/82.
3. *TLS*, 30 Nov. 1922.
4. *Times*, 17 Feb. 1925.
5. *Times*, 26 Apr. 1929.
6. *Greenock Telegraph*, 5 May 1932, Newport RO, Aspinall Papers, 114.
7. *Reynolds Illustrated News*, 1 May 1932, Newport RO, Aspinall Papers, 114.
8. Liddell Hart, *Daily Telegraph*, 8 Mar. 1932, Newport RO, Aspinall Papers, 114.
9. *Times*, 19 Jan. 1932.
10. *Manchester Guardian*, 19 Jan. 1932.

11. *TLS*, 24 Jan. 1935.
12. *Times*, 22 Jan. 1935.
13. Edmonds, *Military Operations: France and Belgium 1917*, Vol. II, p. 61.
14. Edmonds, *Military Operations: France and Belgium 1916*, Vol. I, p. 315.
15. Aspinall-Oglander, *Military Operations: Gallipoli*, Vol. I, p. 343.
16. See Chapter 1.
17. Edmonds, 'Experience Gained in Compiling Official Military Histories of 1914–1918', KCL, Edmonds Papers, VIII/11.
18. Hilton Young to H.A.L. Fisher, 9 Oct. 1922, PRO, Cab 103/73.
19. A. Conan Doyle to Edmonds, 4 Dec. 1929, KCL, Edmonds Papers, II/2/203.
20. E.C. Bentley, cited in Hew Strachan, '"The Real War": Liddel Hart, Cruttwell and Falls', in Bond (ed.), *First World War and British Military History*, p. 49.
21. Hankey memorandum, Oct. 1919, PRO, Cab 103/82 and Cab 103/83.
22. Minutes of meeting of Committee for Control of Official Histories, 23 Mar. 1933, PRO, Cab 16/53.
23. French, 'Sir James Edmonds', in Bond (ed.), *First World War and British Military History*, p. 84.
24. Liddell Hart, 'Talks with Edmonds', 8 Dec. 1930, KCL, Liddell Hart Papers, 11/1930/15.
25. Ibid.
26. Edmonds to Liddell Hart, 8 Mar. 1932, KCL, Liddell Hart Papers, 1/259/46.
27. Edmonds, 'Experience Gained in Compiling Official Military Histories 1914–1918', KCL, Edmonds Papers, VIII/11.
28. Edmonds, *Military Operations: France and Belgium 1918*, Vol. I, p. 257.
29. Edmonds, *Military Operations: France and Belgium 1917*, Vol. II, pp. iv, 387.
30. J.H. Davidson, Letter to *Times*, 16 Feb. 1949.
31. Robertson to Maurice, 1 Dec. 1932, Maurice Papers, 3/5/201, cited in French, 'Sir James Edmonds', in Bond (ed.), *First World War and British Military History*, p. 82.
32. Edmonds, *Military Operations: France and Belgium 1916*, Vol. I.
33. Prior and Wilson, *Passchendaele*, *passim*.
34. Edmonds, *Military Operations: France and Belgium 1917*, Vol. II.
35. Nigel Steel and Peter Hart, *Defeat at Gallipoli* (London: Macmillan, 1994).
36. Aspinall-Oglander, *Military Operations: Gallipoli*, Vol. II, p. 479.
37. Edmonds to Swinton, 21 Mar. 1950, KCL, Edmonds Papers, II/5/1.

Bibliography

PRIMARY SOURCES

Private Papers

Liddell Hart Centre for Military Archives, King's College, London
Sir James Edmonds Papers, boxes II–VIII.
Sir Basil Liddell Hart Papers, 1/259; 11/1927–33.

Newport Record Office, Newport, Isle of Wight
Cecil Aspinall-Oglander Papers, boxes 111–16.

Imperial War Museum
Guy Dawnay Papers, 69/21/1–6.
Orlo Williams Diary.

Official Papers

Public Record Office, Kew
Cab 16/52   Cabinet Official History Committee Minutes 1923.
Cab 16/53   Cabinet Official History Committee Minutes 1924–39.
Cab 27/182   Cabinet Official History Committee Minutes 1922.
Cab 27/212   Cabinet Official History Committee Minutes 1922–23.
Cab 27/213   Memorandum on Use of Official Material in Publications.
Cab 44/20–30   1927 Draft of Loos Chapters Official History and Comments by Haig.
Cab 45/132–8   Post-war Official History Correspondence, Somme.
Cab 45/140–1   Post-war Official History Correspondence, Third Ypres.
Cab 45/182   Post-war Official History Correspondence, Headlam and Jeudwine.
Cab 45/183   Post-war Official History Correspondence, Haig.
Cab 45/184–7   Post-war Official History Correspondence, Third Army.

Cab 45/192–3	Post-war Official History Correspondence, Fifth Army.
Cab 45/238	Notes by Lt-Gen. Sir Gerald Ellison on the History of the Dardanelles Campaign.
Cab 45/241–5	Post-war Official History Correspondence, Gallipoli.
Cab 103/1–21	Progress Report of Historical Section 1915–43.
Cab 103/52	Correspondence, General 1939–41.
Cab 103/53	Correspondence, Edmonds 1939–46.
Cab 103/73–5	Cabinet Official History Committee Correspondence 1922–23.
Cab 103/76	Cabinet Official History Committee Correspondence 1919–21.
Cab 103/77–8	Cabinet Official History Committee Correspondence 1927–28.
Cab 103/79	Cabinet Official History Committee Correspondence 1930–36.
Cab 103/80	Cabinet Official History Committee Correspondence 1920–21.
Cab 103/82	Cabinet Official History Committee Correspondence 1919–22.
Cab 103/83	Cabinet Official History Committee Correspondence 1919–35.
Cab 103/87–93	Cabinet Official History Committee Correspondence 1934–39.
Cab 103/97	Notes on Cabinet Historical Section 1919–21.
Cab 103/102	Cabinet Official History Committee Minutes and Correspondence 1939.
Cab 103/110–13	Post-war Official History Correspondence, Passchendaele.

Official Published Papers

Cd. 8490: *Dardanelles Commission: First Report* (1917–18).
Cmd. 371: *The Final Report of the Dardanelles Commission* (1919).

Published Primary Sources

Brock, M. and Brock, E. (eds), *H.H. Asquith Letters to Venetia Stanley* (Oxford: Oxford University Press, 1982).
Churchill, W.S., *The World Crisis 1911–1918*, 2 vols (London: Odhams Press, 1968).
Ellison, Sir Gerald, *The Perils of Amateur Strategy* (London: Longmans, Green, 1926).
French, Field Marshal John D.P., Earl of Ypres, *1914* (London: Constable, 1919).

Gibbs, P., *The Realities of War* (London: Heinemann, 1920).

Grey, E., *Twenty Five Years, 1892–1916*, 2 vols (London: Hodder & Stoughton, 1926).

Hamilton, Sir Ian, *Gallipoli Diary*, 2 vols (London: Edward Arnold, 1920).

Hankey, M., *The Supreme Command 1914–1918*, 2 vols (London: Allen & Unwin, 1961).

Lloyd George, D., *War Memoirs*, 2 vols (London: Odhams Press, 1938).

Repington, Lt-Col. C. a Court, *The First World War*, 2 vols (London: Constable, 1920).

Spears, Maj.-Gen. Sir E., *Liaison 1914: A Narrative of the Great Retreat* (London: Cassell, 1930).

Williams, O., 'The Gallipoli Tragedy', *19th Century*, 106, July (1929).

SECONDARY SOURCES

Andrew, Christopher, *Secret Service: The Making of the British Intelligence Community* (London: Sceptre, 1985).

Arthur, Sir George, *The Life of Lord Kitchener*, 3 vols (London: Macmillan, 1920).

Bean, C.E.W., *Official History of Australia in the War of 1914–1918*, 4 vols (Queensland: University of Queensland Press, 1942).

Beesly, P., *Room 40: British Naval Intelligence 1914–1918* (London: Hamilton, 1982).

Bond, B., *Liddell Hart: A Study of his Military Thought* (London: Cassell, 1977).

—— *British Military Policy between the Two World Wars* (Oxford: Oxford University Press, 1980).

—— (ed.), *The First World War and British Military History* (Oxford: Clarendon Press, 1991).

Bond, B. and Cave, N. (eds), *Haig: A Reappraisal 70 Years On* (Barnsley: Leo Cooper, 1999).

Cassar, G.H., *The French and the Dardanelles* (London: Allen & Unwin, 1971).

—— *The Tragedy of Sir John French* (London: Associated University Presses, 1985).

Clark, A., *The Donkeys* (London: Pimlico, 1961).

Clausewitz, C. von, *On War*, ed. and trans. M. Howard and P. Paret (Princeton, NJ: Princeton University Press, 1976).

Dewar, G.A.B. and Boraston, J.H., *Sir Douglas Haig's Command, December 19 1915 to November 11 1918*, 2 vols (London: Constable, 1922).

Dixon, N., *On the Psychology of Military Incompetence* (London: Jonathan Cape, 1976).

D'Ombrain, N., *War Machinery and High Policy: Defence Administration in Peacetime Britain, 1902–1914* (Oxford: Oxford University Press, 1973).

Falls, C., *The First World War* (London: Longmans, 1960).

Fergusson, T., *British Military Intelligence 1870–1914: The Development of a Modern Intelligence Organisation* (New York: University Publications of America, 1984).

Freedman, L., Hayes, P. and O'Neill, R. (eds), *War, Strategy and International Politics: Essays in Honour of Sir Michael Howard* (Oxford: Oxford University Press, 1992).

French, D., 'Spy Fever in Britain 1900–1915', *Historical Journal*, 21, 2 (1978).

—— *British Economic and Strategic Planning 1905–1915* (London: Allen & Unwin, 1982).

—— 'Sir Douglas Haig's Reputation 1918–1928: A Note', *Historical Journal*, 28, 4 (1985).

—— *British Strategy and War Aims 1914–1916* (London: Allen & Unwin, 1986).

——*The Strategy of the Lloyd George Coalition 1916–1918* (Oxford: Clarendon Press, 1995).

Fussell, P., *The Great War and Modern Memory* (Oxford: Oxford University Press, 1975).

Gilbert, M., *Churchill*, Vol. III (London: Heinemann, 1971).

Gooch, J., *The Plans of War: The General Staff and British Military Strategy c.1900–1916* (London: Routledge & Kegan Paul, 1974).

Holmes, R., *The Little Field Marshal: Sir John French* (London: Jonathan Cape, 1981).

—— *Riding the Retreat: Mons to the Marne 1914 Revisited* (London: Jonathan Cape, 1995).

Howard, M.E., *The Continental Commitment* (London: Maurice Temple Smith, 1972).

Hynes, S., *A War Imagined: The First World War and English Culture* (London: Bodley Head, 1990).

Keegan, J., *The Face of Battle* (London: Pimlico, 1976).

Liddell Hart, Sir Basil, *The Real War 1914–1918* (London: Faber & Faber, 1930).

Marder, A.J., *From Dreadnought to Scapa Flow* (Oxford: Oxford University Press, 1965).

Maurice, Maj.-Gen. Sir Frederick, *Haldane 1915–1928*, 2 vols (London: Faber & Faber, 1938).

Maurice, Maj.-Gen. Sir Frederick and Grant, M.H., *Official History of the War in South Africa, 1899–1902*, 4 vols (London: Hurst & Blackett, 1906–10).

Middlebrook, M., *The Kaiser's Battle, 21 March 1918: The First Day of the German Spring Offensive* (London: Penguin, 1978).

Philpott, W.J., *Anglo-French Relations and Strategy on the Western Front 1914–1918* (London: Macmillan in association with King's College, 1996).

Prior, R., *Churchill's 'World Crisis' as History* (London: Croom Helm, 1983).

Prior, R., and Wilson, T., *Command on the Western Front: The Military Career of Sir Henry Rawlinson 1914–1918* (Oxford: Blackwell, 1992).

—— *Passchendaele: The Untold Story* (London: Yale University Press 1996).

Rhodes James, R., *Gallipoli* (London: Pan Books, 1965).

Roskill, S., *Hankey: Man of Secrets*, 2 vols (London: Macmillan, 1970).

Royle, T., *The Kitchener Enigma* (London: Michael Joseph, 1985).

Simkins, P., *Kitchener's Army* (Manchester: Manchester University Press, 1988).

Smithers, A.J., *The Man Who Disobeyed: Sir Horace Smith-Dorrien and his Enemies* (London: Leo Cooper, 1970).

Steel, N. and Hart, P., *Defeat at Gallipoli* (London: Macmillan, 1994).

Terraine, J., *Sir Douglas Haig: The Educated Soldier* (London: Leo Cooper, 1963).

—— *White Heat: The New Warfare 1914–1918* (London: Sidgwick & Jackson, 1982).

Travers, T.H.E., *The Killing Ground: The British Army, the Western Front and the Emergence of Modern Warfare 1900–1918* (London: Allen & Unwin, 1982).

—— 'The Hidden Army Structural Problems in the British Officer Corps', *Journal of Contemporary History*, 17 (1982).

Wilson, T., *The Myriad Faces of War* (Cambridge: Polity Press, 1986).

Winter, D., *Haig's Command: A Reassessment* (London: Viking, 1991).

Wolff, L., *In Flanders Fields: The 1917 Campaign* (London: Longmans, 1960).

Woodward, D.R., *Lloyd George and the Generals* (Cranbury, NJ: Associated University Presses, 1983).

OFFICIAL HISTORIES

(All volumes were originally published by Macmillan or HMSO except the Gallipoli volumes which were published by Heinemann. All were recently republished by Imperial War Museum and Battery Press, Nashville, TN.)

Military Operations: France and Belgium

1914

Edmonds, Brig.-Gen. Sir James E., *Military Operations: France and Belgium 1914*, Vol. I, *Mons, the Retreat to the Seine, the Marne and the Aisne, August to October 1914* (London: Macmillan, 1922).

Edmonds, Brig.-Gen. Sir James E., *Military Operations: France and Belgium 1914*, Vol. II, *Antwerp, La Bassée, Armentières, Messines and Ypres, October to November 1914* (London: Macmillan, 1925).

1915

Edmonds, Brig.-Gen. Sir James E., *Military Operations: France and Belgium 1915*, Vol. I, *Winter 1914–15: Battle of Neuve Chapelle: Battle of Ypres* (London: Macmillan, 1927).

Edmonds, Brig.-Gen. Sir James E., *Military Operations: France and Belgium 1915*, Vol. II, *Battle of Aubers Ridge, Festubert and Loos* (London: Macmillan, 1928).

1916

Edmonds, Brig.-Gen. Sir James E., *Military Operations: France and Belgium 1916*, Vol. I, *Sir Douglas Haig's Command to 1st July: Battle of the Somme* (London: Macmillan, 1932).

Miles, Captain Wilfred, *Military Operations: France and Belgium 1916*, Vol. II, *2nd July to the End of the Battle of the Somme* (London: Macmillan, 1938).

1917

Edmonds, Brig.-Gen. Sir James E., *Military Operations: France and Belgium 1917*, Vol. II, *7th June–10th November: Messines and Third Ypres (Passchendaele)* (London: HMSO, 1948).

Falls, Captain Cyril, *Military Operations: France and Belgium 1917*, Vol. I, *German Retreat to Hindenburg Line and Battle of Arras* (London: Macmillan, 1940).

Miles, Captain Wilfred, *Military Operations: France and Belgium 1917*, Vol. III, *The Battle of Cambrai* (London: HMSO, 1948).

1918

Edmonds, Brig.-Gen. Sir James E., *Military Operations: France and Belgium 1918*, Vol. I, *The German March Offensive and its Preliminaries* (London: Macmillan, 1935).

Edmonds, Brig.-Gen. Sir James E., *Military Operations: France and Belgium 1918*, Vol. II, *March–April 1918: Continuation of the German Offensives* (London: Macmillan, 1937).

Edmonds, Brig.-Gen. Sir James E., *Military Operations: France and*

Belgium 1918, Vol. III, *May to July 1918: The German Diversion Offensives and the First Allied Counter-Offensive* (London: Macmillan, 1939).

Edmonds, Brig.-Gen. Sir James E., *Military Operations: France and Belgium 1918*, Vol. IV, *8th August–26th September 1918: The Franco-British Offensive* (London: HMSO, 1947).

Edmonds, Brig.-Gen. Sir James E., *Military Operations: France and Belgium 1918*, Vol. V, *26th September–11th November: The Advance to Victory* (London: HMSO, 1947).

Subsidiary Operations

Aspinall-Oglander, Brig.-Gen. Cecil F., *Military Operations: Gallipoli*, Vol. I, *Inception of the Campaign to May 1915* (London: Heinemann, 1929).

Aspinall-Oglander, Brig.-Gen. Cecil F., *Military Operations: Gallipoli*, Vol. II, *May 1915 to the Evacuation* (London: Heinemann, 1932).

Edmonds, Brig.-Gen. Sir James E. and Davies, H.R., *Military Operations: Italy, 1915–1919* (London: HMSO, 1949).

Edmonds, Brig.-Gen. Sir James E., *Military Operations: Rhineland, 1918–1929* Confidential edn (London: HMSO, 1944).

Falls, Captain Cyril, *Military Operations: Egypt and Palestine*, Vol. II, *From June 1917 to the End of the War* (London: HMSO, 1930).

Falls, Captain Cyril, *Military Operations: Macedonia*, Vol. I, *From the Outbreak of War to Spring 1917* (London: HMSO, 1933).

Falls, Captain Cyril, *Military Operations: Macedonia*, Vol. II, *Spring 1917 to the End of the War* (London: HMSO, 1935).

Horden, Lt-Col. Charles, *Military Operations: East Africa*, Vol. I, *August 1914–September 1916* (London: HMSO, 1941).

MacMunn, Lt-Gen. Sir George and Falls, Capt. Cyril, *Military Operations: Egypt and Palestine*, Vol. I, *From the Outbreak of War with Germany to June 1917* (London: HMSO, 1928).

Moberly, Brig.-Gen. F.J., *Military Operations: Mesopotamia*, Vol. I (London: HMSO, 1923).

Moberly, Brig.-Gen. F.J., *Military Operations: Mesopotamia*, Vol. II (London: HMSO, 1924).

Moberly, Brig.-Gen. F.J., *Military Operations: Mesopotamia*, Vol. III (London: HMSO, 1925).

Moberly, Brig.-Gen. F.J., *Military Operations: Mesopotamia*, Vol. IV (London: HMSO, 1927).

Moberly, Brig.-Gen. F.J., *Military Operations: Persia*, Vol. I, *1914–1919* Confidential edn (London: HMSO, 1929).

Moberly, Brig.-Gen. F.J., *Military Operations: Togoland and the Cameroons, 1914–1916* (London: HMSO, 1931).

Index

233